THE I TATTI
RENAISSANCE LIBRARY

James Hankins, General Editor

FLORENTIUS DE FAXOLIS
BOOK ON MUSIC

ITRL 43

THE I TATTI
RENAISSANCE LIBRARY

James Hankins, General Editor

FLORENTIUS DE FAXOLIS
BOOK ON MUSIC

ITRL 43

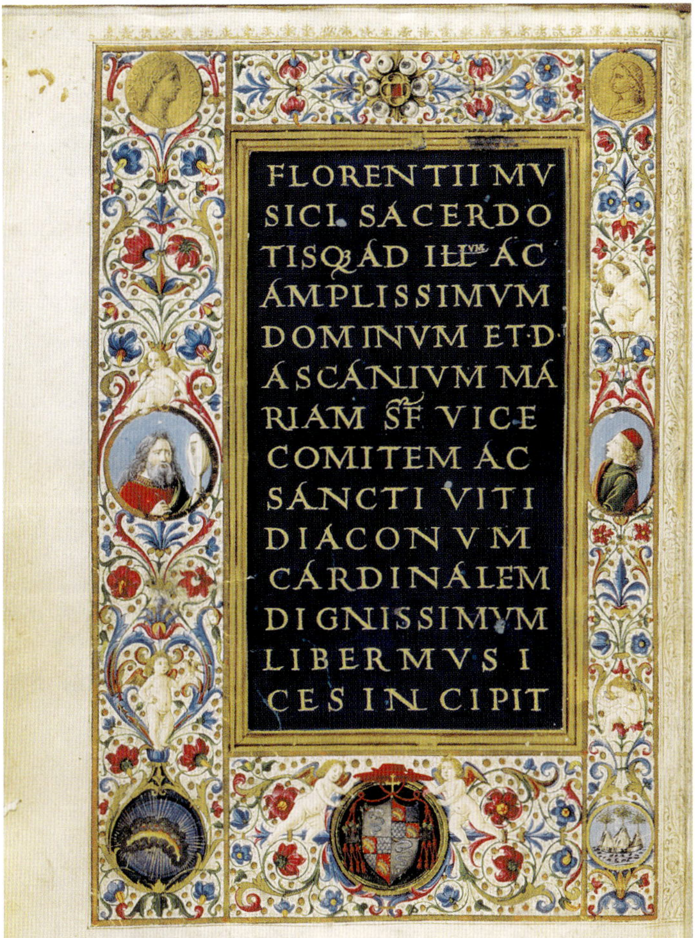

Plate I. Title page to *Liber Musices*. Archivio Storico Civico e Biblioteca Trivulziana, Copyright © Comune di Milano.

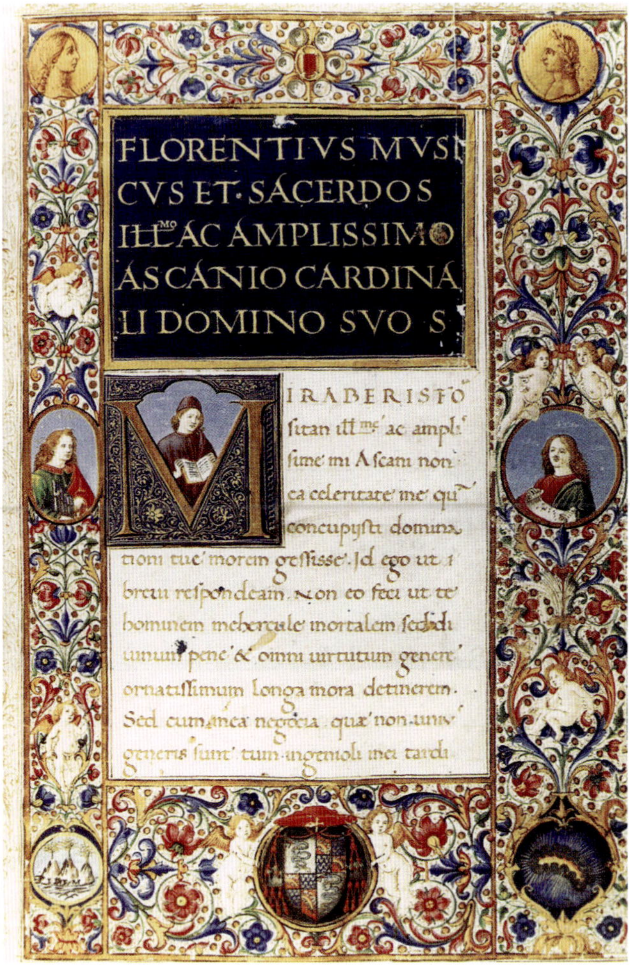

PLATE II. Dedication to *Liber Musices*. Archivio Storico Civico e Biblioteca Trivulziana, Copyright © Comune di Milano.

FLORENTIUS DE FAXOLIS

BOOK ON MUSIC

EDITED AND TRANSLATED BY

BONNIE J. BLACKBURN

AND

LEOFRANC HOLFORD-STREVENS

THE I TATTI RENAISSANCE LIBRARY
HARVARD UNIVERSITY PRESS
CAMBRIDGE, MASSACHUSETTS
LONDON, ENGLAND
2010

Printed in the United States of America

Series design by Dean Bornstein

Library of Congress Cataloging-in-Publication Data

Florentius de Faxolis.
[Liber musices. English & Latin]
Book on music / Florentius de Faxolis ; edited and translated by
Bonnie J. Blackburn and Leofranc Holford-Strevens.
p. cm. — (The I Tatti Renaissance Library ; 43)
Parallel Latin text and English translation.
Includes bibliographical references and index.
ISBN 978-0-674-04943-7 (alk. paper)
1. Music theory — Early works to 1800. I. Blackburn, Bonnie J.
II. Holford-Strevens, Leofranc. III. Title.
MT5.5.F65 2010
781 — dc22 2009042072

Original notation set in Florentius, designed by
Ross W. Duffin expressly for this edition

Contents

Introduction

The *Liber Musices* by "Florentius, musician and priest" is a treatise on music theory presented to the Milanese Cardinal Ascanio Maria Sforza (1455–1505; brother of Ludovico il Moro), a music lover and keen singer. The dedication states that the work was written specifically at the Cardinal's request, and the style, contents, and exposition distinguish it sharply from the usual treatise written for pedagogical purposes by professional musicians; indeed, Florentius's attempts at literary elegance and his parade of learning on music in antiquity bespeak his desire to be recognized as a full-fledged humanist. His work thus takes its place among other testimonies to the rise of practical music as a liberal art in the fifteenth century.[1]

Author and Patron

Who was Florentius Musicus? On 23 July 1482 the Duke of Milan (in fact Ludovico, acting as regent for the young Giangaleazzo) wrote to the archpriest, canons, and chapter of San Fiorenzo at Fiorenzuola d'Arda, which is nowadays in the province of Piacenza but then was under Milanese rule, urging them to confer a newly vacant canonry "Florentio da Fasolis clerico: qui de vitae honestate et moribus apud nos est commendatus" ("on Florentius de Faxolis, cleric, who has been commended to us for his uprightness of life and his conduct"), with a separate letter to his local *economo* with instructions to see that "Florentius de Fassiolis" was elected.[2] The order was obeyed; Florentius remained canon till his death in 1496. However, he did not reside there, for next year the newly vacant chaplaincy of a Milanese church, Santa Maria della Stella outside the Porta Tosa (now Porta Vittoria), was conferred

on "honestum virum et [presbyterum *deleted*] Florentium de Fassolis, clericum Placentinum, Mediolani commorantem" ("the honorable man and [priest] Florentius de Fassolis, cleric of Piacenza, dwelling at Milan").[3] In the record of this transaction, he is more than once described as a priest (*presbyter*), but each time the word is struck out; it was only on 23 May 1484 that he proceeded deacon and priest *per saltum*, at the uncanonical age of 23, by virtue of a papal dispensation secured through the Milanese protonotary Daniele Birago (from 1482 a privy councillor, and from 1489 archbishop of Mytilene),[4] whom he served as administrator and procurator, especially in connection with the church of Santa Maria della Passione, then being constructed by Birago.[5] In his will, dated 9 March 1496, Florentius is "presbiter Florentius de Faxolis filius quondam domini Iacobi" ("the priest Florentius de Faxolis, son of the late Jacobus"), still living in Milan, in the parish of San Nazzaro in Brolio near the Porta Romana, and has added to his canonry the provostship of San Vittore in Porlezza on Lake Lugano; his death on the 18th is noted in the margin.[6] His vernacular name, not attested, will have been Fiorenzo Fasoli.[7]

The identification of our author with the canon of Fiorenzuola, taken for granted since the discovery of the latter's will, has recently been challenged by Francesco Rocco Rossi,[8] who objects that the canon's attested connections are not with Ascanio Sforza but with Daniele Birago, and that he is never spoken of as a musician; he prefers to see the *Liber Musices* as the work of an otherwise unknown Spaniard encountered by Ascanio in Naples, where, as we shall see, its author entered his patron's service. While the discovery that another Josquin was present in Milan before Josquin des Prez arrived there stands as a warning against uncritical identifications,[9] and Florencio (or in the Catalan of the Neapolitan court Florenci) is an unexceptionable Hispanic name, Rossi's argument is far from watertight. Since it was Ascanio who, having set-

tled in Rome in 1484 as cardinal-deacon of SS. Vito e Modesto, proposed Birago as one of two candidates for Milanese ambassador to the papal court,[10] it is not unreasonable to posit a web of patronage, rather than a single thread.[11] Nor was there any occasion in the documents relating to Canon Fiorenzo for mention of his musical ability or learning; indeed, as the preface makes clear, he had much else to occupy his time. Admittedly, there is Hispanic influence in Florentius's Latin, but this, like the elements of Spanish theory in his teachings, could be derived at second hand through the Neapolitan-based Spaniard Blasius Romerus (see below under "Florentius's Sources"); in any case it is outweighed by the Italianisms.[12] Nor would a resident of Naples, in want of an epigram to praise his book, have commissioned it from a Milanese when so many Neapolitan humanists were to hand; but Fiorenzo Fasoli could reasonably have approached the long-standing Sforza dependent, Francesco Tranchedini,[13] who appended one in his own hand following the *Liber Musices*. Above all, only a Lombard was likely to style Anicius Manlius Severinus Boethius "St. Severinus" (Pr. 5, 1.1.29), for his cult (feast day 23 October) was local to Pavia; elsewhere the name would suggest one of several other saints.

In his dedication, Florentius speaks of the time when he was together with Ascanio, then a protonotary apostolic, in Naples and Rome. Following the assassination of Galeazzo Maria Sforza in December 1476, his widow Bona became regent for his young son Giangaleazzo and his brothers were sent into exile, Ascanio being remanded to Pavia. Ludovico returned to Milan in 1479, wresting the government from Bona, but his suspicions of Ascanio led to another period of exile for the protonotary, first to Ferrara in March 1480, then to Naples in September 1481, with a brief stop in Rome. The period in Naples was a most unhappy one for Ascanio, and in June 1482 he escaped to Rome. From there he went to Ravenna, and then to Venice on 11 August, where he col-

laborated in the Republic's plan to conquer Cremona, separating it from the Milanese dominion. Alarmed at this turn of events, and because Ascanio had supporters in Milan, Ludovico grudgingly made peace with his brother, who was readmitted to Milan in September 1482.[14] Florentius was probably a chaplain in Ascanio's entourage during part of his exile; since he makes no mention of Ferrara, he will have already been in Naples, either because (on Rossi's hypothesis) he was a long-standing resident or because he had already come down from the north in the hope of making his fortune, perhaps as a singer. The time he spent with Ascanio in Rome must have been brief, given the turmoil in the cardinal's life, and if Florentius is identical with the canon of Fiorenzuola, the receipt of a benefice in Milanese territory in July 1482 would have come at an opportune moment; otherwise we should have to suppose that, having declined to follow Ascanio beyond Rome, he was attempting to mend fences with his former patron now that the latter was a great man.

Between 3 March 1485, when the Brescian edition of Aulus Gellius finished printing,[15] and August 1492, when Ascanio was made Vice-Chancellor of the Church by Alexander VI,[16] Florentius composed the *Liber Musices,* purportedly at the cardinal's behest; it consists of three books. The first is entitled "on the praises, power, utility, necessity, and effect of music" (a theme much favored in the introductions to works of music theory, though treated much more extensively here), but eventually passes on to the fundamentals of sound, letters and pitches, solmization, and the modes and psalm-tones. Book II (whose title is lost) deals with intervals, counterpoint, and composition, Book III (on "figurative music") with notation, mensuration, and proportions.

Why did the Cardinal wish to have a music treatise? Like all the children of Francesco Sforza, Ascanio grew up in a musical environment at court.[17] We know that he owned a clavichord, because he arranged to have it sent to Ferrara when he was exiled

there in 1480; undoubtedly it followed him to Naples.[18] Indeed it was in Ferrara that he developed his musical talents, under the tutelage of none other than Ercole d'Este himself: according to a conversation with Ascanio in Rome in 1486 reported by the Ferrarese ambassador, it was Ercole who had taught Ascanio to "tenire li libreti in mano" ("hold the books in his hand"), that is, how to read music (Ercole himself was fond of standing amidst his singers and joining in). Ascanio claimed that his two greatest pleasures were hunting when outdoors, and singing at home. The ambassador remarks that the Cardinal was often engaged in music-making when he visited, and that he had recently hired two Spanish boys who sang marvelously. Moreover, in fulfillment of a promise made to Ercole, Ascanio was preparing a polyphonic mass (the *Missa Hercules dux Ferrariae?*) and some other things to send to him.[19] Given the deepening of his musical knowledge in Ferrara, where he became Ercole's "disciple," Ascanio could well have asked Florentius to create a music treatise to complete his education in music theory. No expense was spared in the artistic presentation, which was surely paid for by the Cardinal.

Florentius's Sources

In the dedication, Florentius bids Ascanio not to be put off by his work's length, since he will be induced to read it again and again by "my chosen speakers' harmony and wondrous concord, with which these teachings of mine have been spiced"; these "chosen speakers" are the learned authorities whom he cites. They comprise not only music theorists but classical authors, church fathers, and medieval scholars; moreover, rather than borrow in silence as many other writers did, Florentius prefers to parade his learning by naming his sources and quoting them verbatim. All wrote in Latin except Diogenes Laertius, who compiled his *Lives and Opinions of the Philosophers* in Greek; but the work had long since been

available in Traversari's Latin translation. Indeed, although Florentius occasionally betrays a smattering of Greek (1.5.17, 1.12.6), his failure to cite Greek writers suggests he had little more of the language than Tinctoris or Franchinus Gaffurius.[20]

The extensive citation of classical authors was clearly meant to appeal to a cleric with a humanistic education such as Ascanio had received. The citation of medieval authors reveals that Florentius had much more of a historical orientation than most of his fellow treatise-writers. He is interested not only in the origins of music, but in the development of notation, providing examples from the *Enchiriadis* of ca. 900, from the slightly later Hucbald of St-Amand, and from Guido d'Arezzo (ca. 1030), in addition to his ubiquitous Guidonian hand. Of the fourteenth-century writers he quotes, Marchetto of Padua was a fundamental source for knowledge of the modes, as was Johannes de Muris for notation: these writers are frequently cited in treatises by Florentius's contemporaries. Less often cited is the as-yet unidentified Goschalcus of Paris, the author of part of the "Berkeley Treatise," dating from 1375,[21] and several music theorists whose writings have not been preserved.

We begin to see a pattern in Florentius's citation of more recent authorities, for example, the mysterious "Sanctius geometra" (3.1.4), presumably a Spaniard called Sánchez, and two theorists unknown outside Spanish sources, "Arnaldus Dalps Germanus" and "Abbas Populeti sive magister Blasius." Only for the latter have we any information.[22] The payment list of 27 February 1451 for Alfonso I's court chapel at Naples includes a singer "blay romero";[23] like most of his colleagues, he is not on the next surviving list of 8 November 1455. At some point he became a monk in the great Cistercian monastery of Santa Maria de Poblet in Catalonia, but did not remain there; in 1475 we find him again in Naples, editing the elegant Seneca printed by Matthias Moravus "Sub domino Blasio Romero monacho Populeti philosopho ac

theologo celebri" ("under Blasius Romerus, monk of Poblet, famous philosopher and theologian") He also assisted him in the printing of the Neapolitan grammarian Junianus Maius's lexicon *De priscorum proprietate verborum* (1475) and raised money for his Bible (1476) from the French ambassador Thomas Taqui, before returning to Poblet for the inconclusive abbatial election following the death of Miguel Delgado (r. 1442–78);[24] since Romerus was never abbot, *abbas* appears to be an honorary title.[25] From these documents one would never guess that Romerus was a music theorist, but a "blasius de ro. capitulo ij" was quoted by Cristóbal de Escobar for the statement "Los principios de la musica quanto a nuestro proposito son tres conuiene asaber. letra. boz. y propriedad" ("The fundamentals of music, so far as concerns us, are three, namely letter [= pitch-name], voice [= solmization syllable], and property [=hexachord type]").[26] Since no title is given, one may take it for Romerus's only work, and the source of Florentius's quotations, which are too many and too full to come from oral communication; since none of these is found in Book III, and only one in Book II, it must have been an introductory text; but since so elementary a statement was not made till the second chapter of Romerus's treatise, the first must have been devoted to the praise of music and the place of the art in the intellectual universe. Florentius must have come across the book in Naples. We do not know when the *abbas* died, but he was clearly considered an authority there in the late fifteenth century.[27]

Unsurprisingly, Florentius's first quotation from this philosopher-theologian is scholastic (1.2.6); the next too is a philosophical commonplace on the formation of the voice (1.4.1). But the third raises an important problem of source-criticism: Florentius, having discussed Priscian's treatment of *vox* at the beginning of *De institutione grammatica*, distinguishes the musician's interest in the subject from the grammarian's and the philosopher's (1.4.7–13):

> However, in music we are not speaking about the voice as discussed there, or as the logicians define it, but as the abbot of Poblet does, using these words:[28] Now that we are about to treat of the voice, we must first know that music does not treat of the voice as the grammarian or the logician does, but of the voice that is a sound suitable for harmony, uttered from the shaped mouth of an animate being. Lactantius Firmianus . . . says the following . . . : But what account can we render of the voice? The grammarians and philosophers define the voice as being air struck by breath . . . So he says [*Haec ipse*]. Vergil too . . . says: drawing his voice from the depth of his breast. Aulus Gellius, too, holds the following opinion on the voice: It is an old and standing question argued among the most famous philosophers whether the voice is a body or a thing incorporeal . . . So Gellius.

First Florentius speaks in his own name; next Romerus is cited, and then the Christian apologist Lactantius, followed by *haec ipse*, "these things he (said)," which discharges the function nowadays assigned to closing quotation marks. But who is *ipse:* Lactantius or Romerus? Despite the displacement of the classical philosopher by the medieval logician, Lactantius explains Romerus as Romerus explains Florentius; we may reasonably infer that the first is cited through the second.

We must next ask whether the quotations from Vergil and Gellius also belong to Romerus, or are Florentius's own additions. Whereas the former, in which breath is drawn from the deepest part of the breast, fits adequately with Lactantius's disquisition on vocal physiology, the latter summarizes philosophers' opinions about the nature of the sounding voice, which Romerus has already ruled irrelevant to his purpose; it ought not therefore to come from him, and since it is not separated from the other by any such citation-closing formula as *haec ipse*, neither should that.

Any educated man knew his Vergil, and Gellius is quite a favourite with Florentius, who in 1.1.19–23 copies out verbatim almost a whole chapter of the *Noctes Atticae* (16.19).

The passage just considered follows on from a veritable parade of authorities (1.4.1–6): Papias, Romerus on the formation of the voice, Cicero (or rather the pseudo-Ciceronian *Rhetorica ad Herennium*), Papias again but this time unacknowledged, Nonius, Gregory's *Moralia,* Augustine (in fact a spurious sermon), Isidore, and Priscian. Papias, edited four times in the late Quattrocento and therefore still an author of importance, is cited by name twice in Book I; in Book II there are three explicit quotations, all in chapter 3, where he appears in the company of (Pseudo-) Censorinus, Isidore, and Marchetto, all authors with whom Florentius is familiar. Nor is there is reason to deny him knowledge of the much-read and still supposedly Ciceronian *Ad Herennium.* However, the unacknowledged paraphrase of Papias that follows, though taken from the same complex of entries as the explicit quotation, seems uncharacteristic of Florentius, who likes to parade the owners' labels on his borrowed clothes. Although both Nonius and Priscian had appeared in numerous editions before the *Liber Musices* was written, Romerus knew the former from his work on Maius, and the latter receives a mere passing mention that leads directly into the extract under consideration from the *abbas Populeti.* Priest that Florentius was, he never cites Gregory again except in matters of chant, and the only work of Augustine otherwise cited is *De musica.* It is quite possible, then, that everything from the statement about voice-formation in §1 down to the end of the Lactantian passage in §10 is taken from Romerus. That indeed would explain why Vergil, whose most appropriate place was after Gregory, was instead tacked on to Lactantius: Florentius did not wish to interrupt his master.

Further study appears to suggest that quotations from patristic and scholastic authors are likeliest to come from Romerus;[29] but

that does not exhaust Florentius's debt to him, for it is through Romerus that he is likely to have known the opinions of Sanctius the geometer, Arnaldus Dalps, and Dr. Goschalcus of Paris, who is "Gostaltus francigena" in the Catania copy of the Berkeley treatise,[30] and "Johannes Goscaldus" or "Goscaldo" for Spanish writers.[31] The Catania manuscript bears some textual affinity to Florentius's quotations at 3.3.2–5; it also contains two brief treatises by Jaume Borbó,[32] who was *mestre de cant* of the royal chapel when Romerus sang in it. This cannot be the manuscript that Florentius used, for at 3.8.5 he ascribes to Goschalcus an assertion not found in that or any other surviving copy; rather, we may suppose that Romerus, perhaps through Borbó, knew a fuller text.

At 1.16.1 Florentius cites an apparent echo of Goschalcus from Arnaldus Dalps. Although his epithet "Germanus" suggests an Imperial subject, Dalps is mentioned otherwise only by the Spaniards Durán and Molina;[33] two other passages quoted from him (2.4.7, 2.10.1) seem to be summarized in a manuscript of Catalan origin,[34] and Arnau is a good Catalan name; note that he is Arnaldus not Arnoldus as a German ought to be. It is tempting, though speculative, to identify him with the Arnaldus Dalps named as a representative on 9 July 1415 by the vicar of Serraduy del Pon to convey his resignation to the bishop of Lleida and the prior of Roda de Isábena; all these places lay in the Crown of Aragon.[35] In any case, he appears to be an Iberian writer whom Florentius knew through Romerus, even if he migrated to Imperial territory.[36]

Florentius as a Music Theorist

There is a certain mismatch between the titles of Florentius's three books and their contents. He is somewhat unsystematic in his presentation: for example, *coniunctae*—notes with sharps and flats outside the Guidonian hand—are discussed in three different

places. A whole number of topics are raised, then dropped with the remark that they will be discussed later. This is a mark of self-acquired learning, and of one who has not taught the subject: contrast Johannes Tinctoris, the consummate teacher, who presents his expositions and music examples in precise pedagogical order. In the three manuscripts in which his works are collected the didactic treatises appear in the following order: the fundamentals, comprising the Guidonian hand, pitches, clefs, solmization syllables, properties, hexachords, mutations, and intervals (*Expositio manus*); modes; five separate books on notation; the art of counterpoint; and proportions. Florentius begins with the fundamentals in chapter 5 of Book I ("Why terms were named or instituted by authors even in music," but returns to several of them in chapter 6 ("How the letters and syllables are arranged on the musical hand"). A very condensed description of the modes is also in Book I. Whereas Tinctoris devotes a whole treatise to the imperfection of notes, Florentius is content to give three rules for perfecting and three for imperfecting notes. The discussion of the function of dots is similarly condensed, considering only dots of division and augmentation, not of perfection.

Whereas it is clear from every one of Tinctoris's treatises that his teachings apply to polyphony as well as plainchant, we do not realize that Florentius has polyphonic music in mind until he suddenly drops in two cadential formulas toward the end of Book II. His only other polyphonic examples are those illustrating proportions in Book III. One of the puzzling aspects of the treatise, in fact, is the music examples, which are out of order, and are often gathered at the end of a book rather than placed where they would be most useful to the reader. It would appear that Florentius gave Verrazzano the text and the music examples separately, with inadequate instructions on how to place them.[37] Thus mutation, which is discussed in 1.7–10 on fols. 31ᵛ–37, is illustrated on fol. 43 and on fols. 44ᵛ–45, followed by all the rest of the examples relevant to

Book I. In Book II the examples illustrating cadential patterns in chant and polyphony are written in their proper places (fol. 67^{r-v}), but the rest of the examples follow at the end of the book with the laconic remark "Now let us write out examples of some of the foregoing." "Some of the foregoing" turns out to be only one page (fol. 68), showing intervals from the unison to the octave. Entirely lacking—disastrously for understanding Florentius's rules of counterpoint (see the Commentary to 2.15)—are any examples showing his precepts. Were they left out by accident? There are two blank staves at the top of fol. 68^{v}, suggesting that this indeed was the case, although they would not have sufficed. Florentius does apologize for not illustrating the genera and species of compositions by music examples because "it would take too long" to do so (2.18.4). That is a pity, because in this section he discusses several topics not considered by Tinctoris: fauxbourdon, *fuga*, canon, and imitation. On the other hand, there are music examples for everything covered in Book III, all likewise collected at the end of the book.

Far more than other theorists, as mentioned above, Florentius leans heavily on the writings of others, in their own words, and in particular on the Abbas Populeti. Perhaps he felt that this practice would lend him an aura of authority that he otherwise lacked. Yet we should not be quick to dismiss his treatise as derivative. There is sometimes an overlooked virtue in the self-taught theorist: he will often remark on aspects of musical practice that are not usually discussed by professional theorists. Some of Florentius's more unusual pronouncements, such as the claim that the two semitones in the octave have different sizes, the remark that the words of a composition will assist one in knowing whether to sing *mi* or *fa*, and the mensuration of the maxima and long, are discussed in the Commentary.

We wish to acknowledge the kindness of the staff of the Archivio Storico Civico e Biblioteca Trivulziana in Milan for their assis-

tance during our visit in September 2008 and their prompt responses to e-mail requests, including permission to publish the illustrations. Our warmest thanks go to Ross W. Duffin of Case Western Reserve University, who designed the elegant Florentius font used in the edition, based on the notation of the manuscript. In editorial matter, specific pitches are italicized and named according to the modern Helmholtz system, in which medieval Γ = G and ee (Ela) is *e''*. The Thesaurus musicarum Latinarum, an online database of medieval and Renaissance music theory, at http://www.chmtl.indiana.edu/tml, has been indispensable in the preparation of our edition. Finally we wish to thank James Hankins for his invitation to submit the edition to the Harvard I Tatti series and for his continued interest in it.

NOTES

1. This topic has been investigated especially by Reinhard Strohm: see "Hic miros cecinit cantus, nova scripta reliquit," in *Johannes Ockeghem: Actes du XLe Colloque international d'études humanistes, Tours, 3–8 février 1997*, ed. Philippe Vendrix (Épitome musical, 1; Paris: Klincksiek, 1988), 139–65; "Music, Humanism, and the Idea of a 'Rebirth' of the Arts," in *Music as Concept and Practice in the Late Middle Ages*, ed. Reinhard Strohm and Bonnie J. Blackburn (The New Oxford History of Music, III/1; Oxford: Oxford University Press, 2001), 346–405; "Enea Silvio Piccolomini and Music," in *Uno gentile et sottile ingenio: Studies in Renaissance Music in Honour of Bonnie J. Blackburn*, ed. M. Jennifer Bloxam, Gioia Filocamo, and Leofranc Holford-Strevens (Turnhout: Brepols, 2009), 719–27.

2. Archivio di Stato di Milano, Registro ducale 88, fol. 109^v; cf. fol. 112^r for another letter to the *economo* the next day.

3. Archivio di Stato di Milano, Archivio notarile 1336, 1 Sept. 1483, brought to light by Paul A. Merkley and Lora L. M. Merkley, *Music and Patronage at the Sforza Court* (Studi sulla Storia della Musica in Lombardia 3; Turnhout: Brepols, 1999), 448.

4. Archivio di Stato di Milano, Archivio notarile, 773, 23 May 1484; cf. Paola Modesti, "Sotto il tiburio: Ricerche sulle origini della tribuna di Santa Maria della Passione a Milano," *Annali di architettura* 10–11 (1998–99) (available on http://www.cisapalladio.org, accessed 30 Dec. 2008), 103–30 at 104, and Francesco Rocco Rossi, "Un manuale di musica per Ascanio Sforza: Il *Liber Musices* di Florentius (Ms. 2146 della Biblioteca Trivulziana di Milano)" (doctoral thesis, Università degli Studi di Pavia, Dipartimento di Scienze Musicologiche e Paleografico-Filologiche, 2007), 2:341–42, 409. We thank Dr. Rossi warmly for sending us a copy of his thesis.

5. Rossi, "Un manuale," 2:345, noting that the new-made counselor was sent to Rome on a mission to talk Sixtus IV out of his support for Venice in her war against Ferrara; Modesti, "Sotto il tiburio," 124 n. 52 (cf. 107, 123 n. 67, and 128 n. 149). Florentius wished to be buried in the Passione.

6. Emilio Motta, "Dell'autore probabile di un prezioso codice musicale della Trivulziana," *Bollettino storico della Svizzera italiana* 21 (1899): 76–77.

7. *Fasoli,* stressed on the second syllable (*Fasòli*), is a dialect form of *fagioli,* "beans" (information kindly given by Giovanni Zanovello). Currently, another Fiorenzo Fasoli is politically active in Verona.

8. Rossi, "Un manuale," 2:408–19; idem, "*Auctores in opusculo introducti:* L'enigmatico Florentius musicus e gli sconosciuti referenti teorici del *Liber Musices* (I-Mt 2146)," *Acta Musicologica* 80 (2008): 165–77. The article, which covers much of the same ground as this introduction, appeared when our own work was three months from submission to the publisher (although we had seen and used an Internet version of the pages on Romerus); it was thence that we learned of Florentius's connection with Birago.

9. For the evidence see Merkley and Merkley, *Music and Patronage,* ch. 5.

10. See Marco Pellegrini, *Ascanio Maria Sforza: La parabola politica di un cardinale-principe del rinascimento,* 2 vols. (Rome: Istituto Storico Italiano per il Medio Evo, 2002), 1:149.

11. Indeed, it was Ascanio's brother Ludovico who secured Fiorenzo his canonry, though fraternal relations at the time were strained; had he per-

haps been recommended by Birago, who held a priory *in commendam* near Fiorenzuola (Modesti, "Sotto il tiburio," 115)? However, it is clear from Florentius's preface that he was no longer in Ascanio's household at the time the treatise was completed; perhaps he had already returned to Milan before the reconciliation, when Ascanio left Naples.

12. See below, "Florentius's Language," under "Vernacular Influence."

13. Francesco Tranchedini (b. 1439) served the Sforzas over many decades as secretary and ambassador; see Lydia Cerioni, *La diplomazia sforzesca nella seconda metà del Quattrocento e i suoi cifrari segreti*, 2 vols. (Rome: Il Centro di Ricerca editore, 1970), 1:241–42; cf. Carlo Trivulzio's notes in the manuscript, pp. 2–3, [9].

14. See Pellegrini, *Ascanio Maria Sforza*, 1:78–82.

15. By Boninus de Boninis (Dobrić Dobričević); it introduced two erroneous readings that reappear in Florentius's text.

16. That Florentius wrote between Ascanio's creation as cardinal by Sixtus IV in 1484 and his nomination as Vice-Chancellor, a title not accorded him in the *Liber Musices*, was seen by Edward E. Lowinsky, "Ascanio Sforza's Life: A Key to Josquin's Biography and an Aid to the Chronology of his Works," in *Josquin des Prez: Proceedings of the International Josquin Festival Conference . . . June 1971*, ed. Edward E. Lowinsky with the collaboration of Bonnie J. Blackburn (London: Oxford University Press, 1976), 32–75 at 47–9, correcting Albert Seay, "The 'Liber Musices' of Florentius de Faxolis," in *Musik und Geschichte/Music and History: Leo Schrade zum sechzigsten Geburtstag* (Cologne: Arno Volk, 1963), 71–95 at 74–75.

17. On Ascanio's cultural interests see Giulia Bologna, "Un fratello del Moro letterato e bibliofilo: Ascanio Maria Sforza," in *Milano nell'età di Ludovico il Moro. Atti del Convegno internationale 28 febbraio–4 marzo 1483*, 2 vols. (Milan: Archivio Storico Civico e Biblioteca Trivulziana, 1983), 1:293–332.

18. Edward Lowinsky drew together references to Ascanio's interest in music in "Ascanio Sforza's Life," from his early youth to his patronage of Serafino Aquilano and Josquin des Prez and his personal musicians.

19. The letter (Archivio di Stato di Modena, CA Roma 5, Buonfrancesco Arlotti to Ercole d'Este, 18 October 1486) came to our attention through a reference in Pellegrini, *Ascanio Maria Sforza,* 1:73. We are greatly indebted to Camilla Cavicchi for sending us a photograph of it. The relevant portion reads as follows: "Sigismondo vostro [Ercole's brother] è ritornato qui. Sta per partirse sel non fusse retenuto dal R.^{mo} Car.^{le} Vesconte, el quale prepara una messa cantata, et certe altre cose da mandare a V. Ex. per adimpimento de certa promessa ch'el dice vi fece a Cremona. Sua S. R.^{ma} hora ha conducta [*sic*] in casa doi Garzoneti spagnoli, che è una suavità marevigliosa ad udirli cantare, et cum rasone. Quando vado a visitare S. S. R.^{ma} el più de le volte el trovo suso questa musica, De la qual dice delectarse per exemplo et imitatione vostra, che li incomenzasti a mostrare, et li facevati tenire li libreti in mano, et ch'el vole essere vostro disipulo, et dice ch'el ha ellecto doi piaceri, un, el cazare, quando è fuora, l'altro el cantare, quando sta in casa. Ma Sigismondo copiosamente referirà a bocha como el sia ben fornito per l'un exercicio et l'altro." On Ercole and music, see Lewis Lockwood, *Music in Renaissance Ferrara 1400–1505* (Cambridge, MA: Harvard University Press, 1984), esp. 136.

20. He freely uses the barbarisms *exaden* and *eptaden,* and treats indeclinable *diápente* as if it were a first-declension noun in *-ē,* adding *-s* in the genitive and *-n* in the accusative.

21. *The Berkeley Manuscript: University of California Music Library, MS. 744 (olim Phillipps 4450),* ed. and trans. Oliver B. Ellsworth (Lincoln, NE and London: University of Nebraska Press, 1984). The treatise is unattributed in this source.

22. For fuller accounts, see Leofranc Holford-Strevens, "The Erudition of Florentius de Faxolis and Blasius Romerus," in *Uno gentile et sottile ingenio* (n. 1), 751–59; Rossi, "*Auctores,*" 168–71, and "Un manuale," 2:365–97.

23. See Mariano Fava and Giovanni Bresciano, *La stampa a Napoli nel XV secolo,* 2 vols. (Leipzig, 1911–12), 1:63 n. 1. On his presence in Naples, see Allan W. Atlas, *Music at the Aragonese Court of Naples* (Cambridge: Cambridge University Press, 1985), 32–33.

24. Jaime Finestres y de Monsalvo, *Historia del Real Monasterio de Poblet,* 5 vols. (vols. 1–4 Cervera, 1753–56, vol. 5 Tarragona, 1765, repr. Barcelona: Editorial Orbis, 1947–49), 4:63–4. He was not at Poblet on 10 Sept. 1437 or 3 Dec. 1456 (ibid. 3:273, 279).

25. Rossi's conjecture, "*Auctores*," 169–70 and "Un manuale," 2:371, that Romerus had been sent out in 1442 to deputize for the abbot of Poblet as royal almoner (*lismonero real*) and *ex officio* confessor is disproved by the full list of royal almoners for Alfonso's reign at Finestres 3:272.

26. Escobar, *Esta es una introduccion muy breve de canto llano* ([Salamanca, ca. 1496]), sig. a1^{r}. Rossi, "*Auctores*," 171 identifies him with the humanist Cristóbal de Escobar, canon at Girgenti (now Agrigento), but adduces no evidence.

27. Curiously, he is not mentioned by Tinctoris, who was present in Naples at the time Florentius was; but neither does Florentius mention Tinctoris. Franchinus Gaffurius had been in Naples from November 1478 to 1480, where his first treatise, the *Theoricum opus musice discipline,* was published in 1480; he too does not mention Romerus in his treatises.

28. Quotation marks omitted for reasons that will become apparent.

29. One of these is Aurelian of Réôme, *Musica disciplina,* ch. 20. 1–3, 7, ed. Lawrence Gushee (CSM 21; [Rome]: American Institute of Musicology, 1975), 129, used without acknowledgment at 1.2.1. See Holford-Strevens, "The Erudition of Florentius de Faxolis," for more on this passage.

30. Catania, Biblioteche Riunite Civica e Antonio Ursini Recupero D 39; see Meyer, *The Theory of Music,* 6:466–71. See also *The Berkeley Treatise,* 14–15 for a discussion of this source.

31. He is cited in Domingo Marcos Durán, *Lux bella* (Seville, 1492), sig. a1^{v}; his *Comento sobre Lux bella* (Salamanca, 1498), sig. a3^{v} and e5^{v}; Escobar, *Esta es una introduccion,* four citations on sig. a1^{v}–a3; Bartolomé Molina, *Arte de canto llano llamado lux videntis* (Valladolid, 1503), seven citations on sig. a1^{v}–a6^{r}; Alfonso Spañón, *Introducción de canto llano* (n.p., ca. 1504), sig. a4^{r-v} (two citations). Most of these are marginal notes; only Durán and Escobar refer to part and chapter numbers. He is also known to the Sevillian anonymous of 1480: El Escorial, Real Monasterio de San

Lorenzo del Escorial, Biblioteca y Archivo de Música, MS C. III. 23, fols. 2ᵛ, 7ᵛ, 24ᵛ, as Johannes Goscaldi.

32. One on poetics (fols. 8^r–11^v), the other on proportions (fols. 33^v–34^r); see, respectively, F. Alberto Gallo, "Musica, poetica e retorica nel Quattrocento: *L'Illuminator* di Giacomo Borbo [*sic*]," *Rivista italiana di musicologia* 10 (1975): 72–85, and Prosdocimus de Beldemandis, *Brevis summula proportionum,* ed. Jan Herlinger (Lincoln, NE and London: University of Nebraska Press, 1987), 21, 46–52.

33. Durán, *Lux bella,* five citations on sig. a1–3 ("arnaldus"); *Comento,* in the list of authorities on sig. $e5^v$ ("arnoldo dalpes"); Molina, *Arte de canto llano,* sig. $a3^v$ ("Arnaldus").

34. See note ad loc.

35. See José Miguel Pesqué Lecina, "Documentos del priorado de Roda: Siglos XI al XX," in id. (ed.), *Homenaje a don Antonio Durán Gudiol* (Huesca: Instituto de estudios altoaragoneses, 1995), 675–90 at 681 (no. 9 of 38 documents held by the Ayuntamiento de Roda de Isábena): "Monzón, 9 de julio de 1415. Monsarratus de Valtachar, vicario de la iglesia de Serraduy, nombra como representantes suyos ante el obispo de Lérida y el prior de Roda a Arnaldo Dalps, Berengario de les Lanes y Dominico Madur para renunciar a su vicaría perpetual en Serraduy."

36. A century later one would posit a double surname, Arnau Dalps i Germà, but he lived too early for this to be plausible.

37. Rossi suggests that some of the music examples were added later, explaining their disorder and the appearance of blank staves on fol. 68^v ("Un manuale," 1:7–8).

BOOK ON MUSIC

[o^r] FLORENTII MUSICI SACERDOTISQUE AD ILLUSTRISSIMUM AC AMPLISSIMUM DOMINUM ET DOMINUM ASCANIUM MARIAM SFORTIAM VICECOMITEM AC SANCTI VITI DIACONUM CARDINALEM DIGNISSIMUM LIBER MUSICES INCIPIT

HERE BEGINS THE *BOOK ON MUSIC* OF FLORENTIUS, MUSICIAN AND PRIEST, TO THE MOST ILLUSTRIOUS AND DISTINGUISHED LORD, THE LORD ASCANIO MARIA SFORZA VISCONTI, MOST WORTHY CARDINAL DEACON OF SAN VITO

: [Praefatio] :

[1^r] Florentius Musicus et Sacerdos Illustrissimo ac Amplissimo Ascanio Cardinali Domino suo Salutem

1 Miraberis forsitan, illustrissime ac amplissime mi Ascani, non ea celeritate me qua[1] concupisti dominationi tuae morem gessisse. Id ego ut brevi respondeam, non eo feci ut te hominem mehercule mortalem sed divinum paene et omni virtutum genere ornatissimum longa mora detinerem; sed cum mea negotia, quae non unius generis sunt, tum ingenioli mei tardi[1^v]tas fecit ut diutius quam opinabar, et amplitudo tua optavisset, quod mihi iniunxeras absolverim. Ad hoc accedit quod mihi ipsi non satis fidebam; non enim et de tanta re et ad tantum principem litterarum monumentis, siquid novi dicendum erat, facile erat tradere. Quamobrem anteaquam quicquam ex ingenio meo ederem, diligentissime siquis de arte musicae tractasset indagare volui, ut nihil quod ad eam artem spectaret tuo iussu intentatum relinquerem. Hoc ego te vehementissime credere velim, neque alio nunc animo sum erga dominationem tuam Reverendissimam ac fueram cum Neapoli Romaeque tecum una essemus.

2 Reliquum est ut a tua amplitudine veniam petam, non enim eo ingenio, ea arte, eaque altitudine rerum res edita est, qua ingenii tui acumen et [2^r] admiranda tuae naturae disciplina in legendis emendandisque libris uti soles.

3 Quod opus ut liberali manu dignitati tuae porrigitur, ita quam libentissime ut Florentii tui iugis memoria esse possit, legas velim. Nec te libri nostri longitudo deterreat, cuius suavitas si diligentis-

: [Preface] :

Florentius, Musician and Priest, to the Most Illustrious and Distinguished Cardinal Ascanio, His Lord, Greetings

You may perchance wonder, my most illustrious and distinguished Ascanio, that I have not obeyed your lordship with that alacrity which you desired I should. To reply briefly, I did not take my time in order to delay with a long wait you who are a mortal man to be sure but almost divine and fully graced with every kind of virtue; but on the one hand the variety of my affairs, on the other the slowness of my poor wit, caused me to take more time than I expected, and your distinguished person would have wished, to discharge the task that you had enjoined on me. Added to which, I did not feel sufficient confidence in myself; for it was not easy to put in writing whatever new things there were to say in a written work either on so great a subject or for so great a prince. For which reason, I resolved, before I published anything of my own conceiving, to conduct most careful research into all those who had treated of the art of music, so that I might, at your behest, leave nothing untouched pertaining to that art. This I should most earnestly wish you to believe, nor am I now of another affection towards your most reverend lordship than I was when you and I[1] were in Naples and Rome together. 1

It remains for me to seek forgiveness from your distinguished person, since the work has not been published with that insight, that skill, and that loftiness of subject matter, which your sharp mind and wondrously trained nature[2] are wont to employ in reading and correcting books. 2

As this work is presented to you with open hand, so I should like you to read it with the best will possible, so that it may be a constant reminder of your Florentius. Nor let the length of my book put you off; provided you take all due care to savor my cho- 3

sime eorum quos ego ad dicendum mihi delegi armoniam atque mirum concentum quibus condita sunt haec nostra praecepta perceperis, ad lectionem iure optimo te iterum atque iterum hortari debet. Sed quid multis, amplissime domine? Illud unum est quo ego admirandam humanitatem tuam iudico, scilicet haec quae destinata sunt et perlegere et non ingrata animo tuo fore non aspernaris. Dabis tamen animum mihi ad maiora, ubi primum noverim te his meis ineptiis non nihil oblectari. Quam[2v]obrem ne inter legendum ambigere possis ubi unaquaeque res sit, scribam ordine quodam litterae quicquid tribus libris conscripsimus, atque quicquid in unoquoque eorum capite continebitur pulchra per alphabetum distinctione annotabimus, ut omnia de quibus ambigi possit ampla ac divina tua bonitas sine labore investigare possit.

4 Vale meque dilige.

5 Auctores in opusculo introducti hi sunt: abbas Populeti vel magister Blasius; Hugo; Addon abbas; Augustinus; Aulus Gellius; Guido; Arnaldus Dalps Germanus; Goschalcus Parisiensis; Boethius vel sanctus Severinus; Enchiriades; Brito; Papias; Censorinus; Isidorus episcopus; Lactantius; Marcus Tullius Cicero; Valerius Maximus; Marchettus Paduensis; Macrobius; Iohannes de Muris; Lucius Apuleius.

6 Alteratio. Libro iii, capitulo xii
[3r] Harmonia.[2] Libro ii, capitulo iii
Arsis. Libro ii, capitulo iiii circa finem

7 Bfa♮mi quare non habet[3] mutationem. Libro i, capitulo viiii

8 Cantus quid sit. Libro i, capitulo iiii circa finem
Claves musicales. Libro i, capitulo v

sen speakers'[3] harmony and wondrous concord, with which these teachings of mine have been spiced, its sweetness must have every right to urge you again and again to the reading. But why need I go on at length, most distinguished lord? There is one thing by which I judge your wonderfully civilized nature,[4] namely that you do not refuse either to read through the things that have been sent you or to be pleased with them. But you will give me courage for greater things once I know that you take some pleasure in my triflings. For which reason, so that you may not be in doubt as you read where each topic is, I shall list, ordered by letter, everything covered in the three books, and whatever will be contained in each one of their chapters I shall record by a handsome alphabetical classification, so that all things that may be subject to doubt your distinguished and divine goodness may track down without trouble.

Fare well and love me.[5] 4

The authors introduced in my little work are as follows: the ab- 5
bot of Poblet (Master Blas);[6] Hugo;[7] Abbot Addo;[8] Augustine; Aulus Gellius;[9] Guido [d'Arezzo];[10] Arnaldus Dalps Germanus;[11] Goschalcus of Paris;[12] Boethius (St. Severinus); Enchiriades;[13] Brito;[14] Papias;[15] Censorinus;[16] Bishop Isidore [of Seville];[17] Lactantius;[18] Marcus Tullius Cicero; Valerius Maximus;[19] Marchetto of Padua;[20] Macrobius;[21] Johannes de Muris;[22] Lucius Apuleius.[23]

Alteration, Book III, chapter 12 6
Harmony, Book II, chapter 3
Arsis, Book II, chapter 4, near the end

Why bfa♮mi does not admit mutation, Book I, chapter 9 7

What song is, Book I, chapter 4, near the end 8
Musical clefs, Book I, chapter 5

Recognition of antiphons and other chants, Book I, chapter 14
What a *coniuncta* is and of how many kinds, Book I, chapters 8 and 16
What counterpoint is, where the name comes from, and how it was discovered, Book II, chapter 1
Consonance according to Boethius, Book II, chapter 5
The consonances of the old musicians, Book II, chapter 6
The principal consonances and those formed from them, Book II, chapter 6
The principle of composition, Book II, chapter 16
What a circle is, Book III, chapter 1
What a tail is, Book III, chapter 1
What a centre is, Book III, chapter 1
Color or inked-in figure, Book III, chapter 11

What *diaphonia* is, Book II, chapter 3 9
Diapente or fifth, Book II, chapter 10
What a diameter is, Book III, chapter 1
What dissonance is, Book II, chapter 13
On the modes of plainchant, Book I, chapter 12
On the manner of intoning, Book I, chapter 14

Examples of plainchant, Book I, after chapter 16, that is, of antiphons, psalms, and doxologies 10
Euphony, Book II, chapter 3
Practicing the rules of counterpoint, Book II, chapter 15
Examples of polyphony, Book III, after chapter 21
Afterwards, examples of some proportions

The notation of clefs, Book I, chapter 6, near the end 11
What a figure is, Book III, chapter 1
Why figurative song [= polyphony] is so called, Book III, chapter 2

Figurae cantus quot sint. Libro iii, capitulo ii

Figuratio circulorum et
Figuratio semicirculorum } Libro iii, capitulo iii

Libro iii, capitulo iii

12 Gradus vocum vel notularum. Libro i, capitulo v

H[5]

13 Inventores musicae secundum auctores. Tubal. Amphion. Linus. Zethus. Mercurius. Pythagoras. Item chordarum inventores. Libro i, capitulo i

Indicia proportionum. Libro iii, capitulo xxi

K[6]

14 Litterae septem manus. Libro i, capitulis v et vi

[4v] Linea notularum[7] et spatiorum. Libro i, capitulo v

Lineae et spatia cum notulis. Libro i, capitulo vi

Linea quid sit. Libro iii, capitulo i

Ligaturae notularum. Libro iii, capitulo viii

15 Manus depicta cum suis nominibus. Libro i, capitulo vi in fine

Melodia quid sit. Libro ii, capitulo iii

Modi in plana musica quot sint et quot species eorum. Libro i, capitulo xii

Modorum auctoritas. Libro i.[8] capitulo xiii

Modulatio. Libro ii, capitulo iii

Modus figurativi cantus. Libro iii, capitulo iii

Musicae definitio. Libro i, capitulo ii

Mutatio quid sit et quare instituta sit, et quo in loco fieri possit, et quo ordine. Libro i, capitulo vii

Mutatio diligentissime faciunda et observanda, id est quando in bmolle vel ♮quadro fieri possit iure ipso. Libro i, capitulo x

16 [5r] Neuma et cadentia. Libro ii, capitulo xviii

Nomina litterarum et notularum quo ordine in manu ponantur. Libro i, capitulo vi

Nomina sex vocum ibidem

Notularum figuratio secundum diversa tempora. Libro i<ii>, capitulis xiiii et xv

Numerus sex vocum. Libro i, capitulo v

17 Octava vel diapason. Libro ii, capitulo xii

18 Partitio modi, temporis, et prolationis. Libro iii, capitulo vii

Pausa. Libro iii, capitulo xiii

Praecepta Hubaldi de musica. Libro ii, capitulo ii

Perfectio figurarum quomodo se habeat. Libro iii, capitulo viiii

Proprietas. Libro i, capitulo v

Prolatio. Libro iii, capitulo iii

Proportio cum generibus et speciebus suis. Libro iii, capitulis xv et xvi et xvii et xviii et [5v] xviiii et xx

Punctum quid sit. Libro iii, capitulo i

Punctus augmentationis et alterationis. Libro iii, capitulo x

19 Quare musici terminos in laeva instituerunt. Libro i, capitulo v

Quomodo natura, bmolle, ♮quadrum noscatur. Libro i, capitulo vi

Quadranguli figuratio. Libro iii, capitulo iii<i>

<Q>uot mensurae. Libro iii, capitulo xiiii

20 Regulae contrapunctales iuxta ordinem. Libro ii, capitulo xiiii

21 Species vocis. Libro i, capitulo iiii

Semitonium. Libro ii, capitulo iiii. Item maioris et minoris coniectura et notitia. Libro eodem, capitulo xii

Sexta, vel ditonus et semiditonus <et tonus>, vel [6r] exaden. Libro ii, capitulo xi

Semicirculus quid sit. Libro iii, capitulis i et iii et v

Signa gravitatis et acuminis. Libro i, capitulo viii

Symphonia. Libro ii, capitulo iii

Scriptores ipsius artis quos vidimus:[9] Boethium, Guidonem Arretinum, abbatem Populeti, Enchiriadem, Hugonem, Augustinum, Isidorum, Addonem abbatem, Iohannem de Muris, Goscalchum, Arnaldum, et Marchettum et quosdam alios

22 Tria musices genera. Libro i, capitulo iii

Thesis quid sit. Libro i, capitulo iiii circa finem

Tertia maior et minor. Libro ii, capitulo viiii

Terminus quid sit. Libro iii, capitulo i

Tonus quid sit. Libro ii.[10] capitulo iiii

23 Verba sub notulis ordinanda. Libro i, capitulo xi

[6v] Vox quid sit, et unde dicatur. Libro i, capitulo iiii

Vox aequisona vel unisonus. Libro ii, capitulo viii

The sixth, or ditone and semiditone <and tone>, or [fo. 6^{r}] hexad, Book II, chapter 11
What a semicircle is, Book III, chapters 1, 3, and 5
The signs of low and high pitch, Book I, chapter 8
Concord, Book II, chapter 3
The writers on the art we have seen: Boethius, Guido of Arezzo, the abbot of Poblet, Enchiriades, Hugo, Augustine, Isidore, Abbot Addo, Johannes de Muris, Goschalcus, Arnaldus, and Marchetto, and some others

The three kinds of music, Book I, chapter 3 22
What thesis is, Book I, chapter 4, near the end
The major and minor third, Book II, chapter 9
What a limit is, Book III, chapter 1
What a tone is, Book II, chapter 4

Arranging the words under the notes, Book I, chapter 11 23
What the voice is and why it is so called, Book I, chapter 4
The equal-sounding voice or unison, Book II, chapter 8

· [LIBER I] ·

[7r] DE LAUDIBUS, VIRTUTE, UTILITATE, NECESSITATE, ET EFFECTU MUSICES

: I :

Prooemium caputque primum incipit

1 QUAM laude digna maiorum tempora optimus quisque commentariis elegantissimis ea demonstrat. Namque fundamenta disciplinarum ab his iacta, posteri deinde optimis ingenii acuminibus freti longe meliora reddiderunt. Non enim deerant ea tempestate qui philosophiam partesque eius augerent. Erantque praesertim inter nobiles ducum regumque virtutibus praediti qui maxima cura die noctuque ad ea incumbebant. Nec profecto inter hos defuerunt qui mathematicas disciplinas litterarum monumentis non <indignas> iudicaverint.[1] Mittam alias e quibus peritissimi quam plu[7v]rimi evaserunt, sed solum de musices[2] aliqua memoratu digna, summo caelicolarum redemptore, eiusque genitrice sanctissima Maria semper virgine, meis coeptis divina ope aspirantibus, quam brevisssime potero peritissimorum sententiis comprobata explicabo.

2 Non modo qui astronomiae sive arithmeticae,[3] seu geometriae, aut grammaticae et rhetoricae et poesiae vacantes in ea versabantur, verum qui et rem militarem exercebant, hi agmen aciesque modulatione musices instruebant. Quod Aulus quoque Gellius comprobat:

• [BOOK I] •

ON THE PRAISES, POWER, UTILITY, NECESSITY, AND EFFECT OF MUSIC

: I :

Proem and chapter 1 begin

How worthy of praise the times of our ancestors were is shown by all the best people in their very elegant memoirs; for it was they who laid the foundations of the disciplines. Then their successors, trusting in their admirably sharp intellects, greatly improved them, for there were not lacking at that time those who expanded philosophy and its constituent parts. Among the nobles in particular there were men possessing the virtues of commanders and kings who devoted themselves thereto with the keenest attention day and night. Nor indeed were there lacking among them those who judged the mathematical disciplines with literary texts.[1] I shall pass over the other disciplines in which very many became great experts, but merely expound, as briefly as I can, some facts about music worth mentioning that are established by the opinions of the most expert, if the supreme Redeemer of the heavenly ones and his mother the most holy Mary ever virgin shall inspire my undertaking with their divine assistance. 1

It was not only those who gave their time to astronomy or arithmetic,[2] or geometry, or grammar and rhetoric and poetry, who were familiar with it, but military men too used to form the column of march and the line of battle by the playing of music. This Aulus Gellius too confirms: 2

3 Auctor historiae Graecae gravissimus Thucydides Lacedaemonios summos bellatores non cornuum tubarumve signis, sed tibiarum modulis in proeliis usos esse refert, non prorsus ex aliquo ritu religionum, neque rei divinae gratia, neque autem [8r] ut excitarentur atque evibrarentur animi, quod cornua et litui moliuntur, sed contra ut moderatiores modulatioresque fierent, quod tibicinis numeris temperatur, nihil adeo in congrediendis hostibus atque in principiis proeliorum ad salutem virtutemque aptius rati quam si permulcti sonis mitioribus non immodice ferocirent. Cum procinctae igitur classes erant et instructa acies, coeptumque in hostem progredi, tibicines inter exercitum positi canere inceptabant, et quae ipse pergit.

4 Domi praeterea nec in sacris solum, sed in nuptiis et conviviis hanc non parvi fecerunt. Hinc illud Valerii Maximi:

5 Maiores natu in conviviis ad tibias egregia superiorum opera carmine comprehensa pangebant ut ad ea imitanda iuvenum virtutem alacriorem redderent.

6 Floruit haec in [8v] Graecia magnopere magnique putabantur qui cum philosophia ceterisque scientiis hanc velut quadam insitione conferebant; itaque neglectos imperitosque <habitos> qui hac carebant apud maiores comperii. Illud enim M. Tullius Cicero primo Tusculanarum Quaestionum libro confirmat:

7 Summam eruditionem Graeci sitam censebant in nervorum vocumque cantibus. Igitur et Epaminondas princeps meo iudicio Graeciae fidibus praeclare cecinisse dicitur, Themisto-

> That most venerable authority on Greek history, Thucydides, reports that the Spartans, those foremost warriors, did not employ the calls of horns or trumpets, but the melodies of auloi[3] in their battles. This was not at all due to any religious prescription, nor for the sake of a ritual, nor was it done that [the soldiers'] spirits should be aroused and stirred, which horns and trumpets strive to do, but on the contrary that they should become more moderate and regulated by the calming effect of the aulete's tunes; for they thought nothing more suitable for attacks on the enemy and the beginnings of battles than if they were soothed by gentler sounds and not too immoderately frenzied. Therefore, when the troops were in battle array and the line formed, and the advance on the enemy had begun, the auletes distributed throughout the army began to play, etc.[4] 3

At home too, and not only in religious rituals, but at weddings 4
and banquets they made no small account of it. Hence the passage of Valerius Maximus:

> The elder generation used to tell in songs set to the auloi 5
> about the illustrious achievements of their ancestors so as to make the younger men's courage the readier to imitate them.[5]

This art greatly flourished in Greece and a great reputation 6
was enjoyed by those who combined it with philosophy and the other sciences, much as one grafts trees; in consequence, I have discovered that among our ancestors those who were lacking in it were disregarded and [considered?][6] inexperienced. Cicero confirms that in the first book of the *Tusculan Disputations:*

> The Greeks considered the height of learning to reside in 7
> the music of strings and voice. Hence on the one hand Epaminondas,[7] in my opinion the first man of Greece, is said

> clesque aliquot ante annos cum in epulis recusasset lyram est habitus indoctior. Ergo in Graecia musici floruerunt, discebantque id omnes neque qui nesciebat satis excultus doctrina putabatur. Haec ille.

8 Isidorus enim in musicae laudibus et ex eiusdem effectibus et quam sit necessaria disciplinis aliis hoc dicit:

> 9 Sine musica nulla disciplina [9r] potest esse perfecta, nihil enim sine ipsa; nam et ipse mundus quadam harmonia sonorum fertur esse compositus, et caelum ipsum sub harmoniae modulatione revolvi. Musica vero movet affectus, provocat in diversum habitum sensus. In proeliis quoque tubae concentus pugnantes accendit, et quanto vehementior fuerit clangor, tanto fit ad certamen animus fortior, siquidem et remiges cantus hortatur, ad tolerandos[4] quoque labores musica animum mulcet, et singulorum operum fatigationem modulatio vocis temperat. Excitatos quoque animos musica sedat, sicut de David legitur, qui a spiritu immundo Saulem arte modulationis eripuit. Haec Isidorus.

10 Quintilianus autem vir disertissimus artem dicendi, sive rh<e>toricen, sine musicae minime perfectam fore ostendit. His usus est [9v] verbis.

> 11 Atque ego vel iudicio veterum poteram esse contentus. Nam quis ignorat musicam, ut de hac primum loquar, tantum iam in illis antiquis temporibus, non studii[5] modo, verum etiam venerationis habuisse ut idem musici et vates et sapientes iudicarentur? Mittam alios: Orpheus et Linus, quorum utrumque dis genitum, alterum vero quia rudes quoque atque agrestes animos admiratione mulceret, non feras

> to have been an outstanding lyre-player, on the other Themistocles,[8] a number of years earlier, having declined the lyre at a banquet, was considered something of an ignoramus. Therefore in Greece musicians flourished, and everyone learned it, and the man who did not know it was not thought adequately educated.[9]

Isidore says the following in his praise of music, both on its effects and on how necessary it is for other disciplines: 8

> Without music no discipline can be complete, for nothing is without it. For the very universe itself is said to have been put together with a kind of musical harmony,[10] and the sky itself to rotate to the sound of harmony. Music moves the emotions, it incites the mind to a different mood. In battles, too, the peal of trumpets inflames the fighting men, and the louder the blare has been, the stouter the heart becomes for battle, as surely as song also encourages rowers, and music soothes the mind for enduring[11] toil, and the singing voice moderates the weariness attending every task. Music also calms excited spirits, as is read of David, who rescued Saul from the unclean spirit by the art of playing music.[12] 9

Quintilian, a most eloquent man, shows that the art of speaking, or rhetoric, is[13] in no way complete without music; he has written as follows: 10

> And I could be content even with the judgment of the ancients; for everyone knows that music, to take that first, already in those olden days was paid not only attention, but also veneration, so much so that the same men were accounted musicians, inspired poets, and sages. Others apart, the tradition reached the memory of later ages that both Orpheus and Linus were begotten by gods, and that the former, because he soothed even rough rustic minds with wonder- 11

> modo, sed saxa etiam silvasque duxisse posteritatis memoriae traditum est. Et Timagenes auctor est omnium in litteris studiorum antiquissimam musicam extitisse. Et testimonio sunt clarissimi poetae, apud quos inter regalia convivia laudes heroum ac deorum ad citharam canebantur: Iopas ille Vergilii nonne 'canit errantem lunam solisque labores'? Quibus certe [10r] palam confirmat auctor eminentissimus musicam cum divinarum etiam rerum cognitione[6] esse coniunctam, quod si datur erit etiam oratori necessaria, siquidem ut diximus, et cetera quae ipse pergit.

12 Erat etiam simplex veterum musica quemadmodum et Boethius refert, deinde paulatim virorum ingenia hanc auxerunt. Sic enim Censorinus comprobat:

> 13 Non[7] putes antiquiores cantus esse numeris, sed rusticos[8] et inconditos; postque hos poetica valuit, veluti legitima musica licentior magisque modulata.

14 Haec autem non modo rationabiles homines, sed inrationabilia animalia dum vocem canentium auscultant, ut aves, delectat, et ipsa quoque modulatione quadam concinere videntur. Illud idem et Isidorus confirmat: 'Ipsas quoque bestias necnon et serpentes, volucres, atque delphinos[9] ad [10v] auditum suae modulationis musica provocat.' Hoc et Augustinus sentit. Macrobius quoque haec inquit:

> 15 Et quid mirum si inter homines musicae tanta dominatio, cum aves quoque ut lusciniae et cycni aliaeque id genus cantum veluti quadam disciplina artis exercent?

16 Refert quoque Aulus Gellius de eius virtute utilitateque verba haec:

> 17 Creditum est hoc a plerisque[10] et memoriae mandatum, ischiaci cum maxime doleant, tum si modulis lenibus tibicen

> ment, drew not only wild beasts but rocks and forests after him. And Timagenes avers that music was the oldest of all literary pursuits.[14] This is attested by the most renowned poets, in whom the praises of heroes and gods were sung to the cithara at royal banquets. Does not Vergil's Iopas[15] sing of "the wandering moon and the sun's toils?"[16] With these words the most eminent author gives public confirmation that music is bound to the knowledge even of things divine; grant that, and the orator too will need it, seeing that, as we have said, etc.[17]

The music of the ancients, too, was simple, as indeed Boethius relates;[18] then gradually men's minds made it more complex. This is how Censorinus confirms it:[19] 12

> Do not think[20] that songs predated meter, but [only] rustic and uncouth ones; and after these poetry flourished, being so to speak rule-bound music with greater license and more restrained.[21] 13

This art delights not only rational human beings as they listen to singers' voices, but irrational animals too such as birds, and they too appear to join in, making a kind of music. That is also confirmed by Isidore: "Music incites the very beasts, and also snakes, birds, and dolphins, to hear her playing."[22] Augustine is of the same opinion.[23] Macrobius too says the following: 14

> And why wonder that music should have such power over human beings, seeing that birds too, such as nightingales and swans and others of that kind, practice song as if by some kind of training in the art?[24] 15

Aulus Gellius also reports on its power and efficacy as follows: 16

> It has been believed by many and committed to record that when sufferers from sciatica are at the height of their pain, 17

incinat minui dolores. Ego nuperrime in libro Theophrasti scriptum inveni viperarum morsibus tibicinem[11] scite modulateque adhibitum mederi. Refert et Democriti liber quod inscribitur *περὶ λοιμῶν ἢ λογικῶν κανών*,[12] id est de pestibus aut rationalium regula, in quo docet plurimis hominum morbis medici[11r]nam fuisse incentiones[13] tibiarum. Tanta prorsus est affinitas corporibus hominum mentibusque, et propterea quoque vitiis aut medelis animorum et corporum.

18 Et quoniam delphinos delectare musicam vidimus, ideo eundem Aulum Gellium ex ipso et Arione quaedam notatione dignissima referentem videamus:

19 Celeri admodum et cohibili oratione vocumque filio tereti et candido fabulam scripsit Herodotus super fidicine illo Arione. Vetus inquit et nobilis Ario cantator fidibus fuit. Is loco et oppido Meth<ymn>aeus terra atque insula omni Lesbius fuit. Eum Arionem rex Corinthi Periander amicum amatumque habuit artis gratia. Is inde a rege proficiscitur terras inclutas Siciliam atque Italiam viseret.[14] Ubi eo venit aures omnium mentesque in utriusque terrae urbibus demulsit. In quaestibus istic et voluptatibus amoribusque homi[11v]num fuit. Is tum postea grandi pecunia et re bona multa copiosus Corinthum instituit redire. Navem igitur et nautas, ut notiores amicioresque sibi, Corinthios delegit.

20 Sed eo[15] Corinthios homine accepto navique in altum provecta praedae pecuniaeque cupidos cepisse consilium de necando Arione. Tum illum ibi pernicie intellecta pecuniam ceteraque sua ut haberent dedisse, vitam modo sibi ut parce-

if an aulete then plays gentle melodies, their agony is abated. Just now I found it written in Theophrastus' book[25] that an aulete,[26] skillfully brought in and in good measure, cures adders' bites. Moreover,[27] Democritus' book entitled *On Plagues, or Canon of Logic,*[28] in which he teaches that very many human diseases were treated by playing auloi, reports this. So great, plainly, is the affinity between human beings' bodies and their minds, and therefore also of the failings or remedies of spirits and bodies.[29]

And since we have seen that music delights dolphins, let us 18
therefore see the same Aulus Gellius reporting some things most worthy of record about the dolphin and Arion:

In a very fast-moving and continuously flowing style, and a 19
smooth and delightful sequence of words, Herodotus wrote the story of the famous citharode Arion: "Arion[30] was an ancient and well-known singer to the cithara. By locality and town he came from Methymna, by country and the whole island from Lesbos. This Arion King Periander of Corinth counted as a dear friend[31] on account of his art. From there, leaving the king, he set out to visit the famous lands of Sicily and Italy.[32] When he arrived there he charmed the ears and minds of all in the cities of both countries. He lived profitably and pleasurably and beloved by the people. Then, after that, well supplied with abundant money and much wealth, he decided to return to Corinth. He therefore chose a Corinthian ship and crew as being better known and more kindly disposed to him."

But the Corinthians, having taken him on board, once the 20
ship was on the high seas, greedy for plunder and money, plotted together to kill Arion. Then he, having wind of his destruction, offered them on the spot his money and his other goods to keep, but begged them only to spare his life.

rent oravisse. Nautas precum eius harum commiser<i>tum esse illatenus ut ei necem afferre per vim suis manibus temperarent, sed imperavisse ut iam statim coram desiliret[16] praeceps in mare. Homo, inquit, ibi territus spe omni vitae perdita id unum postea oravit, ut priusquam mortem oppeteret induere permitterent sua sibi indumenta et fides capere, et canere carmen casus illius si[12^{r}]bi consolabile.

21 Feros et immanes nautas prolubium tum[17] audiendi subit; quod oraverat impetrat, atque ibi mox de more cinctus, amictus, ornatus, stansque in summae puppis foro, carmen quod orthium[18] dicitur voce sublatissima cantavit. Ad postrema cantus cum fidibus ornatuque omni sicut stabat canebatque, eiecit[19] sese procul in profundum. Nautae haud quaquam dubitantes quin perisset cursum quem facere coeperant tenuerunt.

22 Sed novum, et mirum, et pium facinus contigit. Delphinum inter undas repente adnavisse, et dorso super fluctus edito vectavisse, incolumique eum corpore et ornatu Taenarum in terram Laconicam devexisse. Tum Arionem prorsus ex eo loco Corinthum petivisse, talemque Periandro regi qualis delphino vectus fuerat sese obtulisse, eique rem sicuti acciderat narravisse.

23 Regem istaec [12^{v}] parum credidisse, Arionem quasi falleret custodiri iussisse, nautas requisitos ablegato Arione dissimulanter interrogasse, ecquid[20] audissent in iis locis unde venissent super Arione. Eos dixisse hominem cum inde irent in terra Italia fuisse, eumque illic bene agitare, et studiis delectationibusque urbium florere, atque in gratia pecuniaque magna fortunatum esse. Tum inter haec eorum verba Arionem cum fidibus et indumentis cum quibus se in salum eia-

The sailors were moved to pity by these prayers of his to the extent that they forbore to inflict death on him by violence with their own hands, but commanded him to leap headlong, at once and in their presence, into the sea. "At this, the terrified man, all hope of life lost, asked only one thing further, that before he went to his death they would allow him to put on his [singer's] robes, and take his cithara, and sing a song of consolation for himself in that sad case.

"At that,[33] the beastly and brutal sailors were overcome by 21
a desire to hear him; he obtained his request, and thereupon, girt, clad, and accoutred in the proper fashion, and standing on the poop deck, sang the song known as *orthios*[34] at the top of his voice. At the end of the song, with his cithara and all his accoutrements just as he stood singing, he threw himself off far into the deep. The sailors, with never a doubt that he had perished, held the course they had begun.

But an unprecedented and marvelous and loving[35] deed 22
took place." A dolphin suddenly swam up to him among the waves, and raising its back above the billows bore him and carried him, body and accoutrements safe, to Taenarum[36] in Laconian territory. Then Arion straight away went from there to Corinth, and showed himself to King Periander in the same state as he had ridden on the dolphin, and recounted the event to him just as it had happened.

The king could not believe it,[37] and ordered Arion to be 23
locked up for deceiving him. He sent for the sailors and with Arion out of the way asked them in pretended ignorance whether they had heard anything in the parts they had come from about Arion. They replied that he had been in Italy when they left there, and was doing well there, and flourishing amid the enthusiastic delight of the cities, and was rich and prosperous in good will and much money. Then, even as they were saying so, Arion burst in with his cithara

culaverat exstitisse. Nautas stupefactos convictosque ire infitias non quisse.

24 Haec Auli Gelli testimonio posui, ut quantae musica Arioni fuerit utilitati salutique notemus.

25 Non modo, ut nos in Dei laudem et sanctorum cantibus in ecclesiasticis caerimoniis utimur, veteres in sacrificiis deorum hymnos adhibebant, verum etiam et in funeribus praecinentes [13r] musicos secum ducebant. Hoc enim Macrobius verbis his ostendit:

26 Ideo canere caelum etiam theologi comprobantes[21] sonos musicos sacrificiis adhibuerunt, qui apud alios lyra et cithara, apud nonnullos tibiis aliisve musicis instrumentis fieri solebant. In ipsis quoque hymnis deorum per stropham et antistropham metra canoris versibus adhibebantur, ut per stropham rectus orbis stelliferi motus, per antistropham diversus vagarum regressus praedicaretur, ex quibus duobus motibus primus in natura hymnus dicandus deo sumpsit exordium.

27 Mortuos quoque ad sepulturam prosequi oportere cum cantu plurimarum gentium vel regionum instituta sanxerunt persuasione hac, qua post corpus animae ad originem dulcedinis musicae, id est ad caelum redire credantur. Nam ideo in hac vita [13v] omnis anima musicis sonis capitur, ut non solum qui sunt habitu cultiores, verum universae quoque barbarae nationes cantus quibus vel ardorem virtutis animentur, vel ad mollitiem voluptatis resolvantur,[22] exerceant, quia in corpus defert memoriam musicae cuius in caelo fuit conscia. Et ita delenimentis canticis occupantur, ut nullum

> and the robes in which he had flung himself into the sea. The astonished sailors, their guilt proved, were unable to deny it.[38]

I have quoted this text of Aulus Gellius as evidence so that we may observe how much music benefited Arion and saved his life. 24

Not merely did the ancients employ hymns in their sacrifices to the gods, just as we make use of vocal music in praise of God and the saints in church services, but they also took singers with them even at funerals. Macrobius demonstrates this as follows: 25

> Therefore the theologians, accepting that the sky made its own music, employed musical sounds at sacrifices; they were made among some peoples with lyre and cithara, among some with auloi or other musical instruments. Even in the hymns to the gods, too, meters with strophe and antistrophe were applied to sung verses,[39] so that the strophe expressed the straightforward motion of the starry sphere, the antistrophe the opposite, backward course of the planets. From those two movements the first hymn in nature to be dedicated to the god[40] drew its beginning. 26
>
> That the dead too should be accompanied to the grave with song has been laid down by the customs of very many nations or countries, persuaded by the belief that after [leaving] the body souls return to the origin of musical sweetness, that is, to the sky. For that is why in this life every soul is captivated by musical sounds, so that not only those who are more civilized in their conduct, but the entirety of the barbarian peoples too practice songs by which they are stirred to the ardor of courage, or relaxed into the softness of pleasure, because it brings down into the body the memory of the music of which it was aware in the sky. And they are so overcome by the comforts of song that no breast is so harsh or so 27

sit tam immite, tam asperum pectus quod non oblectamentorum talium teneatur affectu. Haec ille.

28 Omnia haec de musices[23] laudibus praelibanda putavi, ne quae sentio de ipsa solum a me sentire videar, sed ea peritissimorum virorum sententiis fulcita subtiliterque ab his indagata demonstrarim.[24] Hactenus de his, de scriptoribus inventoribusque disciplinae brevi iam sermone sequamur.

29 Musices igitur praeceptionem summo cum fundamento summaque ratione maiores instituerunt; nam [14r] non modo maiora, sed et minora nequaquam praetermittentes lucidis rationibus ipsius terminos aperuerunt.[25] Non enim desunt qui huius speculationem perspicuo ingenio scripserint. Quorum Divus Severinus (quem Boethium musici vocant) omnium princeps e Graeco sermone in Latinam linguam facundum transtulit opus. Necnon quam plurium musicorum sententias musicos modulos concernentes[26] <cum> eiusdem disciplinae mathematicis exemplis scripto mandabimus.

30 Quibus Guidonem Arretinum et Hucbaldum musicos quidem insignes sonora sui codicis verba legentes praeponendos arbitramur. Aliqua quoque ex Enchiriadis libro notatu dignissima perspiciemus, divique Augustini metricam musicam nostram ad rem spectantem cum his conseremus. Hos ceteris antelaturos diximus, quoniam reliquos hi et facun[14v]dia dicendi et arte excellunt. Praeter hos moderniores etiam meae sententiae cohaerentes hoc in opus transcribam, quid Isidorus iunior, quid Iohannes de Muris, quid doctor Goscalchus Parisiensis, quid Arnaldus Dalps Germanus, quid Marchettus Paduanus, quid abbas Populeti sive magister Blasius, ceterique multi senserunt quorum libris extant, opportunis in locis sua cuiusque dicta collocabo.

rough as not to be enthralled by the influence of such delights.[41]

I have considered it proper to begin with all these praises of music so as not to seem the sole source of my opinions about it, but rather that I may have shown them to rest on those of the most experienced men, the fruit of their subtle research. So much for them; let us now proceed with a few words about the writers on the discipline and its inventors. 28

The teaching of music, then, was established by our ancestors on the soundest foundation and with the utmost rationality. For they laid open its boundaries by lucid reasonings, absolutely not omitting not only greater but even lesser matters. For there are not wanting those who wrote down its theory with clear-sighted intellect; St. Severinus, whom musicians call Boethius, was the first of all to translate their eloquent work from Greek into Latin. We shall also record in writing the opinions of very many musicians concerning musical melodies with mathematical examples of the said discipline. 29

At their head we think it proper to place Guido of Arezzo and Hucbald, certainly distinguished musicians, as we read the resounding words of their text. We shall also look closely at some things from Enchiriades' book that are highly deserving of note. And together with these we shall join St. Augustine's book on meter, *De musica*, which is relevant to our concern. We have said that these will surpass the others, since they excel the rest in both fluency of speech and the art. Apart from these, I shall also copy more modern writers who agree with my opinion in this work: I shall record in appropriate places the respective opinions of Isidore Junior,[42] Johannes de Muris, Dr. Goschalcus of Paris, Arnaldus Dalps the Imperial subject, Marchetto of Padua, the abbot of Poblet, also called Master Blas, and many others whose books are extant. 30

31 Etsi multi inter philosophos de ipsa copiose libros ediderunt (quos Laertius connumerat), tamen illos per hos translatos conspicimus. Non igitur opus esset his addere commentaria, sed hosdem saepe saepiusque perlegisse cuique conduceret. Verumtamen cum librorum paenuria tum obscuritas eorundem novum opus me scripturum coegit.

32 Quis autem ipsam primo adinvenerit Isidorum audiamus:

> 33 Moyses dicit reper[15ʳ]torem musices artis fuisse Tubal, qui fuit de stirpe Cain ante diluvium. Graeci vero Pythagoram dicunt huius artis invenisse primordia ex malleorum sonitu et chordarum extensione percussa; alii Linum Thebaeum et Zethum et Amphionem[27] in musica arte primos claruisse ferunt, post quos paulatim directa est praecipue haec disciplina et aucta multis modis. Haec ille.

34 Hoc idem et Hugo vir quidem egregius comprobat.

35 Sed Mercurius tetrachordum instituisse primum dicitur. Nam simplicem fuisse musicam in initio apud bonos legimus, ita ut quattuor nervis usque ad Orphei tempora tota constaret. Hoc Boethius copiose dicit.

36 Quo modo Pythagoras e caelestibus sphaeris musicam cognoverit, atque deinde ex fabrorum malleis proportiones invenerit, Macrobium peritissimum quidem legamus. Cuius haec sunt [15ᵛ] verba:

> 37 Pythagoras primus omnium Graiae gentis hominum mente concepit et intellexit quidem compositum quiddam de sphaeris sonare propter necessitatem rationis, quae a caelestibus non recedit. Sed quae esset illa ratio vel quibus observanda modis, non facile deprehendebat. Cumque eum frus-

Although many among the philosophers published books about this in abundance (which Diogenes Laertius records), yet we see that the former were translated by the latter. There would therefore be no need to add commentaries to them, but it would be to everyone's advantage to have read them often and more often. However, both the scarcity of books and their obscurity compelled me to write a new work. 31

On its original inventor let us hear Isidore: 32

> Moses says that the discoverer of the art of music was Tubal, who was of the stock of Cain before the flood.[43] But the Greeks say that Pythagoras found out the rudiments of this art from the sound of hammers and the striking of stretched strings. Others report that Linus of Thebes and Zethus and Amphion were the first to have renown in the art of music. After them, little by little, this science above all was set in order and augmented in many ways.[44] 33

This same statement is endorsed by Hugh, an outstanding man to be sure.[45] 34

But Mercury is said to have created the first tetrachord, for we read in good authors that music was simple at the outset, so that it was entirely contained by four strings until Orpheus' time. This Boethius says at length.[46] 35

On how Pythagoras learned music from the heavenly spheres, and then discovered proportions from blacksmiths' hammers, let us read Macrobius, one indeed most expert. His words are these: 36

> Pythagoras was the first of all men of Grecian race who conceived in his mind and indeed understood that something composite sounded from the spheres by the necessity of a rational principle, which never deserts the things of heaven. But what that principle was, or how it was to be observed, he could not easily discover. And when lengthy investigation 37

tra tantae tamque arcanae rei diuturna inquisitio fatigaret, sors obtulit, quod cogitatio alta non reperit.

38 Cum enim casu praeteriret <in> publico fabros ignitum ferrum mollientes ictibus, in aures eius malleorum soni certo sibi respondentes ordine repente ceciderunt, in quibus ita grav<it>ati acumina consonabant, ut utrumque ad audientis sensum statuta dimensione remearet, et ex variis impulsibus unum sibi consonans nasceretur.

39 Hic occasionem sibi oblatam ratus deprehendendi oculis et manibus quod olim cogita[16r]tione quaerebat, fabros adit, et imminens operi curiosius intuetur annotans sonos, qui de singulorum lacertis conficiebantur; quos cum ferientium ascribendos viribus putaret, iubet ut inter se malleos mutent, quibus mutatis sonorum diversitas ab hominibus recedens malleos sequebatur.

40 Tum omnem curam ad pondera eorum examinanda convertit, cumque sibi diversitatem ponderis quod habebatur in singulis annotasset, aliis ponderibus in maius minusve excedentibus fieri malleos imperavit, quorum ictibus nequaquam prioribus similes, nec ita sibi consonantes exaudiebantur.

41 Tunc animadvertit concordiam vocis lege ponderum provenire;[28] collectisque numeris quibus consentiens sibi diversitas ponderum continebatur, ex malleis ad fides vertit examen, et intestina ovium vel boum nervos tam variis ponderibus illi[16v]gatis tetendit, qualia in malleis fuisse didicerat, talisque ex his concentus evenit, qualem prior observatio

of so great and so hidden a matter was wearying him in vain, chance brought him what deep thought did not find.

For when he happened to be passing in a public place some smiths who were softening heated iron by striking it, the sounds of their hammers, answering each other in a fixed order, suddenly fell upon his ears; among them, the high pitches made such consonance with the low that each returned to the listener's hearing at a fixed interval and from the various impacts a single entity, consonant with itself, was produced.[47] 38

Deeming that he had been offered an opportunity of grasping with his eyes and hands what he had long been seeking by thought, he went up to the smiths, peered closely at their work, and observed it with unusual care, noting the sounds that were produced by each man's arms. Thinking that they were due to the strength of the men striking the blows, he bade them change hammers; when they had done so, the difference in sound left the men and followed the hammers. 39

Then he turned all his care to examining their weights, and when he had ascertained the difference of weight there was in each, he ordered hammers to be made that exceeded or fell short of them in weight; their strokes resulted in sounds not at all like the previous ones and not so consonant with each other. 40

Then he realized that the concord in their sound depended on their weights. And having calculated the numbers in which this harmonious disagreement of weights was contained, he turned his examination from hammers to strings, and stretched the intestines of sheep and sinews of cattle by tying to them weights differing in the same ratios as he had discovered in the hammers, and such a concord came from them as his previous apt observation had promised, with the 41

non frustra animadversa promiserat, adiecta dulcedine quam natura fidium sonora praestabat.

42 Hinc Pythagoras tanti secreti compos deprehendit <numeros ex quibus soni sibi consoni nascerentur adeo ut fidibus sub hac>[29] numerorum observatione compositis certae certis aliaeque aliis convenientium sibi numerorum concordia tenderentur, ut una impulsa plectro alia licet longe posita sed numeris conveniens simul sonaret. Haec ille.

43 Fertur quoque a quibusdam tempore quodam Nilum multipliciter redundasse ita ut terrae circa eius litus operire<n>tur, post cuius recessum pisces innumerabiles absque aqua per campos relictos perisse. Acciditque eo tempore Mercurium per hanc pergere harenam cocleamque in qua piscis iam putrefactus erat invenisse, quam cocleam Mercurius accipiens nihil [17^{r}] praeter nervos quattuor eius piscis qui in ea fuerat invenisse dicitur, quos singillatim tangens hoc tetrachordum primus reperisse narratur.

44 Hoc enim tetrachordum usque ad Orpheum (ut diximus) duravit. Quintam chordam deinde Coroebus Atyis filius qui fuit Lydorum rex adiunxit. Hyagnis vero Phryx sextum his apposuit nervum. Sed septimus nervus a Terpandro Lesbio adiunctus est, secundum scilicet vii planetarum similitudinem. Samius Lycaon octavam his adiunxit. Prophrastus autem Pieriotes[30] ad graviorem partem unam addidit chordam ut faceret totum enneachordum. Histiaeus[31] Colophonius decimam in graviorem partem coaptavit chordam. Timotheus Milesius xi^{am} et deinceps ceteri multas coniunxerunt chordas, ut suo libro Boethius auctor est, qui chordarum et ipsorum nomina singulatim ponit.

additional sweetness that the sonorous nature of strings provided.

Hence Pythagoras, being in possession of so great a secret, discovered the numbers from which sounds consonant with each other were generated, so that if the strings were tuned[48] in accordance with the numerical pattern thus observed, given strings were stretched by given numbers, different strings by different numbers, according to the concord of numbers in mutual agreement, so that when one was struck by the plectrum another, far away yet numerically agreeing with it, sounded at the same time.[49] 42

It is reported by some that on a certain occasion the Nile flooded far more than usual, so that the lands about its banks were covered; after its retreat countless fish perished, left without water all over the fields. And it happened at that time that Mercury made his way through this sand and found a shell in which a fish had already rotted; Mercury is said to have taken the shell and found nothing but four tendons of the fish that had been in it; he is reported to have touched them one by one and thus become the first to discover this tetrachord.[50] 43

This tetrachord,[51] as we have said, lasted down to Orpheus.[52] The fifth string was then added by Coroebus,[53] son of Atys, who was king of the Lydians; Hyagnis the Phrygian appended a sixth. But the seventh string was added by Terpander of Lesbos, by analogy, of course, with the seven planets. Lycaon of Samos added an eighth,[54] Prophrastus[55] of Pieria added a string at the lower end to make the whole an enneachord. Histiaeus of Colophon fitted a tenth string at the lower end. Timotheus of Miletus added an eleventh, and then the rest added numerous strings, as Boethius avers in his book; he also gives the names of the strings and their inventors individually.[56] 44

45 [17v] Sunt autem nobis tria musicae genera praeter ea Boethii, quae breviter indicanda esse in huius libri principio statui. Horum enim generum[32] planam primo, deinde contrapunctalem, postremo organicam sive figurativam musicam demonstrabimus. Quae quidem omnia serie ostensa per capitula vel capita finem nostro operi imponent.[33] Quare speculativae primum dicenda aliqua cum auctorum quorundam dictis concinne congrediemur, deinde practicabilis fundamenta suo loco evidenti ratione quam brevissime dici poterit consequemur.

46 Quid igitur Musica sit, undeque dicatur disertos audiamus viros, qui peritissime id definiunt. Deinde quot eius genera sint pergemus.

: II :

Quid sit Musica, undeque dicatur

1 [18r] Musica igitur dicta est *ἀπὸ τῶν* Μουσῶν, id est a Musis,[34] vel *παρὰ τὸ μῶσθαι*, id est a quaerendo, eo quod per illam sonus cuiusque modulationis quaeritur; Graece autem *μουσική* dicitur. Initium autem psallendi ecclesiae extitit vel ad imitationem priscorum, qui inter sacrificiorum exhibitiones Deo laudes persolvere solebant. Vel ab Ignatio beatissimo martyre traditum suscepit, qui voces angelicas domino decantantes audivit, eundemque morem suae ecclesiae tradidit, atque inde in alias ecclesias eadem consuetudo laudabilis inolevit. Apud Latinos autem beatissimus Ambrosius Mediolanensis auctor extitit episcopus, a quo hunc morem omnis occidentalis ecclesia suscepit.

2 Augustinus autem haec dicit:

We have three kinds of music besides those of Boethius,[57] which I have decided need to be briefly indicated at the beginning of this book. Of these kinds we shall first elucidate plainchant, then contrapuntal music, finally organic or figured.[58] The complete explanation in due order of all these by chapters or heads[59] shall conclude our work. Therefore we shall first in due order set about saying some things by way of theory with the sayings of certain authors, then follow with the foundations of practical music in their place by manifest reasoning as briefly as it can be stated. 45

On what music is, therefore, and why it is so called, let us hear the eloquent men who have most expertly defined it. We shall then go on to consider how many kinds of it there are. 46

: II :

What music is and why it is so called

Music, then, was named *apò tôn Mousôn,* that is, "from the Muses," or *parà tò môsthai,* that is, "from [the verb] 'to seek,'" because through it the sound of every melody is sought.[60] In Greek it is called *mousikḗ*. Now singing began for the Church either in imitation of the ancients, who during the performances of sacrifices used to render praises to a god,[61] or [the Church] adopted it as a tradition from the most blessed martyr Ignatius, who heard angelic voices singing to the Lord, and handed down the same practice to his church,[62] and thence the same praiseworthy custom spread among other churches. Among the Latins the most blessed bishop Ambrose of Milan was the authority from whom the entire Western church took up this practice.[63] 1

Augustine says as follows: 2

> 3 Musica est scientia bene modulandi. Igitur modulatio a modo est nominata. [18v] Modus non erit nisi in rebus quae motu aliquo fiunt, et ideo modulatio non incongrue dicitur movendi quaedam peritia. Ergo scientia modulandi scientia est bene movendi.

4 Isidorus haec quoque dicit: 'Musica est peritia modulationis sono cantuque consistens, et inde dicta musica per derivationem a musis.' Quod Papias quoque suo vocabulorum libro affirmat. Hugo autem vir et doctor peritissimus haec etiam de musica: 'Musica ab aqua vocabulum sumpsit eo quod nulla euphonia, id est bona sonoritas sine umore fieri possit.' Brito quoque vir eruditus ita inquit:

> 5 Musica est una de septem liberalibus artibus, dicta a moys quod est aqua, quia olim primo inventa fuit in hydraulis, id est aquaticis instrumentis, et in malleis fabrilibus a Pythagora, vel ideo dicitur a moys, quia tractat de vocibus et de proportionibus vocum, et sine [19r] umoris beneficio nulla cantilenae vel vocis delectatio subsistit.

6 Hoc idem et Uguccio confirmat. Censorinus autem vir profecto disertissimus ita: 'Musica est peritia faciendorum et canendorum modorum.' Abbatis Populeti haec subiungemus: 'Quia musica quae recte canendi ars dicitur, cuius negotium habet consonantiam pro formali subiecto, in artificium et exercitationem dividitur.' Possem autem[35] et multorum prosequi sententias, sed tamen horum nobis eae sufficere[36] possunt. Nunc idcirco quot musicae genera sunt breviter videamus. Et in primis Boethium ipsius disciplinae disertissimum audiamus.

> Music is the science of making melody (*modulandi*) well. 3
> Now *modulatio* is so called from *modus* ["melody, measure"]. There will be no measure except in things that take place by means of some movement. And therefore the name *modulatio* is not inappropriately given to a skill at moving. And therefore the science of making melody is the science of moving well.[64]

Isidore says this too: "Music is the skill of making melody, con- 4
sisting in sound and song. And therefore it is called music by derivation from the Muses."[65] Papias affirms that in his book of words.[66] Hugh, a most expert man and teacher, says this too about music: "Music took its name from water because no euphony, that is, good sonority, can occur without moisture."[67] Brito too, a learned man, says thus:

> Music is one of the seven liberal arts, so called from *moys*, 5
> which is "water,"[68] because of old it was first discovered by Pythagoras in *hydrauli*, that is, water organs, and in blacksmiths' hammers. Alternatively, it is derived from *moys* because it deals with sounds and the proportions of sounds, and without the benefit of moisture there is no pleasure in singing or sounds.[69]

This is also confirmed by Uguccio.[70] Censorinus, assuredly a 6
most eloquent man, speaks thus: "Music is the skill of making and singing melodies."[71] We shall add the following from the abbot of Poblet: "Because music, which is called the art of singing correctly, whose business has consonance for its formal subject, is divided into theoretical system[72] and practice [. . .]." I could continue with many persons' opinions, but those opinions of these writers may suffice us.[73] Therefore let us briefly see now how many kinds of music there are. And first let us hear Boethius, most eloquent in this art.

: III :

De tribus musices generibus

1 In principio igitur de musica disserenti[37] illud interim dicendum videtur quot musicae genera ab eius studi<os>is comprehensa esse noveri[19v]mus. Sunt autem tria: et prima quidem mundana, secunda humana, tertia quae in quibusdam instrumentis constituta, ut in cithara vel in tibiis ceterisque quae cantilenae famulantur. Marcus Tullius Cicero de re publica sive de somn<i>o Scipionis hoc idem confirmare videtur. Nam dicit homines a cursu planetarum sonoro musicam in nervis adinvenisse, his utens verbis:

2 > Illi autem octo cursus in quibus eadem vis duorum septem efficiunt distinctis[38] intervallis sonos, qui numerus rerum omnium fere nodus.[39] Quod docti homines nervis imitati atque cantibus aperuerunt[40] sibi reditum[41] in hunc locum.

3 Boethius vero eadem genera demonstrans his verbis usus est:

4 > Ea quae est mundana in his maxime prospicienda, quae in ipso caelo vel compage elementorum vel varietate temporum visuntur.

5 Deinde, quod in volubilitate siderum sit sonus, [20r] necesse illud probans sequitur: 'Qui enim fieri potest, ut tam velox caeli machina tacito silentique cursu moveatur?'

6 Hoc idem et Macrobius ita affirmat:

: III :

On the three kinds of music

As I begin my exposition on music, then, I think that at this point it must be stated how many kinds of music we know to have been covered by its students. There are three. The first is that of the universe (*mundana*), the second human, the third the kind consisting in certain instruments such as the cithara or auloi and the others that accompany singing.[74] Cicero, in *On the Republic* or *The Dream of Scipio*,[75] appears to confirm this same thing, for he says that human beings discovered stringed music from the sounding course of the planets, using these words: 1

> But those eight courses, of which two have the same force,[76] create seven sounds at distinct intervals; that number is the node of virtually everything. Educated persons, imitating this on strings and in sounds, have opened up for themselves a return to this place [the heavens]. 2

Boethius, setting forth the same [three] kinds, used these words: 3

> That [music] which is of the universe is above all to be sought in those things that are observed in the sky itself, or in the assemblage of the elements, or in the variation of the seasons.[77] 4

Then, proving that there must be sound in the revolutions of the planets, he continues: "For how can it be possible that so swift-moving a celestial mechanism can move in a silent and soundless course?"[78] 5

Macrobius too asserts the same thing thus: 6

7 Ex ipso enim circumductu orbium sonum nasci necesse est, quia percussus aer ipso interventu ictus vim de se fragoris emittit, ipsa cogente natura, ut in sonum desinat duorum corporum violenta collisio. Sed is sonus <qui>[42] ex qualicumque aeris ictu nascitur, aut dulce quiddam in aures et musicum defert, aut ineptum et asperum sonat. Nam si ictu<m> observatio numerorum certa moderetur, compositum sibique consentiens modulamen educitur, at[43] cum increpat tumultuaria et nullis modis gubernata collisio, fragor turbidus et inconditus offendit auditum. In caelo autem constat nihil fortuitum, nihil tumultuarium[44] convenire, sed universa divinis [20v] illic legibus et statuta ratione procedere. Haec Macrobius.

8 De secunda autem musica, ita Boethius verba subiungit:

9 Humanam vero musicam quisque in se ipsum descendit intelliget: Quid est enim quod illam incorpoream vivacitatem rationis corpori misceat, nisi quaedam coaptatio et veluti gravium leviumque vocum quasi unam consonantiam efficiens temperatio? Quid est aliud quod ipsius intra se partes animae coniungat, quae, ut Aristoteli placet, ex rationabili inrationabilique coniuncta est?

10 Lucius vero Apuleius ad Faustinum filium de cosmographia[45] libro de anima loquens hoc dicit:

11 Verum substantiam mentis huius numeris et modis confici congeminatis et multiplicatis <augmentis> incrementisque per se <et>[46] extrinsecus partis, et hinc fieri ut musicae mundus et canore move<a>tur. Haec ille.

> For from the very rotation of the spheres it is necessary for a sound to be generated, since the struck air by the very intervention of the blow releases the force of the clash from itself, Nature herself compelling the violent collision of two bodies to end in sound. But that sound, which is generated from any kind of blow to the air, either brings something sweet and musical to the ears, or sounds uncouth and rough. For if a sure observance of numbers controls the blow, a coherent and harmonious melody is produced, but when the noise comes from a haphazard collision, not governed by any measures, the confused and unregulated clash offends the hearing. Now it is an established fact that nothing accidental, nothing haphazard happens in the heavens, but all things proceed there according to divine laws and fixed proportion.[79] 7

On the second [kind of] music Boethius adds the following: 8

> As for human music, whoever descends into himself shall understand it; for what is it that blends that incorporeal vitality of reason with the body but a kind of fitting together and as it were attuning that makes so to speak a single consonance of low and high[80] pitches? What else is there that should join together the parts of the very soul, which according to Aristotle[81] is joined together out of the rational and the irrational?[82] 9

Lucius Apuleius, addressing his son Faustinus on the subject of soul in his book on cosmography, says the following: 10

> But [Plato says] that the substance of this mind is composed of numbers and measures augmented and multiplied with additions and increases obtained by itself and from outside,[83] and that is why the world moves musically and in song.[84] 11

12 Marcus Tullius Cicero libro etiam de universitate dicit haec: [21r] 'Est autem animus ex omnibus rationis contentionibusque harmonia.'[47] Hugo quoque sic:

13 Musica inter corpus et animam est illa naturalis amicitia, qua[48] anima corpori non corporeis vinculis, sed affectibus quibusdam colligatur, ad movendum et sensificandum ipsum corpus, secundum quam amicitiam nemo carnem suam odio habuit.

14 Item et de tertia haec Boethius inquit:

15 Tertia est musica quae in quibusdam consistere dicitur instrumentis. Haec vero administratur aut intentione, ut nervis, aut spiritu, ut tibiis vel his quae ad aquam moventur, aut percussione <quadam, ut in his quae in concava> quaedam aerea feriuntur, atque inde diversi efficiuntur soni.

16 Has enim tres musicas copiose Boethius suo libro ostendit. Isidorus vero has musicae partes dicit:

17 Musicae partes sunt tres, id est harmonica, rhythmica, et metrica. Harmonica est, quae decernit acutum et grave; rhythmica est [21v] quae requirit incursionem verborum, utrum bene sonus an male cohaereat; metrica est quae mensuram metrorum probabili ratione cognoscit.

18 Et quoniam in musica vocem per ascensum et descensum agimus, idcirco quid ipsa sit explicemus.

Cicero too, in his book *On the Universe,* says as follows: "The soul[85] is and from all contentions of reason a harmony."[86] Hugh too says: 12

> Music is that natural friendship between the body and the soul, whereby the soul is bound to the body not by bodily chains but by certain affections, in order to move the body and make it sensitive, by which friendship "no man hated his own flesh."[87] 13

Furthermore, Boethius says of the third kind: 14

> The third is the music that is said to reside in certain instruments. This is provided either by tension, as on strings, or by blown air, as on auloi or instruments moved in accordance with water,[88] or by a kind of percussion, as in those that are struck against certain concave bronze objects, so that[89] various sounds are produced from them.[90] 15

These three kinds of music are set out at copious length by Boethius in his book. Isidore lists the following parts of music: 16

> There are three components of music, namely harmonics, rhythmics, and metrics. Harmonics is that which distinguishes high and low; rhythmics is that which examines the encounter of words for whether the sound hangs together well or ill; metrics is that which ascertains the measure of meters by scientific proof.[91] 17

And since in music we lead the voice by ascent and descent, let us therefore explain what it is. 18

: IIII :

Quid vox, undeque dicatur, et quot eius species

1 Omnium peritorum de voce eadem fere est sententia. Namque ut Papias inquit, 'vox est materia verborum, verba vero formata vocem indicant.' Ea in corpore animato praesertim rationabili a pulmone per gutturis concavum formata est. Cuius formationi, ut abbas Populeti dicit, haec conveniunt, pulmo, guttur, labia, dentes, et lingua. Hanc enim Marcus Tullius Cicero ita describit:

2 Figura vocis est quae suum quendam possidet habitum ratione et industria comparatum. [22r] Ea dividitur in tres partes, magnitudinem, firmitudinem, et mollitudinem. Magnitudinem vocis maxime comparat natura, nonnihil auget, sed maxime conservat accuratio.[49] Firmitudinem vocis maxime natura comparat,[50] nonnihil adauget et maxime conservat exercitatio declamationis. Mollitudinem vocis—hoc est ut eam torquere pro nostro commodo possimus—maxime faciet exercitatio declamationis. Haec Tullius.

3 Dicunt igitur esse vocem aerem ad linguam ictum auditu sensibilem a verbo Graeco *βοάω βοῶ* dictam. Hoc est voco Latine.

4 Vocare Nonius Marcellus positum pro trahere et ducere dicit; nam ab imo pectore vocem trahimus et deducimus. Hinc illud Gregorii in Moralibus dicitur: 'Nos quippe cum flamus aerem ab exterioribus introrsum trahimus, et introrsus tractum hunc exterius reddimus.' [22v] Vel dicta quod animi voluntatem annuntiet. Augustinus in quodam sermone hoc dicit: 'Vox sonus est, et index

: IV :

What the voice is, why it is so called, and how many species of it there are

All the learned are more or less agreed on the voice. For as Papias says: "The voice is the matter of words,[92] whereas words given form indicate the voice."[93] In an animate body, especially a rational one, it is formed by the lung through the hollow of the throat. For its formation, as the abbot of Poblet says, the following are needed: the lung, the throat, the lips, the teeth, and the tongue.[94] Cicero[95] describes it as follows: 1

> The shape of the voice is that which has a certain character of its own, acquired through method and hard work. It is divided into three parts, volume, firmness, and suppleness.[96] Volume of voice is chiefly provided by nature; taking care of it adds something, but above all preserves it. Firmness of voice is chiefly provided by nature; the practice of declamation adds something, and above all preserves it. Suppleness of voice, that is, the ability to manipulate it at our convenience, will chiefly be created by the practice of declamation. 2

Therefore they say that the voice is air struck against the tongue and perceptible by hearing, so called from the Greek verb *boáō boô*.[97] In Latin that is *voco*.[98] 3

Nonius Marcellus says that *vocare* is used for *trahere* "pull, draw" and *ducere* "lead,"[99] for we draw and lead the voice from the bottom of the chest. Hence Gregory's statement in his *Moralia:* "For when we blow, we draw air in from outside, and having drawn it in let it out."[100] Alternatively, it is so called because it announces the will of the mind.[101] Augustine says in a sermon: "Voice is sound, 4

cogitationum, verbum vero ipsa cogitatio.' Isidorus quoque ita de voce:

> 5 Vox est aer spiritu verberatus, unde et verba sunt nuncupata. Proprie autem vox hominum est seu inrationabilium animalium vel animantium;[51] nam in aliis abusive et non proprie sonitum vocari vocem constat, ut 'vox tubae infremuit,' 'fractasque[52] ab littore voces.' Nam proprium est ut 'littorei sonent scopuli,' 'et tuba terribilem sonitum procul aere canoro.' Haec ille.

6 Priscianus autem pulcherrimam de voce divisionem, ut suo libro liquide inspici potest ostendit.

7 Verum non de voce ut ibi vel quemadmodum logici definiunt in musica dicimus. Sed ut abbas Populeti verbis his utens:

> 8 Tractaturi<s> de voce primo sciendum est quod musica non trac[23r]tat de voce, ut grammaticus aut logicus, sed de voce quae est sonus aptus ad harmoniam prolatus ex ore animalis formato.[53]

9 Lactantius vero Firmianus secundo de ira Dei libro peritissime de voce formanda haec inquit:

> 10 De voce autem quam rationem reddere possumus? Grammatici quidem ac philosophi vocem esse definiunt aerem spiritu verberatum, unde verba sunt nuncupata, quod perspicue falsum est. Non enim vox extra os gignitur sed intra. Et ideo verisimilior est illa sententia, stipatum spiritum cum obstantia[54] faucium fuerit illisus[55] sonum vocis experimere, veluti

and the indicator of thoughts; word is the thought itself."[102] Isidore too says of voice:[103]

> Voice is air struck (*verberatus*) by breath, which is why words 5
> (*verba*) are so called.[104] Properly, voice belongs to human beings or to irrational animals or living creatures;[105] for in other things it is agreed that sound is called "voice" catachrestically[106] and not properly,[107] as "the voice of the trumpet roared,"[108] and "voices broken by the shore."[109] For it is proper that "the rocks of the shore should sound,"[110] and "the trumpet [burst into] a fearful sound far off with singing bronze."[111]

Priscian exhibits a very fine classification of voice, as may be 6
clearly observed in his book.[112]

However, in music we are not speaking about the voice as dis- 7
cussed there, or as the logicians define it, but as the abbot of Poblet does, using these words:

> Now that we are about to treat of the voice, we must first 8
> know that music does not treat of the voice as the grammarian or the logician does, but of the voice that is a sound suitable for harmony, uttered from the shaped mouth of an animate being.

Lactantius Firmianus in his second book *On the Wrath of God* 9
says the following, most expertly, on the formation of the voice:[113]

> But what account can we render of the voice? The grammar- 10
> ians and philosophers define the voice as being air struck by breath, from which words derive their name, which is obviously false, for the voice is generated not outside but inside the mouth. And therefore the other opinion is more probable, that concentrated breath, after being dashed against the obstacles in the throat, gives off the sound of the voice, as

cum in patentem cicutam labroque subiectam dimittimus spiritum, et is cicutae concavo repercussus ac revolutus a fundo dum descendentem occursu suo reddit[56] ad exitum nitens sonum gignit, et in vocalem spiritum resiliens per se ven[23v]tus animatur. Quod quidem an verum sit, Deus artifex viderit. Videtur enim non ab ore, sed ab intimo pectore vox oriri. Denique ex[57] ore clauso ex naribus emittitur sonus qualis potest. Praeterea ex[58] maximo spiritu quo anhelamus, vox non efficitur, et levi et non coartato spiritu quoties volumus efficitur. Haec ipse.

11 Vergilius quoque 'imo trahens a pectore vocem' in Aeneide dicit. Aulus quoque Gellius ita de voce sentit: 'Vetus atque perpetua quaestio inter nobilissimos philosophorum agitata est, corpusne sit vox, an incorporeum,' et quae ipse pergit. Deinde subiungit:

12 Sed vocem Stoici corpus esse contendunt, eamque esse dicunt ictum aera. Plato autem non esse vocem corpus putat: non enim percussus, inquit, aer, sed plaga ipsa atque percussio vox est.

13 Et paulo post ibidem:

14 Democritus ac deinde Epicurus [24r] ex individuis corporibus vocem constare dicunt, eamque ut ipsis eorum verbis utar, *ῥεῦμα λόγων*,[59] id est flumen verborum appellant. Haec Gellius.

15 Vocum species, ut Isidorus ostendit, hae sunt. Suavis, perspicua, subtilis, pinguis, dura, aspera, caeca, vinnolata, et perfecta. Quarum definitionem singulis et is praebet:

> when we let our breath down into an open reed pressed against the lips, and it bounces off the hollow of the reed and turns back from the bottom; in giving back[114] the descending voice by collision with itself, in its struggle to get out it generates sound, and the wind, rebounding by itself, is enlivened into a vocal breath. Whether this be true let God the craftsman determine. For the voice appears to arise not from the mouth but from the inmost breast. In addition, from the closed mouth,[115] from the nostrils, such sound is emitted as is possible. Moreover, voice is not formed by[116] the very strong breath with which we gasp, and is formed by a light and unconfined breath whenever we wish.[117]

Vergil, too, in the *Aeneid* says "drawing his voice from the depth of his breast."[118] Aulus Gellius, too, holds the following opinion on the voice: "It is an old and standing question[119] argued among the most famous philosophers whether the voice is a body or a thing incorporeal,"[120] and so on. He then adds: 11

> But the Stoics contend that the voice is a body, and say that it is struck air. Plato, however, does not think that voice is a body, for, he says, the voice is not struck air, but the blow and striking itself.[121] 12

And a little later[122] in the same place: 13

> Democritus and after him Epicurus say that the voice consists of indivisible bodies, and they call it, to use their very own words, *rheûma lógōn*,[123] that is, a stream of words. 14

The species of voices, on Isidore's showing, are these: sweet, perspicuous, subtle, fat, hard, rough, blind, curly, and perfect. He also provides definitions for each of these: 15

16 Suaves voces sunt subtiles et spissae, clarae atque acutae. Perspicuae voces sunt quae longius protrahuntur, ita ut omnem continuum impleant[60] locum, sicut clangor tubarum. Subtiles voces sunt quibus non est vehemens[61] spiritus, quales sunt infantium, vel mulierum, vel aegrotantium, et[62] sicut in nervis; quae enim subtilissimae chordae sunt, subtiles ac tenues sonos emittunt. Pingues sunt voces quando spiritus multus simul egreditur sicut virorum. Acuta vox est tenuis et alta, sicut in chordis videmus. [24v] Dura vox est, quae violenter emittit sonos, sicut incudis[63] sonus quoties in durum malleus percutitur ferrum. Aspera vox est rauca, quae dispergitur per minutos et dissimiles pulsus. Caeca vox est quae mox ut emissa fuerit conticescit, atque suffocata nequaquam longius producitur, sicut est in fictilibus. Vinnolata verum est quae est mollis atque flexibilis, quae vinnolata dicta a vinno, hoc est a cincinno molliter flexo. Perfecta autem vox est alta, suavis, et clara: alta, ut in sublimis[64] sufficiat; clara, ut aures adimpleat; suavis, ut animos audientium blandiat. Si ex his aliquid defuerit, vox perfecta non erit.

17 Haec de voce satis sint; quid cantus sit animadvertamus.

18 Cantus igitur est inflexio vocis per arsin et thesin. Arsis ut Isidoro et Guidoni placet est vocis elevatio, hoc est in ascensum vocum deduc[25r]tio. Thesis vero vocis positio, id est vocum a fine in pristinum locum reductio. Boethius autem intensionem in nervis et remissionem dicit. Sed abbas Populeti ita inquit: 'Cantus est compositio vocum debitam consequens proportionem.' Haec de cantu sufficiant.

Sweet voices are slender, dense, clear,[124] and high-pitched. Perspicuous voices are those that extend to some distance, so that they fill the entire adjacent area, such as the blare of trumpets.[125] Slender voices are those without vigorous breath, like those of babies, or women, or the sick, and as in strings, for those chords that are slenderest emit slender and thin sounds. Voices are fat when a great deal of breath comes out with them, like those of men. A high-pitched voice is thin and high,[126] as we see in strings. A hard voice is one that emits sounds violently, like the sound of an anvil whenever a hammer is struck against hard iron. A harsh voice is a raucous one, spread by tiny and dissimilar pulses. A blind voice is one that as soon as it has been uttered falls silent, and, being choked, does not reach very far, as in the case of earthenware vessels. A curly (*vinnolata*) voice is one that is supple and flexible; it is called *vinnolata* from *vinnus*, that is, from a softly curved curl. A perfect voice is high, sweet, and clear: high, that it may hold out in the highest [pitches];[127] clear, that it may fill the ears; sweet, that it may soothe the listeners' spirits. If any of these qualities is lacking, the voice will not be perfect.[128] 16

Let this be enough on the voice; let us observe what singing is. 17

Singing, then, is an inflection of the voice by arsis and thesis.[129] 18
Arsis, according to Isidore[130] and Guido,[131] is a raising of the voice, that is, a leading of notes (*vocum*) into ascent. Thesis by contrast is the putting down of the voice, that is, the leading of notes from their final pitch back to their original place.[132] Boethius, however, speaks of "tautening," with reference to strings, and "loosening."[133] But the abbot of Poblet says thus: "Singing is the putting together of notes that achieves due proportion." Let this suffice on singing.

: V :

Quare vocabula in ipsa musica ab auctoribus sint vocitata vel instituta

1 Vocabula planae musices ab ipsis scriptoribus usurpata non frustra notatu digna duxi ponenda. Primum sane in laeva musicales terminos instituerunt, et iure quidem; namque in dextra non libri principium vel cantuum caput conveniret eo ritu quo laeva quadrat, nisi Hebraeorum more scriptum velimus. Distributa sunt autem litterarum et vocum nomina per eius coniuncturas, ut quemadmodum sidera sive planetae in compaginibus caelorum [25v] ob volubilitatem musicum sonum reddunt, ita quoque his iuncturis humana nostrae vocis harmonia comparetur.

2 Litteras deinde septem his nominibus praebuerunt, ut quemadmodum annus ex mensibus, mensis ex hebdomadis, hebdomada de septem dierum numero conficiuntur, sic et tota musica ex eodem litterarum numero consistat. Unde abbas Populeti:

> 3 Littera in cantu idem est quod signum per quod aliud datur ad aliud significari. Nam sicut in corpore materiali continuo aliquae mensurae quibus talis quantitas mensuratur, sic vocum distantia quibusdam litteris demonstratur.

4 Et alio loco:

> 5 Litterae septem ab antiquis assignatae quia septem sunt sphaerae planetarum, volentibus assimilationem inter caelestem et nostram musicam servare.

: V :

Why terms were named or instituted by authors in music itself

I have deemed it my duty to record the vocabulary of *musica plana*[134] used by those writers; it is well worth noting. First of all, they laid out the musical terms on the left hand, and rightly so, for the start of a book or the beginning[135] of songs would not be appropriate on the right in the way that the left fits, unless we would have it written in the Jewish manner. Now the names of the letters and pitches have been distributed through its joints, so that, just as the stars or planets in the heavenly structures yield a musical sound because of their circular motion, so too by these joints the harmony of our human voice may be achieved.[136] 1

Then they have provided seven letters for these names, so that just as the year is made up of months, the month of weeks, and the week of the tally of seven days, so too the whole of music may consist of the same number of letters. Whence the abbot of Poblet says: 2

> The letter in singing is the same thing as the sign whereby one thing is put for another to be signified. For as in the case of a continuous material body there are certain measures by which such and such a quantity is measured, so the distance of pitches is indicated by certain letters. 3

And elsewhere: 4

> Seven letters were assigned by the ancients because there are seven spheres of the planets, since they wished to preserve the resemblance between heavenly music and our own. 5

6 Tullius de re publica de septenario numero hoc inquit: [26r] 'Septem efficiunt distinctos intervallis sonos, qui numerus rerum omnium fere nodus est.'

7 Sex autem voces nec plures nec pauciores eo numero dixerunt, quoniam perfectissimam in eo numero quantitatem arithmetae[65] et geometrae indagantes invenerunt. Nam circulum circino formatum vel circumscriptum, postea mensum a centro per[66] circumferentiam, ea dimensio sextupla[67] per gyrum finita experitur. Hoc inquam quoniam praeter rotundum non datur perfectio figuris aliis, ut quadro et triangulo vel ceteris.

8 De quibus notulis abbas Populeti:

> 9 Ex multiplicatione litterarum et intensione cantus antiqui aequivocantes sex nomina voci,[68] quae est sonus humano ore prolatus, imposuerunt.

10 Quae nomina sunt ut re mi fa sol la, quibus debitis quantitatibus distantibus cantus omnis proponitur.

11 Lineas ad fidium si[26v]militudinem in manu et libro institutas videmus; spatia vero earum intervalla, ut quemadmodum in illis sonus nascitur, ita quoque his vox humana temperetur.

12 Tres postea proprietates, id est naturam, bmolle, et ♮quadrum, quia omnis sive corporum voces sive instrumentorum soni aut dulce vel bmollatice, aut dure vel ♮quadrate, aut naturaliter tempore his dominante sonant vel respondent. Nam bona corporis habitudo dulcem pectori vocem emissam permittit, verum eo minus asperam et laboratam deducendam inde formabit. Sunt quoque qui ciborum vel solis et imbris varietate optimas vel deteriores

Cicero, in *De re publica*, speaking of the number seven, says the 6
following: "They [the courses of the spheres] make seven sounds separated by intervals; that number is the node of virtually everything."[137]

However, they named six pitches,[138] neither more nor fewer 7
than that number, because arithmeticians and geometers on investigation found the most perfect quantity in it.[139] For if a circle has been formed with a compass, or drawn round [a point], and afterwards measured from the center to the circumference, six times that measurement, delimited in circuit, finds it out.[140] I say this because apart from the round [circle], perfection is not given to other figures, such as the square and the triangle and the rest.

Of these notes the abbot of Poblet says: 8

> From the multiplication of letters, and the improvement[141] 9
> of singing, the ancients, by equivocation,[142] imposed six names on the voice, which is the sound produced from the human mouth.[143]

These names are *ut re mi fa sol la*. Every song is performed with 10
them at the due distances.

We see lines defined by the analogy of strings in the hand and 11
the book; the spaces between them are intervals, so that as in them sound is born, so too by them the human voice is controlled.[144]

Next, [we see] three properties, namely nature, *bmolle*, and 12
♮*quadrum*,[145] for all voices produced by bodies or sounds produced by instruments sound or answer either sweetly (or in *bmolle*), or hard (or in ♮*quadrum*), or naturally as time governs them.[146] For a good disposition of the body permits a sweet voice (to be) uttered from the breast, and thence will give it the less harsh and labored a form when it is to be drawn out. There are also those who utter better or worse[147] voices according to the variation of diet or of sun and rain, which are natural because they follow the nature of

emittunt, idcirco naturales, quoniam temporum vel rerum naturam sequuntur. Abbas Populeti haec de his:

13 Omnis recta vocum associatio aut aspere pronuntiatur, aut modulatur lente, vel utrumque reiciens extre[27ʳ]mum mediocriter personatur.[69] Quapropter omnis cantus unius generis istorum necesse est sit aut proprietatis.

14 Tres quoque vocum gradus, id est gravem, acutum, et superacutum, in quorundam scriptis habemus. Nam quaedam corpora imas e sua natura voces exclamant; alia nec profundas, neque satis elatas, sed mediocres tonant; aliqua vero celsiores et magis tenues personant. E quibus Macrobius Saturnalium libro: 'Vides quam multorum vocibus chorus constet, una tamen ex omnibus redditur. Aliqua est illic acuta, aliqua gravis, aliqua media.' Hos gradus litteris Guido demonstrat, ut graves figura maiores sint, acutae mediocri forma, superacutae parva figuratione.

15 In ecclesiasticis vero organis, monochordis, gravichordis, et similibus musicorum instrumentis, plures gradus esse possunt, ut Boethius in fidium [27ᵛ] numero demonstrat. Nam graves gravium, vel gravissimae gravissimarum, infra, et superiores simili augmento, id est acutae acutarum, vel acutissimae acutissimarum augerentur.

16 Duas claves praeterea omnis boni musici noverunt, non autem septem, vel quattuor, vel tres, quoniam maiorum disciplinam sequi libebit.[70] Ipsi enim quattuor lineas suis libris ex atramento signabant, et ut alteram ab altera distinctam cognoscerent, duos super his colores imponebant, id est minium croceumque, per illum F primo, per hunc C secundo in ipsa manu et libro decernebant. Posteritas deinde quattuor lineis ex ipso minio confectis[71] F primum et C secundum loco colorum imposuerunt. Novissime vero hasdem lineas, vel nigras vel alio colore confectas, duabus clavibus

seasons or the universe. The abbot of Poblet says as follows about these matters:

> Every proper association of pitches is either pronounced harshly, or performed gently, or, rejecting both extremes, sounded middlingly. For this reason every song must belong to one kind or property out of those [three]. 13

In some authors' writings we also have three levels of pitches, namely grave, acute, and superacute. For some bodies shout forth very low pitches by their nature; others thunder neither deep nor very[148] high but middling ones; but some sound higher and thinner ones. Of these Macrobius says in his book of *Saturnalia:*[149] "You see how many voices a single choir consists of; yet a single one is yielded from them all. One voice there is high, one low, one middling." Guido indicates these degrees by letters, such that the grave notes are of a larger shape, the acute of middling form, the superacutes of small representation.[150] 14

But on church organs, monochords, clavichords, and similar instruments of musicians, there can be more registers, as Boethius shows in [discussing] the number of strings.[151] For [there could be] lows of the lows, or lowests of the lowests, and the upper notes could be increased by a similar extension, that is, highs of the highs, or highests of the highests.[152] 15

In addition, all good musicians recognize two clefs, not seven or four or three,[153] since it will be my pleasure[154] to follow the teaching of the elders. For they marked four lines in ink in their books, and so that they might recognize one as distinct from the other, they imposed two colors on them, namely red and yellow, marking first F with the former and second C with the latter in hand and book. Then a later generation made all four lines in red and imposed first F and second C on them in lieu of colors. Finally they assigned these same lines, made in black or another color, to two 16

dederunt, altera trium notularum, altera [28r] duarum insignita ad nostram usque aetatem servatae sunt.

17 Nomen vero clavis vocitatum a Graeco vocabulo, hoc est κλισ κλιοσ,[72] per similitudinem dictum.[73] Nam ut ferri clavis aperit ostium, sic quoque ista signa ingenium aperiunt, ut per ea lineas et spatia cognoscamus, alterumque ab altero nominatim distinctum separemus, ut notas in his positas nomine proprio notare possimus. Hactenus de his. Attamen ad practicen nos conferamus.

: VI :

Quomodo in manu musices litterae vocesque ordinantur

1 In laeva haec nomina ordinantur, et primo in pollicis summitate primum, id est Γut ponatur, duo sequentia in eius coniuncturis, id est Are et ♮mi; deinde ab indicis radice usque ad auricularis fundum quattuor sequentia, id est Cfaut, Dsolre, [28v] Elami, et Ffaut ponuntur; postea per eiusdem digiti coniuncturas ascenditur haec nomina, id est Gsolreut, Alamire, bfa♮mi conlocando. Praeterea Csolfaut, Dlasolre, Elami in anularii, medii, indicis summitate positis per ambas coniuncturas huius, hoc est indicis Ffaut et Gsolre secundo deponuntur. Postremo Alamire in media medii coniunctura, bfa♮mi in anularii quoque media relinquimus. Novissime vero Csolfa in anularii, Dlasol medii coniuncturis tertiis ordinatis Ela in medii extrinseca sub ungue iunctura desinit.

2 Haec omnia in manus figuratione non secus manifesta sunt atque in tua instituere poteris. In fine huius capituli depictam[74]

clefs; the one, distinguished as consisting of three notes,[155] and the other of two, have been preserved until our own day.

The name "clef" [i.e. key] is derived from a Greek word, 17
namely *klis klios*,[156] and is used by analogy; for as an iron key opens a door, so too those signs open up the mind, so that through them we may recognize lines and spaces, and separate them distinctly one from another by name, so that we can designate the notes placed in them by their proper names. So much for these; but now let us move on to practice.

: VI :

How the letters and syllables are arranged on the musical hand

These names are arranged on the left hand. To begin with, at the 1
tip of the thumb let the first, that is, Γut, be placed, the next two in its joints,[157] that is, Are and ♮mi. Then from the root of the forefinger to the base of the little finger are placed the next four, that is, Cfaut, Dsolre, Elami, and Ffaut. Then you go up through the joints of the same [little] finger, placing these names, namely Gsolreut, Alamire, bfa♮mi. Furthermore, when Csolfaut, Dlasolre, Elami have been placed on the tips of the ring finger, the middle finger, and the forefinger, descending through the two joints of this last, that is, the forefinger, second Ffaut and Gsolre are placed. Finally we leave Alamire on the middle juncture of the middle finger, and bfa♮mi on the middle juncture too of the ring finger, and last of all, when Csolfa has been arranged on the third juncture of the ring finger and Dlasol on that of the middle finger, Ela ends in the external joint under the nail of the middle finger.

All of these are visible in the representation of the hand in ex- 2
actly the same way as you will be able to set them up on your own

perspicies. Eadem nomina per lineas et spatia sic imposita ut hoc exemplo constat videbis. Nam litterae primo in his, deinde notulae explicantur.

[29r]

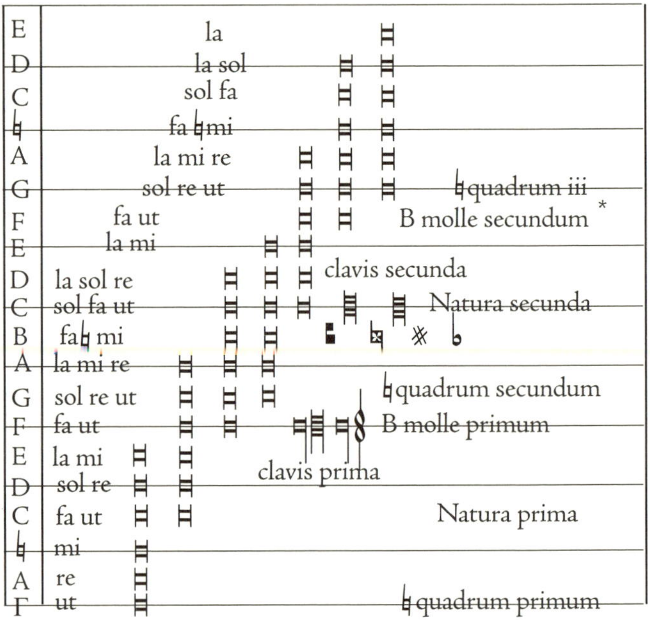

* *secundo* MS

3 In his autem nominibus ut videri potest litteras septem et vocum nomina sex invenies. Illud est autem A B C D E F G, istud vero ut re mi fa sol la. Istud enim vocis agitatum in ascensum et descensum moderatur, illud vero omnem numerum in sese continet. Nam his iterum atque iterum multiplicatis per eundem numerum crementum factum videmus. Sed de hoc alias.

4 Ex his litteris tres, id est C F G, [29v] accipere[75] consuevimus, ut vocum proprietatem ternam hoc est, naturae, bmollis, et ♮qua-

hand; you will observe it portrayed at the end of this chapter. You will see the same names imposed over the lines and spaces just as is laid down in this example. For first the letters are explained in what follows, then the notes.

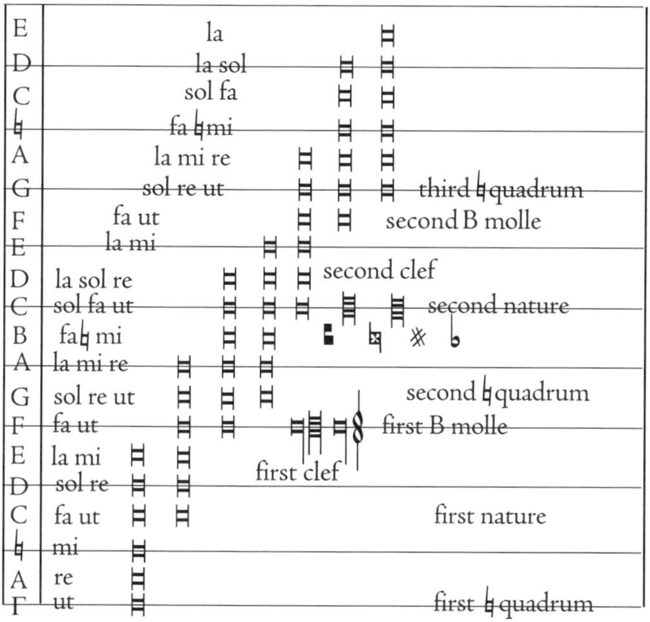

In these names, as can be seen, you will find seven letters and six names of pitches: the former set comprises A B C D E F G, the latter *ut re mi fa sol la*. The latter governs the upward and downward movement of the voice, the former contains all number in itself, for when these are multiplied again and again by the same number we shall see that an increase has been made. But of this I treat elsewhere.[158] 3

Of these letters, we are accustomed to take three, namely C F G, so that they may indicate the three properties of pitches, namely [those of] nature, *bmolle*, and ♮*quadrum*. For where there is 4

dri hae indicent. Namque ubi C naturae initium id est ut, ubi F bmollis, ubi G ♮quadri ibidem dicimus. Post hunc hae quinque, hoc est re mi fa sol la, seriatim sequuntur. Dicemus igitur in Γut ♮quadrum, nam Γ apud Graecos id quod apud nos G denotat, in Cfaut naturam quoniam ibi C repertum videmus, in Ffaut bmolle, quia F ibi id demonstrat. Hasdem primas proprietates vocamus, nam in manus vola vel palma in primis ipsas habemus.

5 In ceteris deinde ♮quadrum, naturam, et bmolle (ubi eorum litterae sunt) secundas dicemus proprietates, utpote Gsolreut, Csolfaut, et Ffaut secundo. Postremo Gsolreut secundum ♮quadrum tertium vocitabimus. Nota igitur ordinem sic sese habere.

6 Mandatis memorie his nominibus, reductisque ab Ela [30r] in Γut, iterum in pollicis summitate, deinde in Cfaut, postea in Ffaut, ♮quadrum, naturam, et bmolle primo dicemus. Deinde in Gsolreut, in Csolfaut, in Ffaut alterum, ♮quadrum, naturam, bmolle secundo subiungemus. Novissime in alterum Gsolreut tertium ♮quadrum terminabimus.

7 Quare autem primo et secundo vel tertio has proprietates dicimus? Quoniam illud in serie constat. Praeterea ab eodem pollice lineam, deinde spatium, et item quousque ad Ela perveneris deducemus.

8 Postremo notandum quod ubicumque natura<m>, bmolle, et ♮quadrum diximus, ibidem deductionem et reductionem, id est ut re mi fa sol la la sol fa mi re ut, ordinatim per coniuncturas formare debemus.

9 Posteriori loco notatione digno animadvertendum videtur, ut his summa cura notatis, quibusque proprietatibus notis optime repertis, [30v] et voce propria per ascensum et descensum in his notulis experimento habito pronuntiata, †lineas et spatia altero ab altero distincto nec cognoscimus quidem†.[76] Ideo claves duae ponuntur in linearum principio, quarum[77] figura[78] haec est . Ea<e>dem in figurativo[79] non coloris id est atramento plenae,

C, we say the beginning of nature, that is, *ut*, where F, of *bmolle*, where G, of ♮*quadrum*. After this these five, that is, *re mi fa sol la*, follow in order. We shall therefore say ♮*quadrum* on Γut, for Γ among the Greeks means what G means among us; on Cfaut [we shall say] nature because we see C found there, on Ffaut *bmolle*, because F shows it there. These we call the first properties, for we have them at the start in the flat or palm of the hand.

Among the rest, we shall then call ♮*quadrum*, nature, and *bmolle* 5
(on the appropriate letters) second properties, for example Gsolreut, Csolfaut, and second Ffaut. Finally we shall call second Gsolreut the third ♮*quadrum*. Note therefore that the arrangement is thus.

Having committed these names to memory, and brought them 6
back from Ela to Γut, once more at the tip of the thumb, and then to Cfaut, after that to Ffaut, we shall say first ♮*quadrum*, nature, and *bmolle*. Then on Gsolreut, Csolfaut, and second Ffaut we shall add second ♮*quadrum*, nature, and *bmolle*. Finally, on second Gsolreut we shall round off third ♮*quadrum*.[159]

But why do we call these properties first, second, and third? 7
Because that is manifest in the sequence. Furthermore, from the same thumb we shall draw a line, then a space, and so on until you have reached Ela.

Lastly, it must be noted that wherever we have said nature, 8
bmolle, and ♮*quadrum*, there we should form the ascending and descending sequences, namely *ut re mi fa sol la, la sol fa mi re ut*, in order through the joints.

As a notable postscript[160] it seems needful to remark that even 9
when we have marked these with the utmost care, discovered all the known properties to perfection, and learned by experience to utter the proper syllable in ascent and descent in these notes, we [still] cannot even tell the lines and spaces clearly one from another.[161] That is why two clefs are placed at the beginning of the lines. Their shape is this . The same clefs may in polyphony be

sed vacuae figurantur, ut hic ♮ ♮. Quarum prima in Ffaut primo, secunda in Csolfaut reperitur.

Per claves has autem inferiores superioresque lineas et spatia notabimus, hisque recte cognitis notulas proprio nomine vocitabimus in talibus existentes. Hactenus de his. Nunc vero ipsam manum pingamus.

[31r]

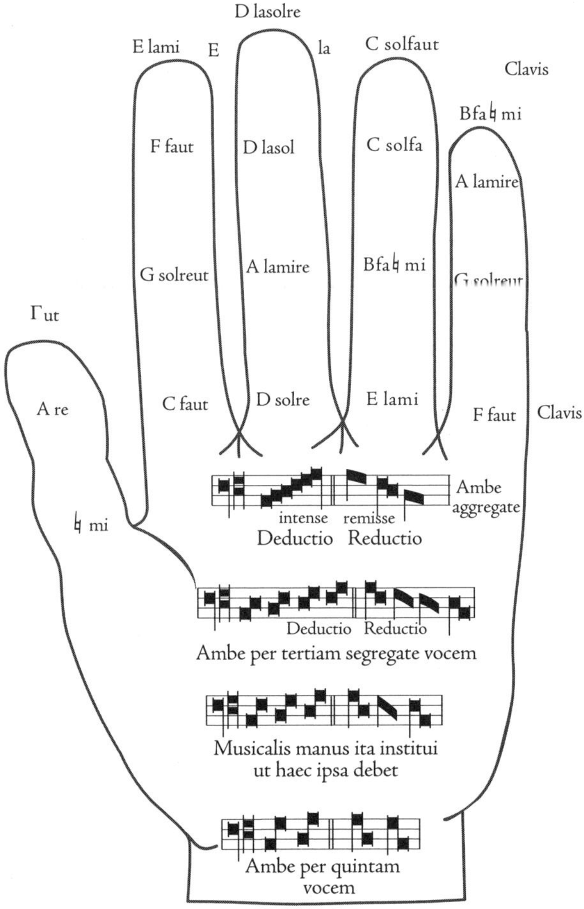

drawn not filled with color,[162] that is, ink, but empty, as here. Of these the first is found on first Ffaut, the second on Csolfaut.

By these lower and higher clefs we shall identify the lines and spaces, and once these are properly known we shall call the notes on or in[163] them by their proper names. So much for them. Now let us depict the hand itself.

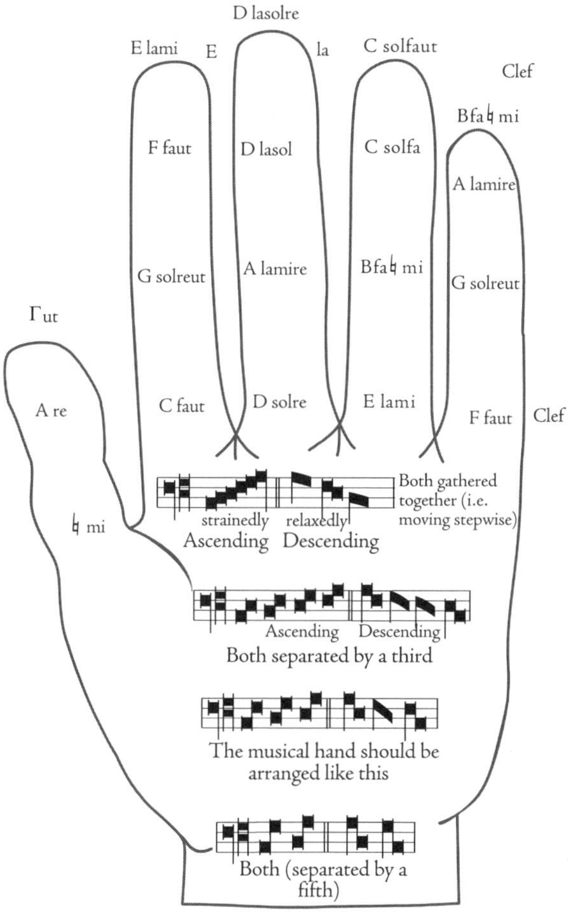

Quisquis has notulas recte deducet reducetque absque trepidatione libri, quas reperiet, eas concinet secure.

: VII :

[31ᵛ] *De mutationibus*

1 A principio pollicis ad Ela sine mutatione perveniri non potest, namque sex vocum nominibus finitis ultra extrema transeundum non esset. In ascensu la[80] dicimus extremum, in descensu vero illud in ut, hoc idem et cantibus universis accideret; illi enim octo aut decem vel ultra vocum curriculum habent, ut suo loco videbimus.

2 Idcirco nunc de mutatione sermonem explicemus. Mutatio est per ascensum aut descensum de proprietate in proprietatem invicem conexa decessio. Iure ergo nos ut et maiores mutationem dicimus, namque ex proprietate in proprietatem (ut diximus) ascendimus aut descendimus, et ideo nomina vocum et proprietatem mutamus, non autem vocem ipsam. Mutatio igitur aut ubi duae aut tres voces sunt cogente extre[32ʳ]morum necessitate fieri debet. Sic abbas Populeti inquit:

3 Qualiter ex una deductione in aliam cantus extendatur mutatio signat. Quae facta in eadem littera in qua voces diversarum proprietatum eundem possunt habere sonum, nec quantitatem augeat, neque idem vocis nomen retineat.[81] Fit autem ipsa mutatio solum ascendendi et descendendi vel tritoni evitandi causa. Haec ille.

Whoever shall correctly follow these notes' ascent and descent without trepidation of the book[164] will sing those he finds without a worry.

: VII :

On mutations

From the base of the thumb it is impossible to reach Ela without mutation, for once the six pitch names had been traversed there would be no crossing beyond the bounds. In ascending [through the hexachord] we say *la* last, in descending that is the case on *ut*. The same thing would also happen in all songs, for they have ranges of eight or ten or more pitches, as we shall see in the appropriate place. 1

Therefore let us now unfold our discourse on mutation. Mutation is the departure by mutual linkage,[165] in ascent or descent, from property to property. Therefore we rightly call it mutation as our predecessors also did, for we ascend or descend, as we have said, from property to property, and therefore change the pitch names and the property, but not the pitch itself. Mutation therefore should take place when there are either two syllables or three, and necessity [caused by] the limits [of the hexachords] compels. Thus the abbot of Poblet says: 2

> Mutation marks how the song is extended from one hexachord to another. Made on the same letter on which pitches of different properties may have the same sound, it neither increases quantity nor retains the same pitch name.[166] This mutation takes place only in order to ascend, descend, or avoid a tritone. 3

4 Loca autem duarum vocum, ubi mutatio fit ipsa, sunt in Cfaut, Dsolre, Elami, Ffaut, Csolfa, et Dlasol. Trium vero Gsolreut, Alamire, Csolfaut, et Dlasolre. Dixi 'cogente necessitate,' quia ob extrema quae impenetranda essent, et signorum gravitatis et acuminis figurationem, mutatio fit. Secus si necessitas horum non impellat. Signa autem acuminis et gravitatis suo loco explanabimus.

5 Dixi quoque non vocem mutari, sed proprietatem [32v] et notulae nomen, quoniam ubi mutatio fit, cum vocis nomen in alius[82] nomen mutabimus, ea duo nomina in vocis aequalitate servamus. Hinc sequetur in bfa♮mi non fieri mutatio ob inaequalitatem notularum, ut suo loco diffuse dicemus. Nunc autem ad propria mutationis dicenda redeamus.

6 Mutatio duorum locorum[83] hoc pacto fit. Primae notulae nomen in secundae nomen[84] conversum sequentes libri notulas ascendentes facit, quod inde contra temptatum, statim hasdem videbimus descendentes, id est secundae nomen in primae reductum. Hoc autem aeque his locis notarum paribus atque in uno ipsorum eveniet, ut mox in exemplis videre poterimus. In Cfaut, Dsolre, et Elami igitur de primi ♮quadri proprietate in naturam primam mutationes ascendunt, i<bi>demque contra de natura in ♮quadrum descen[33r]dent [see Exx. 1.1, 1.2, 1.4]. In Ffaut e natura in bmolle et e bmolle in naturam [Ex. 1.3]. In Csolfa et Dlasol e bmolle in ♮quadrum tertium vel contra ordine dicto, ut in ceteris fieri videtur.

7 In his autem locis trium notularum unius series ceteros sequetur. Nam primam et secundam, deinde primam et tertiam, postea secundam et tertiam accipiemus, hisdemque versis e contrario (ut iam dictum est) sex hinc mutationes extrahemus. In Gsolreut id-

The two-syllable locations where mutation takes places are on Cfaut, Dsolre, Elami, Ffaut, Csolfa, and Dlasol, the three-syllable ones Gsolreut, Alamire, Csolfaut, and Dlasolre. I have said "when necessity compels," since mutation takes place because of the bounds that could not [otherwise] be breached, and the marking of flat and sharp signs, but not in the absence of necessity. We shall explain sharp and flat signs in due course. 4

I have said too that it is not the pitch[167] that is mutated but the property and the name of the note, since where mutation takes place, when we change the name of the pitch into that of another, we keep those two names on an equality of pitch. Hence it will follow that mutation does not take place on bfa♮mi owing to the inequality of the notes, as we shall state at length in due course. But for now let us return to stating the proper features of mutation. 5

Mutation of two places takes place as follows.[168] The name of the first note, changed into that of the second, makes the following notes of the book ascending; when this is tried in reverse, we shall see the same notes descending, that is, the name of the second brought back to that of the first. This will happen equally in these places to pairs of notes, and in one of the places,[169] as we shall soon be able to see in the examples. On Cfaut, Dsolre, and Elami, therefore, the mutations ascend from the property of the first ♮*quadrum* to the first nature, and conversely in the same places they will descend from nature to ♮*quadrum* [see Exx. 1.1, 1.2, 1.4]. On Ffaut from nature to *bmolle* and from *bmolle* to nature [Ex. 1.3]. On Csolfa and Dlasol from *bmolle* to third ♮*quadrum* or vice versa in the said order, as is seen to happen in the rest. 6

But in the places with three note names the sequence of one place will follow the others. For we shall take the first and second, then the first and third, afterwards the second and third, and having turned these round (as has already been said) we shall extract six mutations from them. Therefore on Gsolreut the first, that is, 7

circo prima, id est solre e natura in bmolle ascendit [Ex 1.5], resol vero secunda e bmolle in naturam revertitur. Solut tertia e natura in ♮quadrum subit [Ex. 1.6], utsol quarta, e ♮quadro in naturam descendet. Reut quinta e bmolle in ♮quadratum, utre e ♮quadrato in bmolle gradum revocabit [Ex. 1.7]. Itidem in Alamire servabis. Verum his duobus locis notandum[85] sextam mutationem tam ascendentem quam descenden[33v]tem quis offendet, ceteris vero semper descendentem viderit [Ex. 1.8]. In Csolfaut et Dlasolre, quibus proprietatibus eae notulae deducantur cognito, mutationem inde factu facilem noverimus [Ex. 1.9]. Haec quoad extremorum mutationis necessitatem diximus. Nunc autem signorum eiusdem necessitatem prosequamur.

: VIII :

De signis acumen gravitatemque significantibus, et eorum officio

1 Signa quae in cantibus ad mutationem inducunt cantantem sunt duo, id est gravitatis alterum, alterumque acuminis, sic sane planae musicae sive ecclesiastico cantui insignita ᵬ ♮. Ea cantu organico hoc modo figurata videbis, ♭ ⋇. Prima quorum unam bfa♮mi litteram, cetera vero secundam eiusdem ostentant. Illa gravitate vocem deprimunt, ista acumine eandem extollunt. Quo in loco [34r] reperta fuerint, id est et lineis et spatiis, fa vel mi ob ea vox ipsa sonabit. E tono quoque in semitonium, sive de semitonio in tonum, vox ab his transfertur.

sol re, ascends from nature to *bmolle* [Ex. 1.5]; *re sol*, the second, returns from *bmolle* to nature. *Sol ut*, the third, climbs from nature to ♮*quadrum* [Ex. 1.6]; *ut sol*, the fourth, will descend from ♮*quadrum* to nature. *Re ut*, the fifth, will retrace its steps from *bmolle* to ♮*quadratum*, *ut re* from ♮*quadratum* to *bmolle* [Ex. 1.7]. You will do the same on Alamire. But in these two places it must be noted that one will find the sixth mutation as well ascending as descending, but in the others will always see it descending [Ex. 1.8]. On Csolfaut and Dlasolre, once we have recognized in what properties those notes proceed in hexachordal sequence, we shall know that the mutation is easy to perform [Ex. 1.9]. So much for the necessity of mutation caused by the limits; now we shall proceed to the necessity of mutation caused by signs.

: VIII :

On the signs indicating sharpness and flatness, and their function

The signs that in songs induce the singer to mutation are two, one of flatness, the other of sharpness, marked thus in plainsong or ecclesiastical chant ♭ ♮. In polyphony you will see them shaped thus, ♭ ♮. The first signs in these pairs indicate one letter of bfa♮mi, the others the second. The former lower the notes by flatting, the latter raise them by sharping. Where they are found, that is, both on lines and in spaces, the voice will sound [respectively] *fa* or *mi* on their account. They also change the pitch from tone to semitone, or from semitone to tone. 1

2 Haec ipsa maius sive minus semitonium, hoc est toni partes inaequales causantia, faciunt hunc vel in id maius vel minus dimidiatum. Marchettus et abbas Populeti in his mutationem dicunt permutationem. Hoc enim abbas:

> 3 Aliquando permutatio quae nominis est variatio et[86] quantitatis, aliquorum scriptis coniuncta, eo quod accidentalis sit cantus attributio, fitque signorum impositione aut coloris causa. Imponit apotome<n>, quod maius semitonium dicitur, aut abstulit inde, vel minus. Haec ille.

Hinc enim Boethius disertissime tonum in aequali parte nec divisum quidem, neque dividendum dixit. Verumtamen alio loco de hoc. Nunc autem ad id quod [34^{v}] orsi sumus redeamus.

4 Quidam minus inter musicos periti eadem signa clavis locum bmollis[87] tenere credunt, quod nullo modo nec tenere nec defensare ausim. Nam verae claves sunt duae, ut dictum suo loco cumulatissime.

5 Coniunctae enim per hosdem caracteres per exempla ostensae[88] non deerunt[89] inferius, quam fictam musicam quidam quoque dicunt. Nobis autem potius coniunctam nominatam placet quoniam desueta notularum nomina diversis in locis suetas voces, id est ut re, mi fa, sol la coniungunt. Hinc enim coniunctae nomen musici praecessores dixerunt. Abbas Populeti disiunctam ex officii ratione figuram appellat. Quae et quot et quibus locis sint, infra exempla dabunt. Et quoniam ut supra dixi haec signa de bfa♮mi principaliter oriri videntur, ideo de ipso aliqua duxi ponenda.

These same signs, producing the major or the minor semitone, that is, the unequal parts of the tone, cause it to be halved into that greater or lesser portion. Marchetto and the abbot of Poblet call mutation at these places permutation. For thus speaks the abbot: 2

> Sometimes permutation, which is a variation in the name and quantity, called *coniuncta* in certain persons' writings, as being the accidental attribute of a song, is brought about through the imposition of signs, or for the sake of color.[170] It imposes, or has taken away thence, the apotome, which is called the major semitone, or else the minor [semitone].[171] 3

That is why Boethius most eloquently stated that the tone neither had been divided nor could be divided equally; but of that elsewhere. Now let us return to our theme.

Certain less expert musicians think that the same signs occupy the place of a *bmolle* clef, which I should not venture in any way either to think or to defend.[172] For the true clefs are two, as has been stated in great detail in the proper places. 4

Coniunctae shown by these characters in examples will not be lacking below; some people also call them *musica ficta*, but we prefer the name *coniuncta* because unusual note names conjoin the usual pitches, that is, *ut* and *re*, *mi* and *fa*, *sol* and *la*, in various places. That is why our musical predecessors used the name *coniuncta*. The abbot of Poblet calls it a disjunct figure by reason of its function.[173] How many of them there are, and in what places, the examples will state below. And since, as I said above, these signs seem principally to arise from bfa♮mi, I have therefore deemed that some things should be said about it. 5

: IX :

[35r] Quare in bfa♮mi non fit commutatio

1 In bfa♮mi duae voces inaequales sunt natura ipsa id ordinante. Nam mi cum fa non eandem aequalitatem habet, quoniam illud isto sonum acutiorem habens facit, nec ibidem mutationem fieri posse <constat>. Nam ut iam dictum est, mutatio in notarum aequalitate semper est faciunda. Non enim duo diversi soni, id est acutus et gravis, in uno eodemque loco convenirent, namque inter sese repugnant.

2 Quidam dicunt bfa♮mi non secus habendum ac si esset locus unius litterae vocisque. Nam in eo notulam in notulam mutatam non conspicimus, quia unica est, ita bfa♮mi notulae per litteras separatae mutationem ob id a<d>mittunt.

3 Aliqui mutationem tono non autem semitonio faciundam indicarunt. [35v] Alii nunquam fa in mi mutari oportere asserunt. Sed tamen magis diserti quod prius dixeram, id comprobarunt. His enim rationibus etsi ibi duae sunt notulae, tamen nullo modo mutatio fieri potest, nisi coniuncta illud fieri iubeat. Non enim tunc mi in fa <mutabimus>, sed alio pacto utrumque permutabimus.

: X :

De mutationibus dubie faciundis solutio claret

1 Mutationem persaepe dubie faciundam trium notularum locis offendemus. †Hoc praesertim necne mutari de proprietate in alteram vel alteram sit necesse nos deprehendere poterit.†[90] Quod

: IX :

Why commutation does not take place on bfa♮mi

On bfa♮mi there are two unequal pitches at nature's own command. For *mi* has not the same equality with *fa*, since the former has and makes a sharper sound than the latter, and it is certain that mutation cannot be made there. For as has been said, mutation is always to be made on an equality of notes. For two different sounds, that is, a high and a low, could not agree together in one and the same place, since they repel each other. 1

Some say that bfa♮mi should be treated just as if it were the place of one letter and pitch,[174] for there we do not see one note changed into another, since it is single; the notes bfa♮mi, being separated by their letters, allow[175] mutation on that account.[176] 2

Some have indicated that mutation should take place on a tone but not a semitone. Others say that *fa* should never be changed into *mi*. But the more skilled have approved what I said before. For on these principles, although there are two notes there, yet in no way can mutation take place except at the command of a *coniuncta*. For we shall not change *mi* into *fa*, but permute each in another way. 3

: X :

On ambiguous mutations the solution is clear

Very often we shall encounter doubt as to the mutation to be made in three-note places. We shall not be certain whether or not we ought to mutate from one property into one or other of the 1

quidem quam saepissime in Gsolreut Alamireque eveniet. Non enim duarum notularum locis ambiguam, sed manifestam mutationem conspicimus, ex qua in quam mutari debeant notulae. Sed tamen [36r] his solum locis trium quomodo mutari debeant advertamus.

2 Communis enim musicorum responsio sic se habet, ut puta in Gsolreut et Alamire. Quoties ibidem in mutationem inciderimus ascendentibus in libro notis ad bfa♮mi tantum, postea inde inferiora petentibus, sive per signa supradicta demonstratum sit sive non, de naturae proprietate in bmollis proprietatem semper mutatio fiat. Secus si bfa♮mi eaedem notae excellant, nam tunc omnino de natura ipsa in ♮quadrum mutatio quadrat. Huius enim primae regulae suo loco exempla patebunt [Exx. 1.3, 1.4].

3 Secunda regula haec est. In Csolfaut et Dlasolre, cum ibi bmollis notulas cantaremus, notulis inde Elami usque ascendentibus, tunc in ♮quadrum gressum torqu<e>amus [Ex. 1.5]. Sin autem ad Ffaut vel ultra progressus earundem esset, tunc naturae notulas accipiamus [Ex. 1.9]. [36v] Quoad ascensum hoc diximus. In descensu vero primo notandum hoc quoque censui. Cum in Alamire et Gsolreut ventum fuerit pro ♮quadri proprietate cantantes in aliquibus modis potius bmollis proprietatem ingredi quam naturae debemus. Hoc in primo et sexto modo sive tono, et quinto et octavo.

4 Secunda regula descensus hoc notat in Dlasolre et Csolfaut. Si inde gradatim ad Ffaut notae descendant, quocumque modo id acciderit, in bmollis proprietatem nos ingressuros oportet [Ex. 1.9]. Sin autem secus, ♮quadrum adeundum arbitrabimur. Sed tamen non semper in organicis cantibus hoc consequimur, nam signa gravitatis ibi vel acuminis scripta reperiemus; in plana musica vero ut exempla monstrabunt quod ostendimus faciundum, suademus id observandum.

5 In cunctis enim [37r] modis attendenda sunt verba saepissime sub notulis posita. Nam cantari eas molle vel dure notulas bfa♮mi,

remaining two.[177] This happens very often on Gsolreut and Alamire. For in two-note places we observe no ambiguous mutation, but one in which it is obvious from which to which the notes must be mutated. But, just in these three-note places, let us take note of how they ought to be mutated.

The common reply of musicians is as follows, for example on Gsolreut and Alamire. Whenever we run into a mutation when the notes in the book ascend only to bfa♮mi, and after that descend,[178] whether it has been shown by the signs aforesaid or not, the mutation should always be made from the natural property to that of *bmolle*. It is otherwise if the notes rise above bfa♮mi. For then mutation from nature to ♮*quadrum* is unconditionally appropriate. Examples of this first rule will be shown at the appropriate place [Exx. 1.3, 1.4]. 2

The second rule is this. On Csolfaut and Dlasolre, when we have sung the notes of *bmolle*, if the melody rises as far as Elami, let us bend our step to ♮*quadrum* [Ex. 1.5]. But if the progession be to Ffaut or further, then let us take the notes of nature [Ex. 1.9]. This applies to ascent. In descent the first thing to be noted is this. When we have reached[179] Alamire and Gsolreut, singing according to the property of ♮*quadrum,* in some modes we should go into the property of *bmolle* rather than nature. This is the case in the first and sixth mode or tone, and the fifth and eighth. 3

The second rule of descent prescribes the following on Dlasolre and Csolfaut. If the notes descend stepwise from them to Ffaut, however that comes about, we should go into the property of *bmolle* [Ex. 1.9]. But if it is otherwise we shall think we must go to ♮*quadrum*. But we do not always achieve this in polyphony, for there we shall see flat or sharp signs written. But in plainsong, as the examples will demonstrate, we urge that what we have shown should be done is the practice to be observed. 4

In all modes, attention must be paid to the words very often underlaid to the notes. For they show very well that those notes 5

sive sint signa sive non, per sonum fa vel mi optime demonstrant. Hucusque de his; pauca de verbis sub notis collocandis subiungamus.

: XI :

Quo pacto verba mi vel fa sonent

1 Verba igitur quocumque cantu aptanda, vel plano, vel organico, perlegi primum debent, deinde syllabae legitimae singulis notulis vel pluribus sortitae graviter aut acute, ut supra ostendimus sonent. Notandum quoque cantu ab initio ad finem inspecto non minimam nobis ex hoc utilitatem consequemur. Namque inter canendum quam saepissime ut modus adimpleatur per ascensum aut descensum in linearum medio claves alterum locum tenentes [37v] pergendi inscitiam nobis obtulerint, et eo magis in errorem nos id deducet quod amissis linearum et spatiorum nominibus verba cum notulis vel fa vel mi sonantia nesciremus. Hinc incassum hoc incognito basse vel alte nimis voce delirata canendi iter prosequemur. Hactenus de canendo. Quo ritu cantus initiari queant ima vel alta voce videamus.

: XII :

De modorum nomine numeroque

1 Modi sive tropi quos improprie tonos quidam vocant octo sunt iuxta modernos, id est primus, secundus, tertius, quartus, quintus, sextus, septimus, et octavus. E quibus Guido:

bfa♮mi are sung as *fa* or *mi* whether there are signs or not.[180] So much for this; let us add a little about the words to be underlaid to the notes.

: XI :

How the words mi and fa sound

The words, then, to be fitted to any song, whether plain or polyphonic, must first be read through; then let the proper syllables assigned to one or more notes each be sung low or high, as we have shown above. It should also be noted that when we have examined the song from beginning to end, we shall achieve no small benefit from this.[181] For very often while we are singing, a different placement of the clefs in mid-staff, to let the melody[182] be completed whether rising or falling, will have left us ignorant of how we should continue, and all the more will it lead us into error because, if we lose the names of the lines and spaces, we shall not know the words sounding with the notes *mi* or *fa*. Hence, if we do not know this, we shall pursue our course of song in vain with voice astray too low or high. So much for singing. Let us see in what way songs can be started in low voice or high. 1

: XII :

On the names and number of the modes

The modes or *tropoi*, which some improperly call tones, are eight according to the moderns, namely the first, second, third, fourth, fifth, sixth, seventh, and eighth, of which Guido says: 1

2 Hi sunt quattuor modi vel tropi quos abusive tonos nominant, qui sic ab invicem naturali sunt diversitate disiuncti, ut alter alteri in sua sede locum non tribuat, alterque alterius neumam aut transferat, vel[91] trans[38r]formet, aut nunquam recipiat. Haec ipse.

3 Hi autem multae speciei primitivi per arsim thesimque diversas neumas ordiuntur. Nam (ut videri potest in ecclesiasticis beati Gregorii cantibus) non eundem concentum habent inter sese, sed diversum. Et hoc pacto quodlibet horum tanquam genus ex se species mittit. Non enim a principio ad finem sine difficultate improvisos recte quis percurret, nisi prius ipsorum propriam naturam noverit, quoniam quilibet horum ultra suum finem vel in altum vel in imum eundi potestatem habebit. Quare authenticos aut plagales hos fore oportebit, quorum ab altero alterum hoc modo dissentire nostri dixerunt: quot impares sunt, patres sive magistros authenticos, quot vero pares,[92] filios sive discipulos plagales quidam vocitarunt.

4 Impares [38r] sunt primus, tertius, quintus, et septimus, pares secundus, quartus, sextus, et octavus, quorum proprium alterius est ascensus, alteriusque descensus. Quorum definitionem abbas Populeti breviter ostendit: 'Tonus, modus proprie appellatus, est certa cantus regula quae in fine communiter qualis sit cantus diiudicat.' Hos autem tropos sive modos Dorium, <Hy>podorium, Phrygium, <Hy>pophrygium, Lydium, <Hy>polydium, Mixolydium, <Hy>pomixolydium[93] Boethius vocitat.

5 Authenticus igitur ultra suam finalem litteram adminus septem voces in altum effert. Plagalis vero sub eadem duos tonos descendit. Sunt autem finales littere quattuor, hoc est D E F G primo [Ex. 1.10]. In una quarum primus et secundus desinunt, in altera tertius et quartus, in tertia quintus et sextus, in quarta septimus et octavus. Eae quoque [38v] A B C D confinales, id est secundas vel

These are the four modes or tropoi which they catachrestically call "tones." They are so much separated from each other by their natural diversity that the one cannot grant space to another in its own seat, and one [mode] either transfers or transforms the other's *neuma*,[183] or never receives it.[184] 2

But these primary modes of many a species weave various 3
neumae by arsis and thesis. For as can be seen in the ecclesiastical chants of Blessed Gregory, they have not the same concord among themselves, but a different one. And in this manner every one of them sprouts species like a genus. For one will not run through them from beginning to end without difficulty at first sight, unless one knows their nature beforehand, for each of them will have the power of going beyond its final either upwards or downwards. Hence they will need to be authentic or plagal, the difference between which our people stated as follows: the odd-numbered ones some have called fathers or authentic masters, the even-numbered sons or plagal pupils.[185]

The odd-numbered modes are first, third, fifth, and seventh, 4
the even second, fourth, sixth, and eighth. The property of one group is ascent, of the other descent. The abbot of Poblet defines them briefly: "Tone, properly called mode, is a fixed rule of singing that at its end commonly determines of what kind the chant is." These tropes or modes Boethius calls Dorian, Hypodorian, Phrygian, Hypophrygian, Lydian, Hypolydian, Mixolydian, and Hypomixolydian.

Now the authentic rises at least seven pitches above its final let- 5
ter, the plagal descends two tones beneath it. There are four final letters, namely first D, E, F, G [Ex. 1.10]. On the first of these the first and second [modes] end, on the second the third and fourth, on the third the fifth and sixth, on the fourth the seventh and eighth. They [the modes] also have A, B, C, D as cofinals, that is,

acutas habent. Hae in acuto gradu, illae in gravi sunt. Hos autem modos protum, deuterum, tritum, et tetartum[94] Graece dictos solum maiores habebant. Verum Gregorium maximum pontificem hos quos diximus pares ex his dirimisse didicimus.

6 Genera ex talium generibus haec sunt. Antiphona, invitatorium, introitus, graduale vel tractus, alleluia, sequentia, offertorium, et postcommune. Item hymnus, Kyrieleyson,[95] Gloria in ex,[96] Credo in unum, Sanctus, Agnus Dei. Namque ista modorum omnium alternis neumis componi possunt. Sed de hoc alias. Verumtamen ad orsa nunc redeamus.

: XIII :

Facultas ascendendi descendendique modorum

1 Sunt autem qui in cantuum primordiis cuius modi[97] sint ostendisse conantur. Quas regulas [39^v] ob ambiguitatem non ponemus. Nam Guido, Marchettus, abbas Populeti, et plures musici id scribunt. Ex his Addon abbas non imperitus, de modis breviter haec inquit:

> 2 Primus tonus finitur in voce iiii, proceditque usque ad xii et etiam ad xiii, et descendit ad vocem tertiam et etiam ad primam. Secundus tonus finitur in voce iiii, proceditque usque ad ix et etiam ad x, descenditque ad primam et etiam ad gammam. Tertius tonus finitur in voce v, proceditque usque ad xii et etiam ad xiii, descenditque usque ad iiii. Quartus tonus finitur in voce v, proceditque usque ad ix et ad x, de-

the second or high [letters]. The latter are in the high range, the former in the low. But the older writers had only the modes protus, deuterus, tritus, and tetrardus, named in Greek. But we have been told that Pope Gregory separated from them the even modes we have mentioned.

The genres formed from the genera of such modes are these: antiphon, invitatory, introit, gradual or tract, alleluia, sequence, offertory, and postcommunion. Also hymn, Kyrie, Gloria, Credo, Sanctus, Agnus Dei. For these may be composed in alternating *neumae* of all the modes. But of this elsewhere. However, let us return to our theme. 6

: XIII :

The modes' faculty of ascending and descending

There are some who attempt to show at the outset of chants of what mode they are. We shall not state these rules owing to their ambiguity. For Guido,[186] Marchettus,[187] the abbot of Poblet, and numerous musicians write about the matter. Of these the experienced abbot Addo makes the following brief remarks about the modes:[188] 1

> The first tone ends on the 4th pitch [*d*], and proceeds as far as the 12th [*e'*] and even the 13th [*f'*], and descends to the 3rd pitch [*c*], and even the 1st [*A*]. The second tone ends on the 4th pitch, and proceeds as far as the 9th [*b♭*][189] and even the 10th [*c'*], and descends to the 1st and even Γ [= G]. The third tone ends on the 5th pitch [*e*], and proceeds as far as the 12th and even the 13th, and descends as far as the 4th. The fourth tone ends on the 5th pitch, and proceeds as far as 2

scenditque usque ad iii et etiam ad primam. Quintus tonus finitur in voce vi, proceditque usque ad xiii et etiam xiiii, descenditque usque ad vocem sextam. Sextus tonus finitur in voce vi, proceditque ad x et etiam ad xi, descenditque [40r] ad vocem tertiam. Septimus tonus finitur in voce vii, proceditque usque ad xv et etiam xvi, descenditque usque ad vocem vi et etiam iiii sed raro. Octavus tonus finitur in voce vii, proceditque usque ad xii et etiam xiii, et descendit ad vocem iii. Haec Addonis verba.

3 Sunt et item qui breviter in finalibus et clarius indicarunt; quorum brevitatem nos quoque secuti hoc modo normam edemus.

: XIIII :

De cognoscendis antiphonis et aliis cantibus ecclesiasticis

1 Antiphonis primi, quarti, et sexti modi euouae psalmorum quod est saeculorum amen principium in Alamire Gregorius instituit, tertii, quinti, et octavi in Csolfaut, secundi vero et septimi alterius in Ffaut primo, alteriusque in Dlasolre saeculorum composuit [Ex. 1.11]. Hinc enim tracta sunt [40v] verba scilicet:

2 Primus ad quintam re la
Secundus ad tertiam re fa
Tertius ad sextam mi fa
Quartus ad quartam mi la
Quintus ad quintam fa fa
Sextus ad tertiam fa la

the 9th and 10th, and descends as far as the 3rd and even the 1st. The fifth tone ends on the 6th pitch [*f*], and proceeds as far as the 13th and even the 14th [*g*′] and descends as far as the 6th pitch. The sixth tone ends on the 6th pitch, and proceeds to the 10th and even the 11th [*d*′], and descends to the 3rd pitch. The seventh tone ends on the 7th pitch [*g*], and proceeds as far as the 15th [*a*′] and even the 16th [*b*♮′], and descends as far as the 6th pitch, and even the 4th, but rarely. The eighth tone ends on the 7th pitch, and proceeds as far as the 12th and even the 13th and descends to the 3rd pitch.

There are also some who have indicated [the chant mode] more briefly and clearly by the finals. Imitating their brevity, we too shall state the rule in this fashion. 3

: XIV :

On recognizing antiphons and other ecclesiastical chants

In antiphons of the first, fourth, and sixth modes Gregory set the beginning of the *euouae* of psalms, which means *saeculorum amen*, on Alamire; in those of the third, fifth, and eighth on Csolfaut; in those of the second and seventh he set *saeculorum* in the one on first Ffaut, the other on Dlasolre [Ex. 1.11]. For hence are drawn the words: 1

The first at the fifth, *re–la*. 2
The second at the third, *re–fa*.
The third at the sixth, *mi–fa*.
The fourth at the fourth, *mi–la*.
The fifth at the fifth, *fa–fa*.
The sixth at the third, *fa–la*.

Septimus ad quintam ut sol
Octavus ad quartam ut fa

3 Hoc est antiphonae finis, et initium euouae vel saeculorum.

4 Ex his autem versiculis quidam breviores delegeru<n>t, scilicet

5 Pri re la. Se re fa. Ter mi fa. Quar mi la.
Quin fa fa. Sex fa la. Sep ut sol. Oc ut fa.

6 Quod idem dicunt. His cognitis principium cantandi psalmos sic sese habet, unde versus:

7 Primus cum sexto fa sol la semper habeto [Ex. 1.12].
Tertius et octavus ut re fa [Ex. 1.13], sicque secundus [Ex. 1.14].
La sol la quartus [Ex. 1.15], ut mi sol sit tibi quintus [Ex. 1.16].
Septimus fa[98] mi fa sol [Ex. 1.19], sic omnis esse recordor.

8 Quos versus Arnaldus Dalps et quam plurimi beatum Gregorium fecisse autumant.

9 [41^r] Ad quorum declarationem haec verba ipsius Arnaldi supposui:

10 Quibus sic itaque dispositis, dico quod primus et sextus modi intonantur sive principiantur per tres solfales notas fa sol la secundae deductionis sive proprietatis ad differentiam aliarum deductionum sive proprietatum, quae septem existunt, pro quibus intonationibus do istam regulam maximam et veram, quod ultima solfa intonationis situatur ubi toni sive modi sua saeculorum faciunt principia. Secundus, tertius, atque supremus sive octavus intonantur per alias tres solfales notas, videlicet ut re fa. Verumtamen non sunt eiusdem deductionis sive proprietatis, quia[99] secundi existunt per

The seventh at the fifth, *ut–sol.*
The eighth at the fourth, *ut–fa.*

This is the end of the antiphon and the beginning of the *euouae*, or *saeculorum*. 3

From these little verses some people have selected shorter ones, namely: 4

Pri re la. Se re fa. Ter mi fa. Quar mi la. 5
Quin fa fa. Sex fa la. Sep ut sol. Oc ut fa.

Which say the same thing. Once these are known, the basis for singing psalms is thus obtained, whence the verses: 6

Let the first [mode] with the sixth always have *fa sol la* [Ex. 1.12], 7
The third and the eighth *ut re fa* [Ex. 1.13], and so the second [Ex. 1.14];
Let *la sol la* be the fourth [Ex. 1.15], *ut mi sol* the fifth for you [Ex. 1.16],
The seventh *fa mi fa sol* [Ex. 1.19], so I recall they all are.

Which verses very many people, including Arnaldus Dalps, maintain that St Gregory composed. [190] 8

To explain them I have given below Arnaldus's own words: 9

> Once they have been thus disposed, I say that the first and sixth modes are intoned or begun by the three notes solmized *fa sol la* of the second *deductio* or property to distinguish it from the other *deductiones* or properties, which number seven; for these intonations I give this supreme and true rule, that the last note of the intonation is situated where the tones or modes make the beginnings of their *saeculorum*. The second, third, and last or eighth are intoned by three other solmized notes, to wit *ut re fa*. But they do not belong to the same *deductio* or property because [those of] the second are 10

secundam deductionem, tertii vero pariter et octavi per quartam deductionem. Quartus namque suam facit intonationem per tres solfales voces, vi[41v]delicet la sol la, quae sunt secundae deductionis sive proprietatis. Quintus vero intonatur per tres solfales voces, scilicet ut mi sol, quae tertiae deductionis sive proprietatis existunt. Sed et septimus suae intonationis facit principium per solfales quattuor voces, videlicet fa mi fa sol, quae sunt quartae deductionis, quibus inspectis et memoriae commendatis faciliter ad cognitionem intonationis meruerit pervenire. Haec Arnaldus.

11 Hunc ipsum ordinem fere Venite exultemus, invitatorii, et psalmi introituum habent, ut exempla monstrabunt. Ex horum brevitate atque obscuritate in ecclesiis inter clericos mala consuetudo canendorum psalmorum orta est; namque non eodem modo notis ligatis syllabas in sexto velut primo damus, et in ceteris item, ut suo loco videbimus.

12 Et ut brevius responsori<or>um introituum[42r]que rem ipsam ostenderim, ipsorum Gloria Patri de versibus quemadmodum extrahi debeant notatione ipsa exempla patebunt.[100] Nam hi versus alter ab altero inter sese quoquo modo differunt. Quorum differentia<m> finitis responsoriis iidem versus in eorum initio, medio, et fine neumis propriis compositi demonstrant [Exx. 1.22–35]. Iam sequentur omnium capitum exempla quae necessaria erunt de rebus his quas ubique diximus.

13 Sed prius de modo notulas figurandi pauca absolvamus. Primo Boethii aliquas notulas monstrabimus, deinde Enchiriadis, postea Guidonis, deinde Hucbaldi, postremo modernorum.

in the second *deductio,* the third and likewise the eighth in the fourth *deductio.* The fourth makes its intonation by three solmized notes, to wit *la sol la,* which are of the second *deductio* or property. The fifth is intoned by three solmized notes, namely *ut mi sol,* which are of the third *deductio* or property. But the seventh makes the beginning of its intonation on four solmized notes, to wit *fa mi fa sol,* which are of the fourth *deductio;* once these things have been reviewed and committed to memory [the student] will easily have deserved to attain knowledge of intonation.

This is very much the order kept by *Venite exultemus* [settings], invitatories, and introit psalms, as the examples will show. Their brevity and obscurity has given rise in churches to a bad habit among clerics in psalm singing. For we do not assign[191] [text] syllables to ligated notes in the same way in the sixth mode as the first, and likewise in the others, as we shall see in due course. 11

And in order that I may show with some brevity the very nature of these responsories and introits, the manner of extracting the doxologies from their verses[192] will be demonstrated in the examples. For these verses are different from one another in every way; once the responsories are over, the difference is demonstrated by these verses, composed in their own *neumae,* at their beginning, middle, and end [Exx. 1.22–35]. There will now follow examples pertaining to all the chapters, which will necessarily concern the things we have said in each of them. 12

But first let us get a few things out of the way on the manner of forming notes. First we shall show some of Boethius's notes, then of Enchiriades's, next of Guido's, then of Hucbald's, lastly of the moderns'.[193] 13

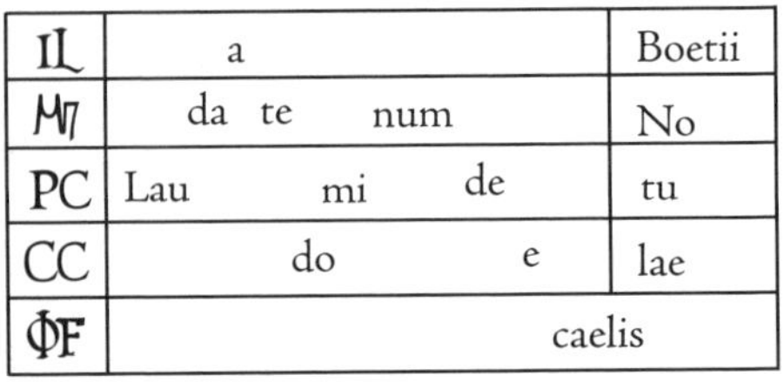

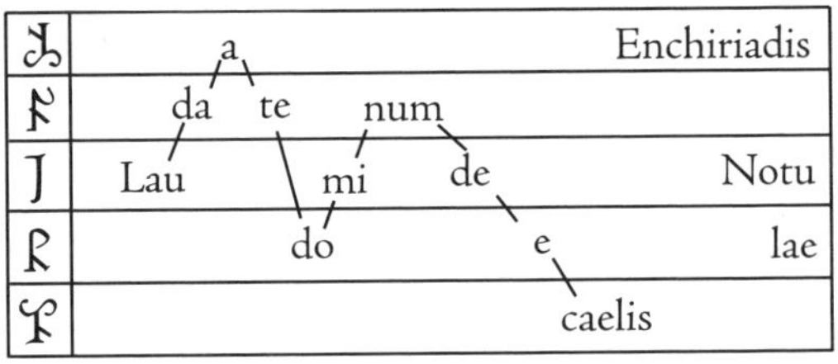

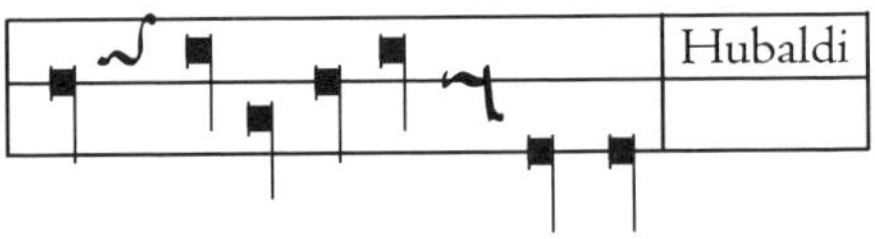

: XV :

[42v] De modo figurandi notulas

1 Omnis peritus scriptor has notulas modernae institutionis figurandas hoc pacto notet, quarum nomina periti sic vocitari dixerunt, id est primam , longam , [43r] brevem , correptam , al-

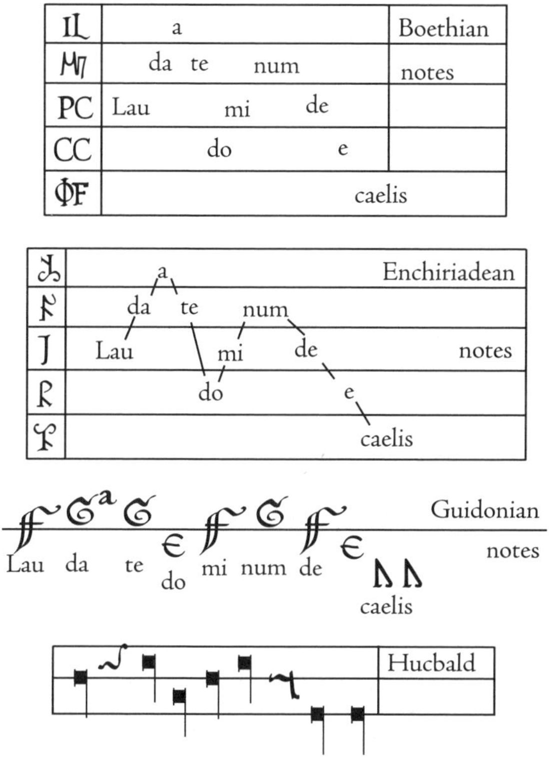

: XV :

On the manner of forming notes

Every expert scribe should write these notes of the modern system 1
in the following way. The experts have said that their names are called as follows: *prima*[194] ⊐, long ⊐, breve ⊐, *correpta*[195] ◊, *alpha*[196] ▶,

pham, tochatam, unchatam, finalem. Quae sub his syllabae collocari debent Abbatem audiamus:

2 Duae primae syllabam longam recipient, tertia vero brevem; quarta vero nec syllabam recipit, nec sola esse potest, sed[101] bis duplicata. Quinta in principio capit syllabam tantum; sexta et septima dipthongon[102] sonat, octava, vel novissima completam sententiam finit. Sed tamen paenultimam cum notula syllabam semper producere debemus.

EX. 1.1 *Mutatio de ♮quadro in naturam per ascensum et contra per descensum in Cfaut*

EX. 1.2 *Mutatio ad sol re ascendens et descendens in eodem*

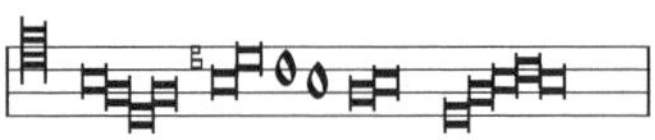

EX. 1.3 *De natura in bmolle*

EX. 1.4 *De natura in ♮quadrum*

toccata[197] ∩, *uncata*[198] ∪, *finalis* . Concerning the syllables to be set under them let us hear the Abbot:

> The first two receive a long syllable, the third a short; the 2
> fourth neither receives a syllable nor can stand alone, but twice, doubled. The fifth at the beginning receives only one syllable. The sixth and seventh sound a diphthong. The eighth, or last, ends the complete sentence. But we ought always to lengthen the penultimate syllable with its note.

EX. I.1 *Mutation from* ♮quadrum *to nature by ascent and conversely by descent to Cfaut*

EX. I.2 *Mutation ascending to sol re and descending taken together*

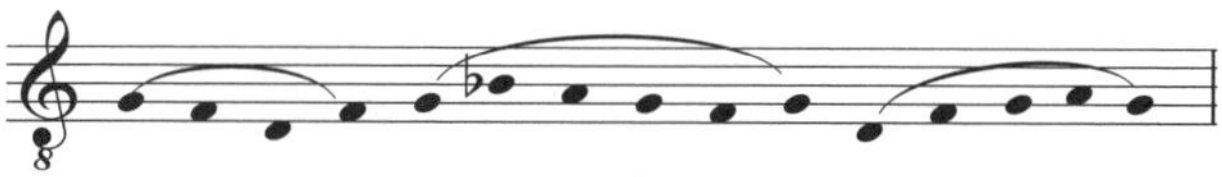

EX. I.3 *From nature to* bmolle

EX. I.4 *From nature to* ♮quadrum

: XVI :

[43ᵛ] De coniunctis caput

1 Illud profecto quod iam de verbis sub notulis acumen vel gravitatem demonstrantibus diximus, coniunctarum musicam deductionem[103] conectemus. Ubique locorum deductio formari potest, sed tamen his locis quibus optimi musici dicunt eas esse, ut nos instituemus. 'Est enim coniuncta'[104] (ut Arnaldus inquit) 'quaedam acquisita canendi[105] actualis attributio, in qua licet de tono facere semitonium, et econtra.' Vel sic: 'coniuncta est alicuius proprie[44ʳ]tatis seu deductionis de loco proprio ad alienum locum sub vel supra intellectualis transpositio.'

2 Prima quarum sub Γut vocibus duabus incipit, finitque in Cfaut, ponitque fa in Are. Secunda initium sub Γut habet, finemque in Dsolre, fa concipiendo in ♮mi. Tertia primordiat in Are, finitque in Ffaut, sonans in Dsolre fa. Quarta suum initium in ♮mi, finem vero in Gsolreut habet, sonans suum fa in Elami. Quinta in Dsolre initiat, finitque in bfa♮mi, suum vero fa in Gsolreut sonans. Sexta in Elami primo incohat, desinitque in Csolfaut, fa in Alamire primo tenens. Septima primordiatur in Alamire primo, terminaturque in Ffaut secundo, suum fa in Dlasolre sonans. Octava in bfa♮mi primo initium, finemque in Gsolreut secundo habet, fa in Elami secundo observans. Nona init caput in Dlasolre, desinitque in bfa♮mi secundo, suum fa in [44ᵛ] Gsolreut resonans. Decima caput habet in Elami secundo, terminationem vero in bfa♮mi secundo, fa in Alamire secundo formans. Undecima in Alamire secundo principium, finemque supra[106] Ela habet, fa sonans in Dlasol. Duodecima et ultima in bfa♮mi secundo initiatur, terminaturque supra[107] Ela vocibus duabus, fa suum in Ela resonando.

3 Possem quam plurimas inscribere; sed hae sufficiant.

: XVI :

On coniunctae

To what we have already said about words under notes showing high or low,[199] we shall append the musical *deductio* of *coniunctae*. A *deductio* can be constituted everywhere, but in those places in which the best musicians say they are,[200] as we shall expound. "For a *coniuncta*[201] (as Arnaldus says) is an acquired actual attribute of singing, in which one may make a semitone out of a tone, or vice versa." Alternatively: "a *coniuncta* is the intellectual transposition of some property or *deductio* from its proper place to that of another below or above." 1

The first of them begins two pitches below Γut, and ends on Cfaut, and places *fa* on Are. The second has its beginning below Γut, and its end on Dsolre, conceiving *fa* on ♮mi.[202] The third commences on Are, and finishes on Ffaut, sounding *fa* on Dsolre. The fourth begins on ♮mi, and has its final on Gsolreut, sounding its *fa* on Elami. The fifth begins on Dsolre, its final is on bfa♮mi, its *fa* on Gsolreut. The sixth starts on first Elami, and ends on Csolfaut, keeping *fa* on first Alamire. The seventh is commenced on first Alamire, and is terminated on second Ffaut, sounding its *fa* on Dlasolre. The eighth has its beginning on first bfa♮mi, and its end on second Gsolreut, observing *fa* on second Elami. The ninth enters its head on Dlasolre, and ceases on second bfa♮mi, resounding his *fa* in Gsolreut. The tenth has its head on second Elami, its termination on second bfa♮mi,[203] forming *fa* on second Alamire. The eleventh has its head on second Alamire, and its end above Ela, sounding *fa* on Dlasol. The twelfth and last is initiated on second bfa♮mi and terminated two pitches above Ela, resounding its *fa* on Ela. 2

I could list very many. But let these suffice. 3

EX. 1.5 *Mutatio de natura in bmolle et de bmolle in ♮quadrum*

EX. 1.6 *Mutatio de natura in ♮quadrum et de ♮quadro in bmolle*

EX. 1.7 *Mutatio e ♮quadro in bmolle*

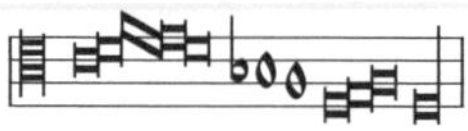

EX. 1.8 *Mutatio e natura in bmolle*

[45r] 

EX. 1.9 *In Csolfaut eodem modo mutationes*

EX. 1.10 *Finales modorum notulae*

EX. 1.5 *Mutation from nature to* bmolle *and from* bmolle *to* ♮quadrum

EX. 1.6 *Mutation from nature to* ♮quadrum *and from* ♮quadrum *to* bmolle

EX. 1.7 *Mutation from* ♮quadrum *to* bmolle

EX. 1.8 *Mutation from nature to* bmolle

EX. 1.9 *Mutations in the same manner on Csolfaut*

EX. 1.10 *The final notes of the modes*

EX. 1.11 *Euouae modorum principia*

EX. 1.12 *Primi modi intonatio*

EX. 1.13 *Secundi intonatio*

[45v]

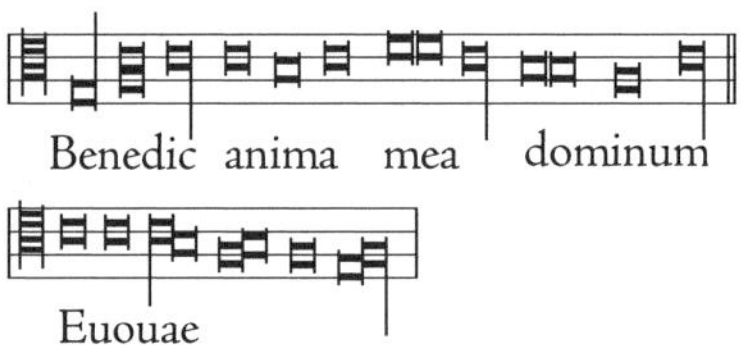

EX. 1.14

EX. I.11 Euouae: *The beginnings of the modes*

EX. I.12 *The intonation of the first mode*

EX. I.13 *The intonation of the second*

EX. I.14

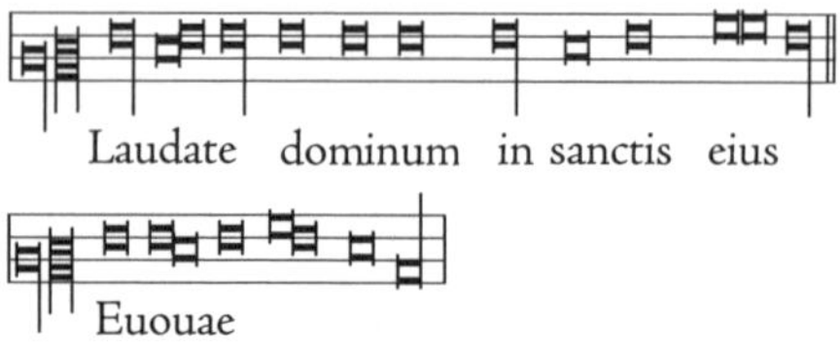

EX. 1.15

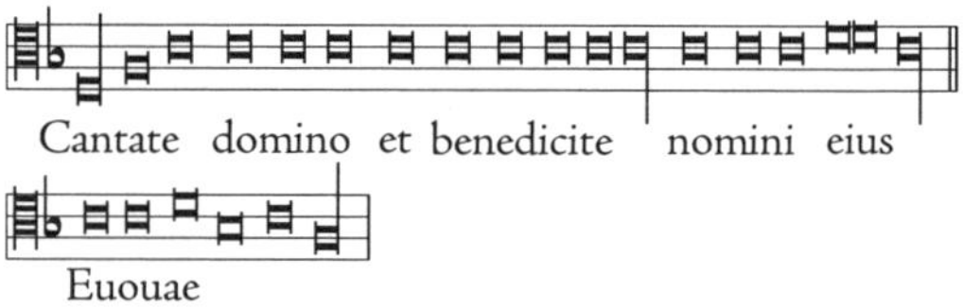

EX. 1.16

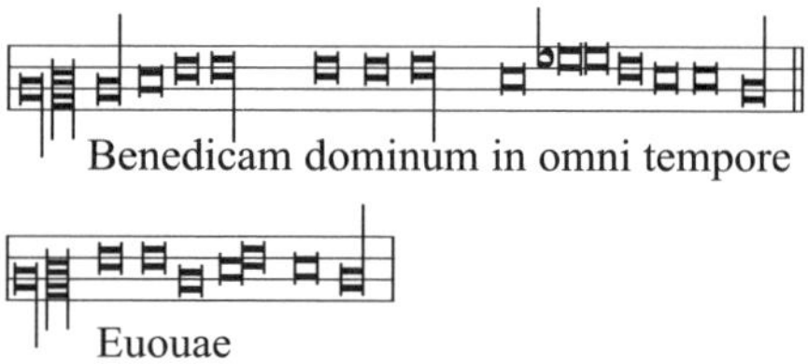

EX. 1.17

EX. 1.15

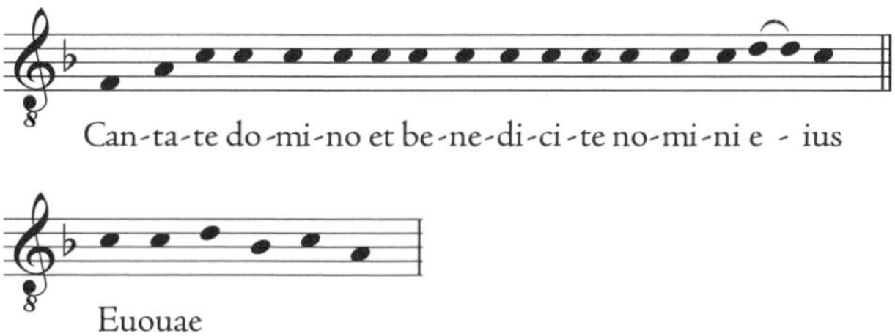

EX. 1.16

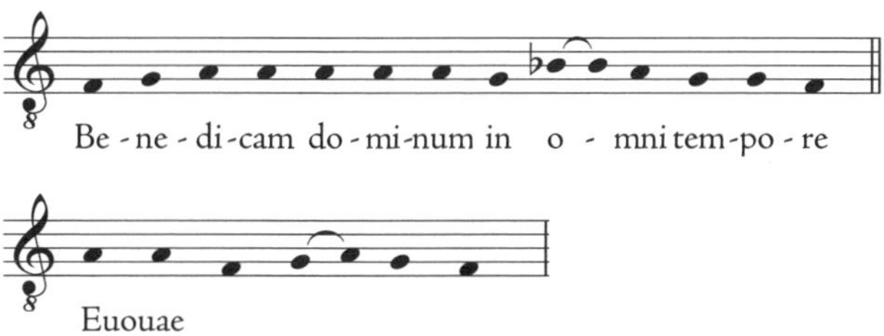

EX. 1.17

EX. 1.18

[46r]

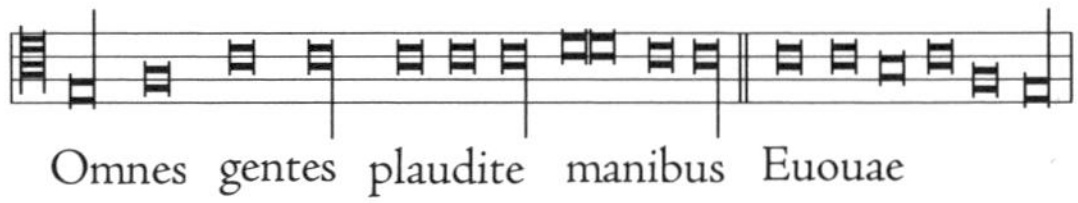

EX. 1.19

4 Consueverunt quoque musici tres psalmos, id est Magnificat, Benedictus Dominus, et Nunc dimittis, in his modis solemniter intonare, et praesertim in octavo, quamvis etiam et in omnibus per duplicationem quarundam[108] notularum illud idem effici possit. Exemplum quorundam:

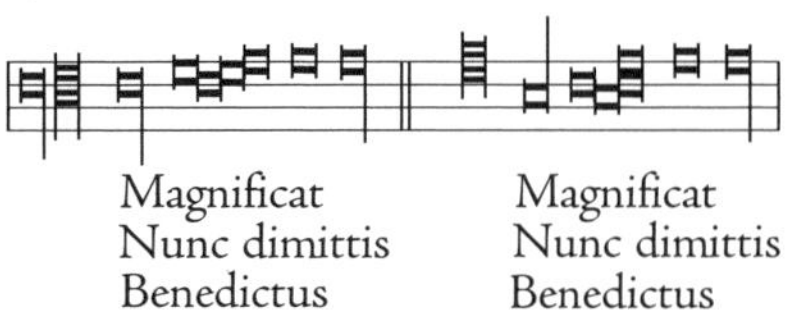

EX. 1.20

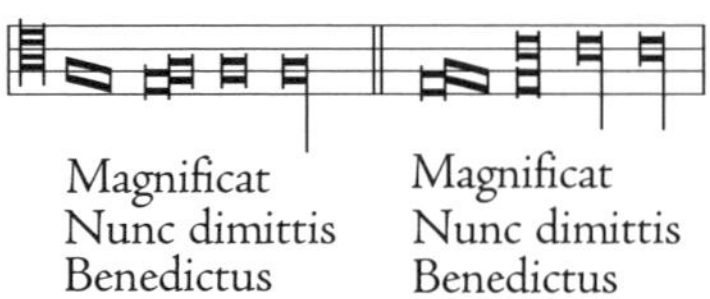

EX. 1.21

EX. I.18

EX. I.19

Musicians are also accustomed to solemnly intone three psalms, 4
namely the *Magnificat, Benedictus dominus,* and *Nunc dimittis,* in these modes, and especially in the eighth, although the same effect may also be achieved in them all by doubling certain notes. An example of some:[204]

EX. I.20

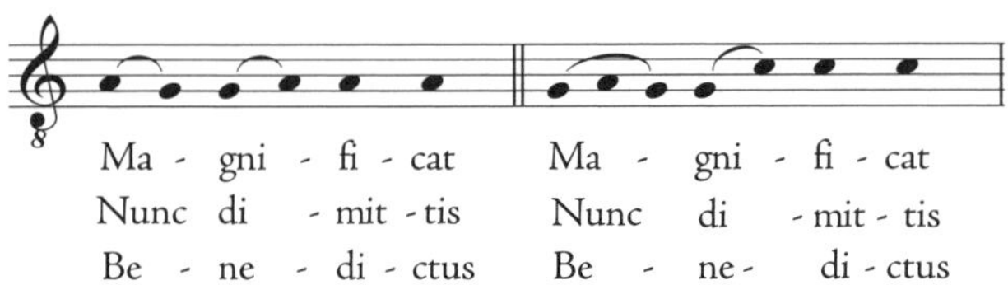

EX. I.21

5 [46v] Nunc autem Gloria Patri ex responsoriorum versibus proficiscentes sequuntur seriatim octo modorum.

EX. 1.22

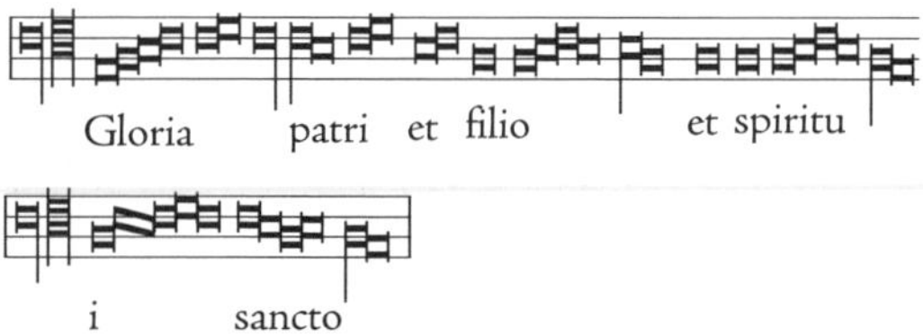

EX. 1.23

EX. 1.24

There follow now in order settings of the doxology in the eight modes, taken from the verses of responsories.[205]

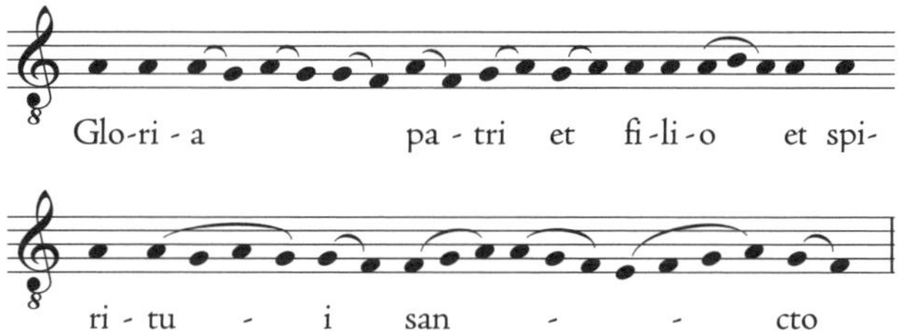

EX. I.22

EX. I.23

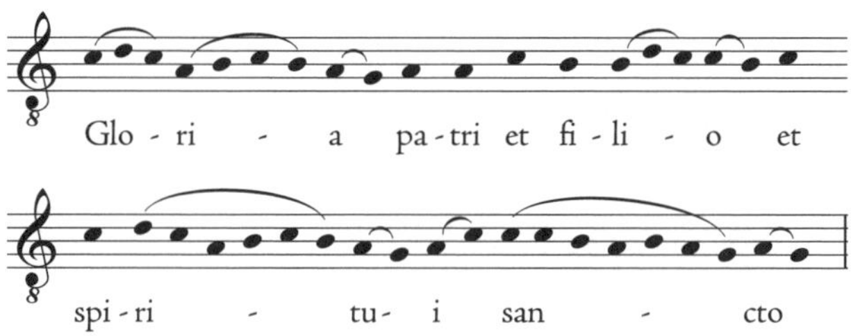

EX. I.24

[47r]

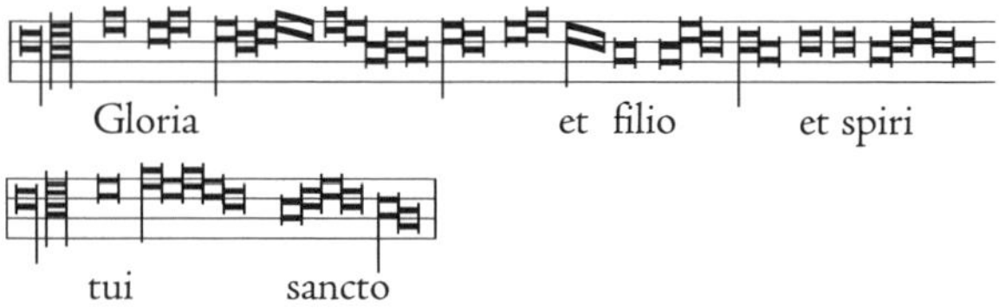

EX. 1.25

EX. 1.26

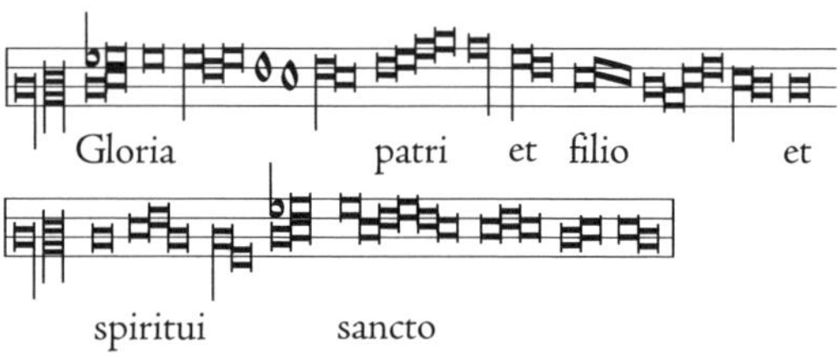

EX. 1.27

EX. I.25

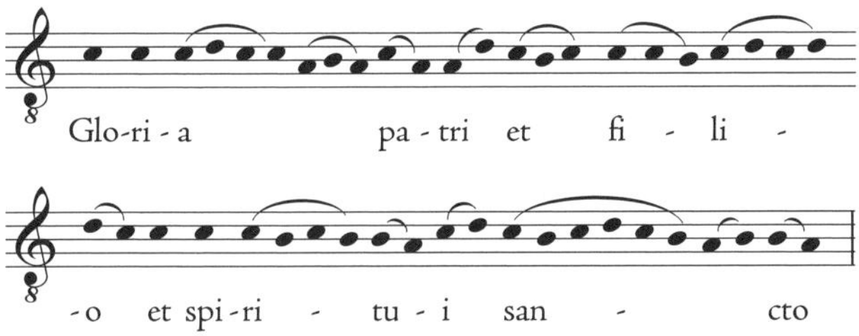

EX. I.26

EX. I.27

[47v]

EX. 1.28

EX. 1.29

6 <Sequuntur Gloria Patri ex versibus introituum proficiscentes itidem seriatim octo modorum>

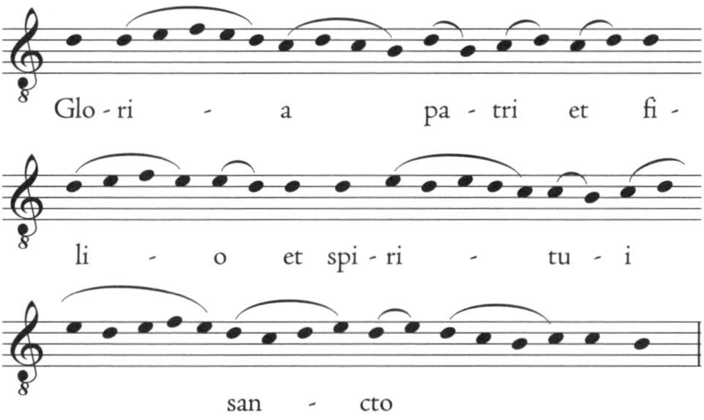

EX. I.28

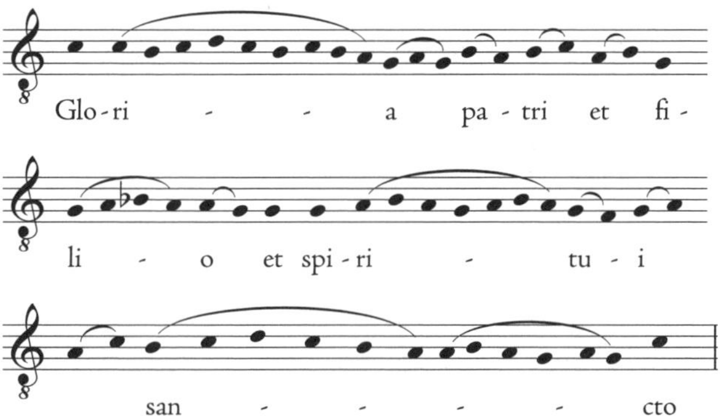

EX. I.29

<The doxologies taken from the verses of introits follow, like- 6
wise in the order of the eight modes.>[206]

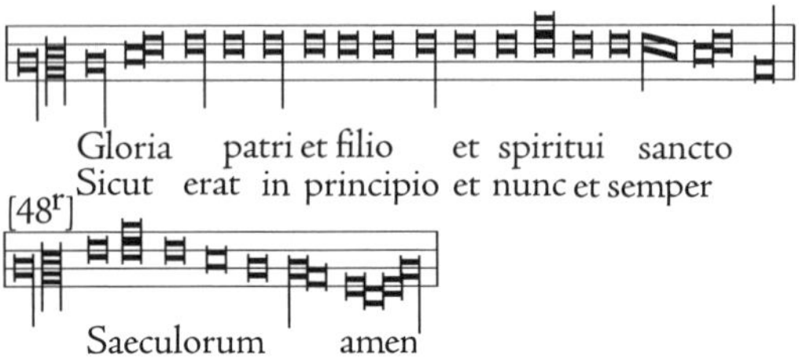

EX. 1.30

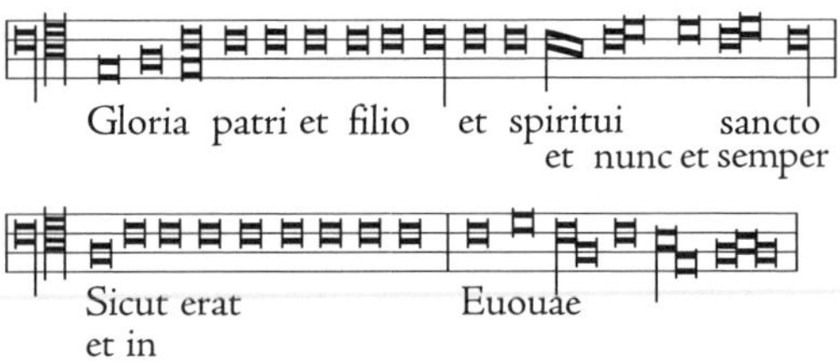

EX. 1.31

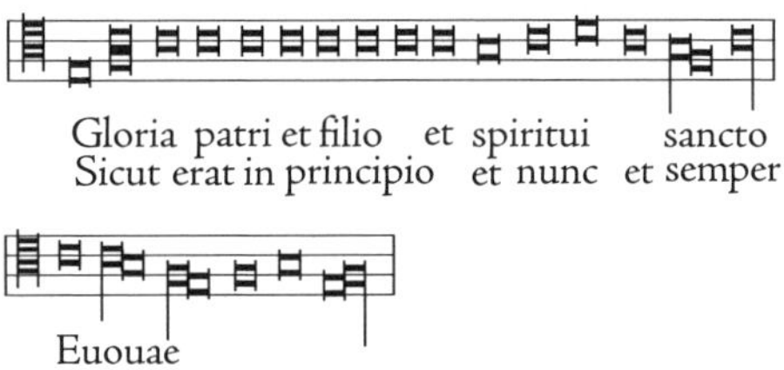

EX. 1.32

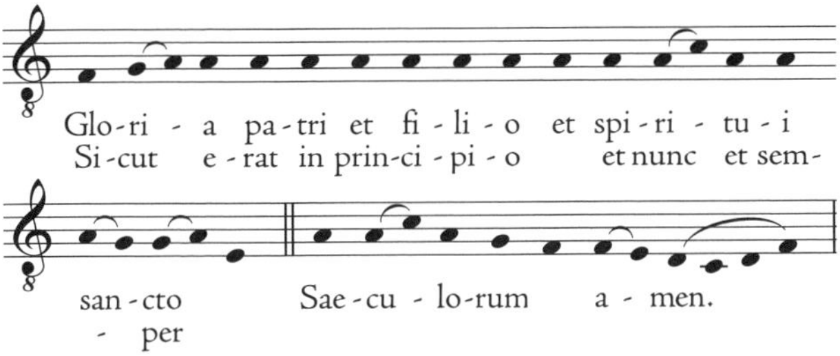

EX. 1.30

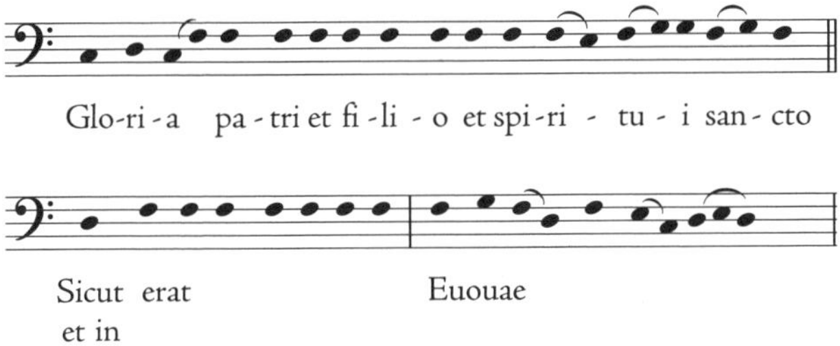

EX. 1.31

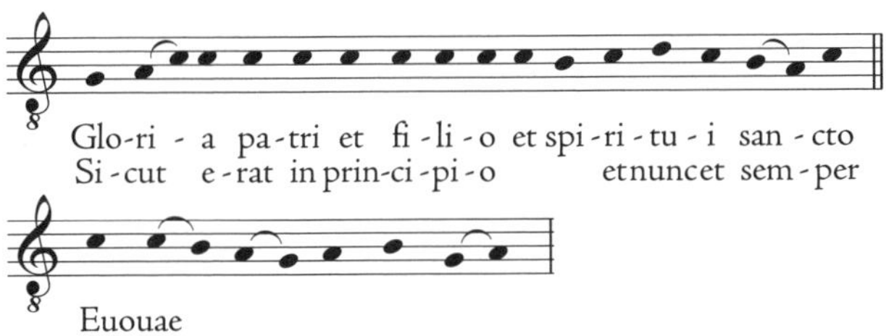

EX. 1.32

[48v]

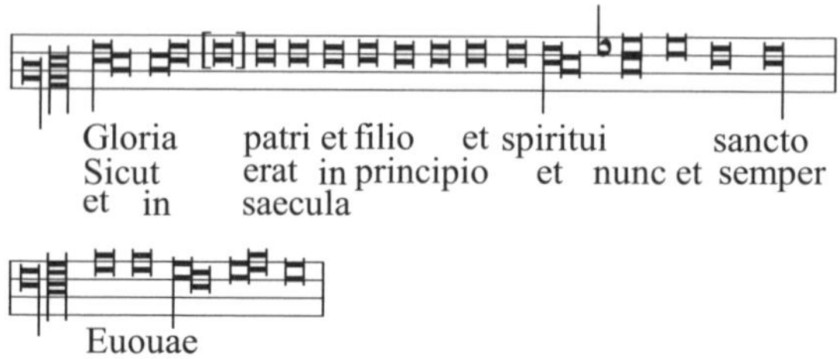

EX. 1.33

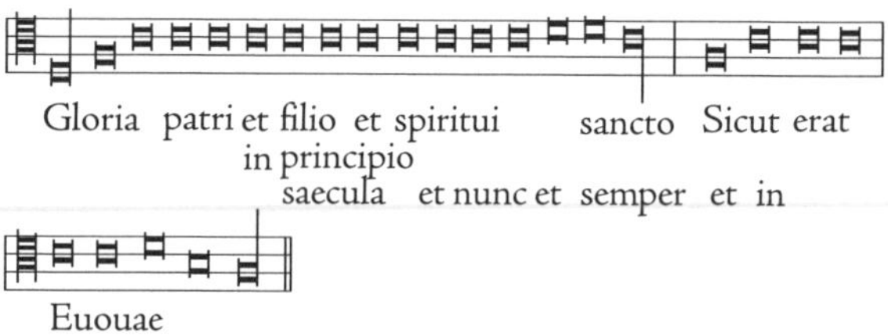

EX. 1.34

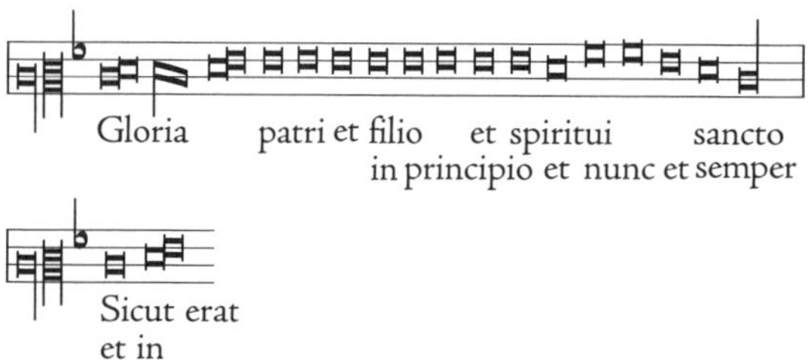

EX. 1.35

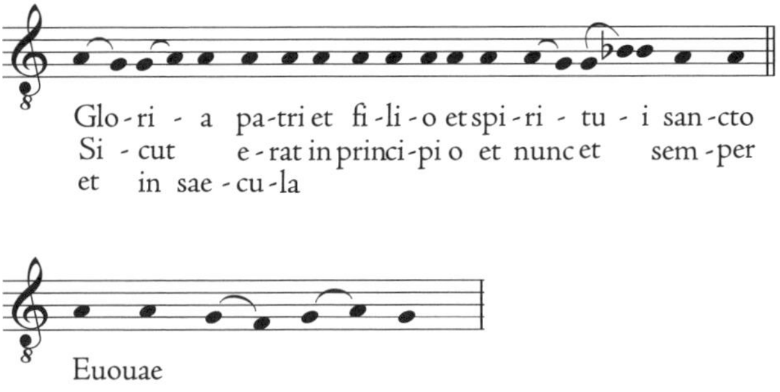

EX. I.33

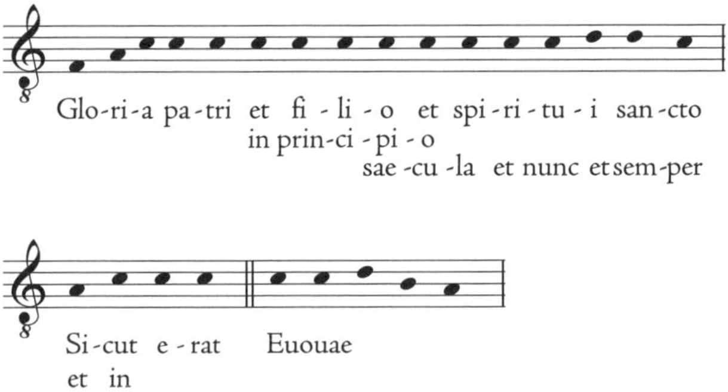

EX. I.34

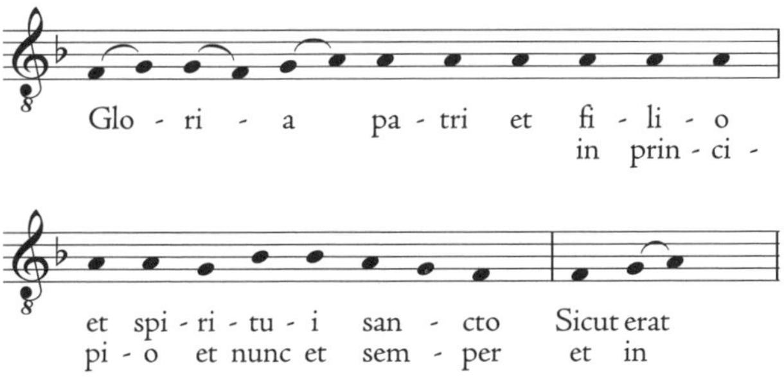

EX. I.35

• [LIBER II] •

: I :

<*Contrapunctus quid sit, unde dicatur, et quomodo inventus fuerit*>[1]

1 [49^{r}] . . . putavimus, quoniam super puncta ii comperierunt, nobis quoque eodem modo super notulas investigatam concinne per consonantias et perfectas et imperfectas operandam eandem esse.

2 Simplicem fuisse musicam principio musici insignes autumant, adeo ut quattuor nervis tota constaret, hoc quoque ad Orphei tempora permansisse. Primus enim nervus et quartus diapason, id est octavam consonantiam resonasse, medii ad se invicem <tonum> atque ad extremos diapenten, id est quintam ac diatessaron, hoc est quartam, sonabant, ut nihil in his inconsonum esset ad mundanae musices instar quae ex quattuor elementis constat, id est aere, igni, aqua, et terra. Cuius quadrichordi Mercurium dicunt fuisse auctores inventorem, eandem[2] comparasse. Paulatim postea singuli musici (ut Boethius ostendit) auxerunt. Quae documenta [49^{v}] igitur dentur his qui se praeparant ad musicam praesertim contrapunctalem, peritissimum Ubaldum audiamus.

✦ [BOOK II] ✦

: I :

[What counterpoint is, where the name comes from, and how it was discovered][1]

. . . we thought, since they learned it on the basis of points, that in the same way we too, having studied it on the basis of notes, should exercise it artistically through perfect and imperfect consonances.[2] 1

Outstanding musicians aver that music in the beginning was simple, so much so that it was entirely contained within four strings, and further that this state of affairs lasted until Orpheus's times.[3] The first string and the fourth sounded the diapason, that is, the consonance of the octave. The middle two sounded a tone against each other and the diapente, that is, the fifth, and the diatessaron, that is, the fourth, against the outer strings,[4] so that nothing in them should lack consonance, on the pattern of the music of the universe, which consists of four elements, that is, air, fire, water, and earth. The authors say that the inventor of this tetrachord was Mercury, and that he procured it [music].[5] Afterwards individual musicians (as Boethius shows) gradually augmented it. On the materials given to those who prepare themselves for music, in particular contrapuntal, let us hear the most expert Hucbald. 2

: II :

Quid investiget qui musicam scire[3] cupit

1 Ad musicae initiamenta quemlibet ingredientem qui aliquam scilicet interim cantilenarum percipere intelligentiam quaerit, qualitatem sive positionem quarumcumque vocum diligenter advertere oportebit. Et primo quae sint aequales <voces atque uniformiter sibi consimiles; quae deinde inaequales>[4] et quibusdam spatiis a se discrepantes, ipsorum denique spatiorum quanta habeantur discrimina, quotque etiam varietatibus ea moderari contingat; post et praeterea quot vel quibus sonis, qui vice habentur elementorum, tota regatur cantilena.

2 Iam vero his non parvi temporis exercitiis tamquam pro foribus assuetum, ad ipsius demum penetralia disciplinae, acie quodammodo visus obtusi paulatim summota caligine radiata, ad[50r]mitti forte donabitur, quomodo scilicet haec omnia, vel vis[5] de quibus ea tractat consonantiarum, rationabilitate congruentissima disponantur numerorum, atque ad eorundem sint exemplar universa composita atque compacta.

3 Et de aequalibus quidem vocibus quoniam ipsae per se patent, nihil aliud dicendum nisi quod continuo vocis impetu proferuntur in modum soluta oratione legentis; et quod una tantum vox est quotiescumque repetantur,[6] veluti si unam quamlibet litteram saepius scribas aut proferas, ut a a a; et quod nulla inter eas est consonantia. Sunt enim aequisonae non consonae. Nam in consonantia duae voces a se

: II :

What he should study who desires to know music

Anyone embarking on the rudiments of music, that is, any- 1
one who seeks to receive for the moment some understanding of songs, ought to observe attentively the quality or position of all the pitches. And first, which pitches are equal <and uniformly consistent, then which are unequal> and at certain distances from each other,[6] and how great the gaps between the intervals are, and also in how many varieties they are to be measured; after that, and in addition, by how many and which sounds, which are taken as the primary components,[7] the whole song is directed.

Then, it may perchance be granted that, having become 2
accustomed to these time-consuming exercises while so to speak [waiting] before the door, he is granted entry at last to the sanctum of the discipline proper, the sight of his blunted vision having gradually been as it were made radiant by removal of the darkness, namely [to see] how all these things, or the power[8] of the consonances that it treats of, are arranged with a most well-matched proportionality of numbers and how without exception they are made up and fitted together on the pattern of the same [i.e. numbers].

And of equal pitches, since they are obvious by them- 3
selves, nothing else need be said except that they are uttered by a continuous flow of voice in the way that one reads prose; and that there is only one and the same pitch, however often they are repeated, as if you were to write or utter any one letter several times, as *a a a;* and that there is no consonance between them, for they are equal-sounding, not consonant. For in a consonance it is in all cases voices at an

> omnimodo distantes simul concorditer sonant; in his autem vocibus etiam si a pluribus[7] eaedem promantur, nullo tamen a se spatio distant. Haec ille.

4 Et quoniam hac in arte consonantia<m> tenere principatum dicimus, [50v] idcirco ipsam partesque eius primo notabimus.

: III :

De harmonia, euphonia, simphonia, melodia, modulatione

1 Harmonia, ut Papias indicat, est 'vocis modulatio et plurimarum vocum consonantia, quae in ipsa musica acutum et grave discernit.' Isidorus de eadem: 'Harmonia est modulatio vocis et concordantia vel coaptatio plurimorum sonorum.' Marchettus vero auctores adducens, hoc de ipsa refert:

> 2 Harmonia (ut Hucbaldus refert) est diversarum vocum apta coadunatio, dicitur enim ab armos Graece, quod Latine est adunatio, inde harmonia coadunatio vocum dicitur. Et Philosophus: 'Harmonia est ratio numerorum in acuto et gravi.' Haec ille.

3 Euphonia est vocis sonus suavis. Haec melos dici potest, id est suave. Isidorus: 'Euphonia est suavitas [51r] vocis.' Haec a melosa suavitate, id est a melle et eu Graece, id est bonum deducta. Marchettus: 'Euphonia bona sonoritas dicitur. Nam eu bonum et pho-

> interval from each other that sound together in concord, but in the case of these pitches, even if the same ones are uttered by several people, there is nevertheless no interval between them.[9]

And since we say that in this art consonance holds the primacy, therefore we shall first describe it and its parts. 4

: III :

On harmony, euphony, concord (symphonia), melody, modulatio

Harmony, as Papias indicates, is the "*modulatio* of the voice, that is to say,[10] the consonance of very many pitches, which in music distinguishes high and low."[11] Isidore says of it: "Harmony is the *modulatio* of the voice, that is to say, the concord or fitting together of very many sounds."[12] Marchetto, citing authorities, has this to say on it: 1

> Harmony (as Hucbald says) is "the apt uniting of different pitches,"[13] and is so called from *armos* in Greek, which in Latin is *adunatio,* hence harmony is called the uniting of pitches. And the Philosopher: "Harmony is the ratio of numbers in high and low."[14] 2

Euphony is the sweet sound of the voice. It may be called *melos,* that is, sweet. Isidore: "Euphony is sweetness of voice."[15] It is derived from melodious sweetness, that is, from *mel* [Latin for "honey"] and *eu* in Greek, that is, "good." Marchetto: "Euphony is the name for good sonority. For *eu* means 'good' and *phonia* 'sonor- 3

nia sonoritas interpretatur.' Aulus Gellius libro primo: 'Sonus qui εὐφωνία, id est voculatio.'

4 Symphonia (ut Papias dicit) 'est consonantia plurimorum[8] sonorum et modulationis temperamentum ex gravi et acuto concordantibus sonis in voce, flatu, et pulsu.' Marchettus:

> 5 Symphonia (ut dicit Augustinus) est concordia vocum in quibus non est absurdus vel dissonus sonus. Ex definitionibus supradictis colligere possumus quod euphonia, harmonia, symphonia, et consonantia unum quodammmodo sint. Haec Marchettus.

6 Isidorus:

> 7 Symphonia est modulationis temperamentum ex gravi et acuto concordantibus sonis sive voce, [51ᵛ] sive flatu, sive impulsu.[9] Per hanc quippe voces acutiores gravioresque concordant, ita ut quisquis ab ea dissonuerit, sensum auditus offendat. Cuius contrarium est diaphonia, id est voces discrepantes vel dissonae. Haec ille.

8 Melodiam 'cantus dulcedinem' Papias dicit, 'vel vocis suavitatem, a convenientia chordarum tanquam membrorum dictam. Graeci τὰ μέλη dicunt.' Nam 'melos suave, hoc est sonus dulcis cantilenae a suavitate et melle dictus.' Mel quoque ab apibus derivatum dicimus, nam μέλισσα apis dicta est a Graecis. 'Modulatio (ut Censorinus dicit) est modorum prudens dispositio. Eius tres species διάτονος, χρῶμα, ἁρμονία.'

9 Et quoniam consonantiae ut videbimus e tonis semitoniisque componuntur, ideo quid ii, scilicet tonus et semitonium, sint [52ʳ] videamus.

ity.'"[16] Aulus Gellius, Book I: "Sound, which is *euphonia,* that is, accent."[17]

Concord [*symphonia*] (as Papias says) "is the consonance of very many sounds and the blending of *modulatio* from low and high with concordant sounds in voice, wind, and percussion."[18] Marchetto: 4

> *Symphonia* (as Augustine says)[19] is "a concord of pitches in which there is no sound out of tune or dissonant." From the above definitions we may infer that euphony, harmony, concord, and consonance are in a certain sense the same.[20] 5

Isidore: 6

> Concord is the blending of *modulatio* from low and high with concordant sounds whether by voice, by wind, or by percussion. For by this, higher and lower voices are in concord, so that whoever is in dissonance with it offends the sense of hearing. Its contrary is *diaphonia,* that is, discrepant and dissonant voices.[21] 7

Papias calls melody "the sweetness of singing, or the pleasantness of voice, so called from the symmetry of strings as if of the limbs, which the Greeks call *tà mélē.*"[22] For "*melos suave,* that is, the sound of sweet song,[23] is so called from *suavitas* [sweetness] and *mel* [honey]."[24] *Mel,* moreover, we say is derived from bees, for the bee was called *mélissa* by the Greeks.[25] "*Modulatio,*" as Censorinus says, is the "prudent arrangement of *modi*. Its three species are diatonic, chromatic, and enharmonic."[26] 8

And since consonances, as we shall see, are made up of tones and semitones, let us see what they—tone and semitone—are. 9

: IIII[10] :

De tono et semitonio

1 Tonus (ut Isidoro placet)

2 est acuta vocis enuntiatio. Est enim harmoniae differentia et quantitas, quae in vocis accentu vel tenore consistit, cuius genera in xv partibus musici diviserunt. E quibus Hyperlydius novissimus et acutissimus, <Hy>podorius omnium gravissimus est. Hoc ille de tono.

3 Ex nostris ita quidam de tono definitionem dederunt: 'Tonus est legitimum spatium a sono in sonum per arsim vel thesim, utpote ut re, re ut.' Semitonium vero imperfectum spatium dicunt, sicut est mi fa vel fa mi.

4 Hoc de his Abbas Populeti:

5 Tonus autem est legitimum spatium a sono in sonum, id est ut re et aliae praeter spatium mi fa. Semitonium est a sono in sonum non plena positio, id est mi fa.

6 Arnaldus Dalps haec quoque de his:

7 Tonus etenim est duarum [52v] vocum ascendentium sive descendentium collectio omni medio postposito plenum intervallum emittentium existit. Et dicitur de tono, -as. Et capitur ubicumque est intervallum duarum vocum coniunctarum, mi fa excepto, quoniam mi (sine fa videlicet) cum re, et fa (sine mi videlicet) cum sol, faciunt tonum. Semitonium vero est collectio duarum vocum ascendentium sive descendentium absque aliquo medio interposito non plenum inter-

: IV :

On the tone and semitone

The tone (as Isidore holds) 1

is a high utterance of the voice; for it is the difference and quantity of harmony, which consists in the accent or tenor of the voice; its kinds have been divided by musicians into fifteen parts, of which the Hyperlydian is the last and highest, the Hypodorian the lowest of all.[27] That is what he says on the tone. 2

Among our people,[28] some have given a definition of the tone thus: "The tone is the proper interval from pitch to pitch,[29] rising and falling, for example *ut re, re ut.*" "Semitone" is their name for the imperfect interval, as *mi fa* or *fa mi.* 3

The Abbot of Poblet has this to say of them: 4

Now the tone is the proper interval from pitch to pitch, that is, *ut re* and the others, apart from the interval *mi fa.* The semitone is a less than full position from pitch to pitch, that is, *mi fa.* 5

Arnaldus Dalps too says the following about them:[30] 6

For the tone is the combination of two ascending or descending pitches, with no middle pitch between them,[31] emitting a full interval. And it is so called from *tono, -as.*[32] And it is observed wherever there is an interval of two conjunct pitches, except *mi fa,* since *mi* (i.e., without *fa*) with *re,* and *fa* (i.e., without *mi*) with *sol,* make a tone. A semitone, on the other hand, is the combination of two ascending or descending pitches, without any middle pitch between them, hav- 7

vallum habentium, sicuti est mi fa vel fa mi, et dicitur a semus, quod est imperfectum, id est non bene plenum. Quod a Boethio, <qui> fons et origo <est>[11] scientiae musicalis, dyesis nuncupatur.

8 Guido autem sic: 'Maius quidem spatium tonus dicitur, minus vero semitonium, semis videlicet, id est non plenus sonus sive tonus.' Hoc maius et minus in consonantia diapason invenitur. De quibus [53r] Boethius suo opere fecundas speculative causas reddit.

9 Macrobius autem de his hoc pacto sermonem explicat:

10 Epogdous est numerus qui intra se habet minorem et insuper[12] octavam partem, ut novem ad octo, quia in .viiii. octo sunt et insuper octava pars eorum, id est unum. Hic numerus sonum parit quem tonon musici vocaverunt. Sonum vero tono minorem veteres quidem semitonium vocitare maluerunt. Sed non ita accipiendum est, ut dimidius tonus putetur, quia nec semivocalem in litteris pro medietate vocalis accipimus. Deinde tonus per naturam sui in duo dividi sibi aequa non poterit. Cum <enim>[13] ex numero novenario constet, novem autem nunquam aequaliter dividantur, tonus in duas dividi medietates recusat. Sed semitonium vocaverunt sonum tono minorem, quem tam parvo dista[53v]re a tono deprehensum est quantum hi duo numeri inter se distant, id est <ccxliii et>[14] cclvi. Hoc semitonium Pythagorici quidem veteres diesim[15] nominabant. Sed sequens usus sonum semitonio minorem diesim constituit[16] nominandum. Plato semitonium limma vocitavit. Haec ille.

11 Ex his autem infinitas consonantias perfectas formatasque inspiciemus. At iam quid Boethius de consonantia inferat audiamus.

> ing an interval that is not full, such as *mi fa* or *fa mi,* and is so called from *semus,* which is "imperfect,"[33] that is, not properly full. Boethius, who is the fount and origin of musical science, called this *diesis.*[34]

Guido speaks thus: "The greater interval is called the tone, the lesser the semitone, namely the *semis,* that is, not a 'full' pitch or 'tone.' "[35] These greater and lesser intervals are found in the consonance of the octave. Of them Boethius offers in his work a rich theoretical explanation. 8

Macrobius unfolds the following discourse about them: 9

> The epogdous is a number that has within it a smaller number and its eighth part in addition, as 9 : 8, since in nine eight is contained and in addition its eighth part, that is, one. This number begets the sound that musicians have named the tone. The sound less than a tone the ancients preferred to call a semitone. But it is not to be so taken as to be thought half a tone, for neither do we understand a semivowel[36] in the alphabet[37] as being half a vowel. Furthermore, the tone by its nature cannot be divided into two equal parts: since it is made from the number nine, and nine is never divided equally,[38] the tone refuses to be divided into two halves. But they called "semitone" a sound less than a tone, which was found to differ from the tone by as small an interval as these two numbers differ, namely 243 and 256. This semitone the ancient Pythagoreans called a *diesis,* but later usage determined that it was a sound less than a semitone that should be so called. Plato called the semitone *leimma.*[39] 10

But we shall examine the infinite consonances framed[40] and formed from them. Now let us hear what Boethius states on consonance. 11

: V :

Quid consonantia

1 Consonantia quae omnem musicae modulationem regit praeter sonum fieri non potest. Sonus vero praeter quendam pulsum percussionemque non redditur, pulsus vero atque percussio nullo modo esse potest nisi praecesserit motus. Si enim cuncta sint immobilia non poterit alterum alteri concurrere, ut alterum impellatur ab altero. Sed cunctis stantibus motuque carentibus nullum fieri [54^{r}] sonum necesse est. Idcirco definitur sonus percussio aeris indissoluta usque ad auditum, et quae ipse pergit.

2 Verum enim vero consonantiam in plana musica tonum, semitonium, diatessaron, omnisque et singulas a consequendo, non autem a consonando musici dicunt. Sed hic in contrapuncto et figurativo a consonando ea<n>dem a con et sono, -as compositam vocitamus. Quo pacto hanc Boethius distinxerit, nunc videamus:

3 Vocum aliae sunt unisonae, aliae minime. Unisonae sunt quarum sonus unus est vel in gravi vel in acuto. Non unisonae vero quando est alia gravior, alia acutior.

4 Alio quoque loco is ipse:

5 Oportet vero has omnes consonantias rite esse animo atque auribus notas. Frustra enim haec ratione et scientia colliguntur, nisi fuerint usu atque exercitatione notissima.

: V :

What consonance is

> Consonance, which governs every realization of music, cannot be created without sound. Sound is not rendered without a striking and beating, nor can striking and beating exist at all without a preceding motion. For if all things are immobile, nothing will be able to run into anything else for the one to be impelled by the other; but if all things are standing and bereft of motion, it follows of necessity that no sound is produced. Therefore sound is defined as a beating of air not broken up till it reaches the hearing, etc.[41] 1

However, in plainchant musicians apply the name "consonance" 2
to the tone, semitone, fourth, and all and each of them, from *consequor* ["follow"], not from *consono* ["sound together"];[42] but here in counterpoint and in mensural music we use the word because they sound together, as a compound of *con* ["with"] and *sono, -as* ["I sound, thou soundest"]. Let us see now how Boethius made the distinction:

> Of pitches, some are in unison, some not. In unison are 3
> those that have a single sound, whether low or high. They are not in unison when one is lower, one higher.[43]

Elsewhere too he says: 4

> All these consonances ought to be properly known to the 5
> mind and the ears. For it is no use deriving these from reason and theory if they have not become thoroughly familiar by experience and practice.[44]

6 Hactenus de his. Nunc autem contrapuncti seriem [54ᵛ] sequamur.

: VI :

E quibus numeris consonantiae componuntur, et quomodo inventae fuerunt

1 Super planam musicam igitur maiores nostros contrapunctum adinvenisse constat, idque paulatim experti viam rationemque consonantiarum per tonum semitoniumque compositarum posteris aditum dederunt. Solum diatessaron, diapenten, et diapason celeberrimas e tonis semitonisque confectas ipsi noverant.[17] Verum posteri ditonum, semiditonum, diapenten cum tono vel exaden indagantes his addiderunt.

2 Quam ob causam de consonantiarum numero inter se multi dissentire videntur: nam quidam septem, quidam novem, aliqui plures aut his pauciores suis rescriptis ostendunt. Nos vero numerum septenarium spectantes, quem sola singularitas generat, solum quattuor principales ab hisque infinitas [55ʳ] per crementum derivatas habemus. Nam ut Boethio placet, quid duo, nisi bis unum? quid tria, vel quattuor, vel quinque, vel sex, vel septem, nisi totidem[18] unum? Unde Macrobius: 'Tam paris quam imparis numeri monas origo est.'

3 Cum ad octonarium numerum veniemus unius reiterationem noverimus; sic quoque reliquorum, et deinceps. Quare consonantias huiusmodi de singulis deductas principalibus legitima descriptione pangemus.

So much for them. Now let us follow the course of counterpoint. 6

: VI :

From which numbers consonances are made up, and how they were discovered

Over plainchant, then, it is established fact that our forebears de- 1
vised counterpoint, and having little by little found out the path and principle of consonances made up of tones and semitones, they opened the way to their successors. They themselves recognized only the fourth, fifth, and octave, the best-known [consonances] made up of tones and semitones. However, their successors researched further and added the major and minor third and the fifth plus tone or major sixth.

For this reason many of them are observed to disagree over the 2
number of consonances: some point to seven, some nine, some more or fewer than these in their writings.[45] But we, taking note of the number seven, which unity alone generates,[46] recognize only four principal consonances and an infinite number derived from them by addition. For as Boethius has it,[47] what is two, but twice one? what is three, or four, or five, or six, or seven, but so many times one? Whence Macrobius: "Unity is the origin as well of the even number as the odd."[48]

When we come to the number eight we shall recognize that one 3
is being repeated, and likewise that the rest are, and so forth.[49] Therefore we shall set forth such consonances derived from each of the principals in a regular table.

: VII :

De consonantiis primitivis ceteras formantibus

1 Erunt igitur consonantiae principales quattuor, id est aequisona vox, quam unisonum musici vocant; tertia, quam ditonum vel semiditonum dicunt; quinta vel diapente; sexta, quam exaden vel diapenten cum tono nominant. Quarum duae per[55v]fectae, id est unisonus et quinta, imperfectae tertia et sexta sunt. E quibus multae deduci possunt et formari. Quae vero a perfectis vel imperfectis proficiscentur, hae primitivarum naturam sequentur; nam ab unisono et quinta perfectas, a tertia et sexta imperfectas extrahemus. Igitur:

2

ab unisono	viii xv xxii xxviiii xxxvi xliii la
a tertia	x xvii xxiiii xxxi xxxviii xlv liia
a quinta	xii xviiii xxvi xxxiii xl xlvii liiiia
a sexta	xiii xx xxvii xxxiiii xli xlviii lv

3 Omnes hae consonantes, per septenarium numerum de unis in ceteras auctae cumulataeque, in organis aut monochordis vel quovis instrumento augeri possunt, pectori autem humano superfluae pronuntiatuque minus possibiles sunt. Nam cum ab ima, id est graviori vel inferiori, voce ad altiorem per vicesimam quartam vel sextam citra manum consonan[56r]tiam petere conabimur, acutiores inde consonantias nec posse quidem[19] absque labore pectoris maximo id consequi. Sed in instrumentis longe plures his convenirent.

4 Hoc de consonantiarum multiplicatione per augmentum septenarii numeri inquam. Nunc vero quibus tonis semitoniisque conficiantur edemus.

: VII :

On the primitive consonances that form the others

There will thus be four principal consonances, that is: the equal-sounding pitch, which musicians call the unison; the third, which they call the ditone or semiditone; the fifth, or diapente; the sixth, which they call the hexad or diapente plus tone. Of these two are perfect, namely the unison and the fifth; the third and sixth are imperfect. From these many consonances can be derived and formed; but those that issue from the perfect and imperfect will follow the nature of the [respective] principals: from the unison and the fifth we shall extract perfect [consonances], from the third and the sixth imperfect ones. Thus: 1

from the unison	octave, 15th, 22nd, 29th, 36th, 43rd, 50th	2
from the third	10th, 17th, 24th, 31st, 38th, 45th, 52nd	
from the fifth	12th, 19th, 26th, 33rd, 40th, 47th, 54th	
from the sixth	13th, 20th, 27th, 34th, 41st, 48th, 55th	

All these are consonant, increasing and accumulating by sevens from one to the other, and may be expanded on organs, or monochords, or any instrument, but they are excessive for the human chest and not so capable of utterance. For when from the bottom, that is, the deepest or lowest pitch, we try to reach the highest[50] by a twenty-fourth, or the sixth consonance that dispenses with the hand,[51] we shall not even be able to reach any higher consonances without the greatest toil of the chest. But far more than these would be appropriate for instruments.[52] 3

This is what I have to say on the multiplication of consonances by increase in sevens; now we shall state by what tones and semitones they are formed. 4

: VIII :

De prima consonantia

1 Vox aequisona vel unisonus e pluribus in unitate vocibus, vel aequalitate perfecta consonantia conficitur [Ex. 2.4]; non enim sibi toni vel semitonii compositio quadrat, sed ea tantum binae vocis vel plurimae consentaneum sonum vel acutum vel gravem habet. De duabus ad minimum vocibus coadunatio est, uniusque soni plurimarum vocum conexio dicitur, et ubique locorum formari potest, dummodo inter se voces [56ᵛ] coaequentur, id est ut ut, re re, et in ceteris tam ascendendo quam descendendo. De hac Arnaldus Dalps:

2 Porro unius sonus fundamentum, fons, et origo consonantiarum omnium existit, praesertim cum sicut in numero ab unitate incipiendum est licet numerus non existat potissime, quia numerus in pluralitate consistit, attamen ab ipso indubitanter incipiendum est. Haec ille.

: IX :

De secunda consonantia

1 Tertia est duplex, maior scilicet et minor. Hanc semiditonum musici vocitarunt, illam vero ditonum. Constat autem maior e tonis duobus componi, quod est ut mi vel fa la [Ex. 2.5]. Hoc idem in descensum res ipsa postulat, id est mi ut, vel la fa. Minor autem

: VIII :

On the first consonance

The equal-sounding voice or unison is made up of several pitches in unity, or equality, by perfect consonance; for the addition of a tone or semitone is incompatible with it, but it involves only the concordant sound, high or low, of two or many voices. It is the uniting of at least two voices, and it is called the conjunction of one sound in many voices; and it may be formed everywhere, provided the voices are made equal, that is, *ut ut*, *re re*, etc., ascending or descending [see Ex. 2.4].[53] Arnaldus Dalps says of it: 1

> Indeed the sound of one is the foundation, fount, and origin of all consonances, especially since, as in number, we must begin from unity even though properly speaking it is not a number, since number consists in plurality; nevertheless, we must undoubtedly start from it. 2

: IX :

On the second consonance

The third is twofold, namely major and minor; musicians have called the latter the semiditone, the former the ditone. It is well known that the major is made up of two tones, that is, *ut mi* or *fa la* [see Ex. 2.5]. Inevitably this also applies in descent, that is, *mi ut* or *la fa*. The minor comprises a tone and a semitone, whether ma- 1

tono et semitonio vel maiori vel minori conficitur [Ex. 2.6]. Quid sit semitonium maius vel [57r] minus suo loco videbimus. Cum minori ab A primo vel secundo vel tertio in C primo, vel secundo vel tertio, hoc est re fa. Idem a ♮ primo vel secundo vel tertio in D primo vel secundo, vel tertio, hoc est mi sol, tantundem in descensum. Cum maiori vero a D primo vel secundo vel tertio in F primo vel secundo vel tertio, id est re fa, idem ab E primo vel secundo vel tertio in G primo vel secundo vel tertio, id est mi sol, et in descensum hisdem conversis. De hac Arnaldus Dalps:

2 Tertia etenim quae etiam imperfecta consistit, et simplex numero, tamen incipiendo ab unitate respectu tonorum et semitonorum duplex existit, una quidem maior, reliqua vero minor, et quae ille pergit.

: X :

De tertia consonantia

1 Diapente vel quinta constat composita de tonis tribus unoque semi[57v]tonio vel maiori sit vel minori [Ex. 2.7];[20] non ad rem spectat, nam per vocis acuitionem illud minus maius reddetur contrapunctanti id iudicante. Quod haec minus semitonium et non maius habeat (ut Arnaldo placet), hoc mihi perspicue falsum videtur. Nam si huic vel ceteris perfectis quid addatur sive auferatur, non ea solum turpe sonaret, sed penitus discreparet.

jor or minor [see Ex. 2.6]. What the major and minor semitone are we shall see in due course.[54] With the minor [semitone, the third is the interval] from first, second, or third A to first, second, or third C, that is, *re fa*. The same from first, second, or third ♮ to first, second, or third D, that is, *mi sol;* the same quantity in descent. With the major, [it is that] from first, second, or third D to first, second, or third F, that is, *re fa*, the same from first, second, or third E to first, second, or third G, that is, *mi sol*, and vice versa in descent. Arnaldus Dalps says of it:

> For the third, which also exists in an imperfect form, although simple in number, nevertheless, beginning from unity, is twofold in respect of tones and semitones, one kind major, one minor, and so forth. 2

: X :

On the third consonance

The diapente or fifth is well known to be made up of three tones and a semitone [see Ex. 2.7], irrespective of major or minor, for by the sharping of the voice the minor will be rendered major when the contrapuntist deems fit. Arnaldus's opinion that it contains the minor semitone and not the major seems to me manifestly false.[55] For if anything were added to or taken from this or the other perfect consonances, it would not only sound ugly, but be utterly dissonant.[56] 1

: XI :

De quarta consonantia

1 Diapenten cum tono vel exaden quam et sextam dicimus maiorem minoremque habemus. Maior illud idem quod diapente et tonum habet, hoc est, semitonium et quatuor tonos [Ex. 2.9]. Minor vero tres tonos et duo semitonia quorum alterum maius est, alterum vero minus [Ex. 2.10]. Quam formationem quo in loco semiditonus haec ipsa quoque habet.

: XII :

[58r] De diapason et notione semitonii maioris et minoris

1 Diapason vel dupla quam octavam dicimus consonantiam de omnibus dicitur. Nam de diatessaron et diapente conficitur, quae tonos quinque et semitonia duo continent [Ex. 2.11], quae semitonium alterum maius alterum vero minus esse, Boethius ostendit. Haec[21] enim ab unisono per duplam proportionem numero septenario addito deducitur, quod iam supra ostensum est cumulatissime. Verum quomodo in consonantiis semitonium maius vel minus appareat, quid breviter ex his explicabimus.

2 Tonum Boethius et Macrobius duas partes habere autumant, id est apotomen, quod est maius semitonium, et dyesin, quod est minus, isque in proportione sesquioctava divisionem habet [Ex. 2.14], qui numeri viii et viiii ea semitonia conficiunt.[22] In promptu veri[58v]tas experimento disputationis tam peritorum virorum exa-

: XI :

On the fourth consonance

1 The diapente plus tone, or hexad, which we also call the sixth, we have in major and minor. The major contains the equivalent of diapente and a tone, that is, a semitone and four tones [see Ex. 2.9]; the minor three tones and two semitones, of which one is major, the other minor [see Ex. 2.10]. It has this formation in the same place as the semiditone.[57]

: XII :

On the diapason and the notion of the major and minor semitone

1 The diapason or duple proportion, which we call the octave consonance, is named from "all."[58] For it is made up of the diatessaron and diapente, which contain five tones and two semitones [see Ex. 2.11], of which Boethius shows one to be a major semitone and the other a minor;[59] for it is derived from the unison by duple proportion by adding the number seven, which has been shown above in very great detail.[60] But as to how the major or minor semitone appears among the consonances, we shall offer a brief explanation.

2 Boethius and Macrobius maintain that the tone has two parts, namely the apotome, which is the major semitone, and the diesis, which is the minor;[61] it [the tone] involves division in sesquioctave proportion [see Ex. 2.14], which numbers 8 and 9 create these semitones.[62] The truth is ready to hand, having been subjected to

minata constat, fidibus id praesertim intensione vel remissione indicantibus.

3 Verum quoniam in manu quidam non ea noverunt, idcirco de his aliqua dicenda duxi. Semitonium mi fa dici constat ubique, tamen id quandoque maius, quandoque vero minus; quo in loco sit pauci hauserunt. Nam magni interest mi fa ♮ c quam e f; ratio totum hoc dictitat. Notulae autem in ♮ et b non aequales ut in e sunt, licet eadem linea vel spatio sint, ideo semitonium elatius [Ex. 2.15] ibi minus intervalli ad fa quam alibi naturaliter efficit, hic vero depressius est, ex quo maius intervallum sequatur necesse est [Ex. 2.16].

4 Sunt etiam qui dicunt inter b et ♮ semitonium esse, sed spatio multo minori. Quod a nobis iure creditur; [59r] nam in lyrae vel citharae fidibus hoc evidentius saepe novimus. Pauca de semitonio attigi, quoniam quidam minus idonei cantores non intellexisse musicam Boethium opinantur, quod perspicue falsum inscii crediderunt sibi. Sed iam de dissonantia pauca subiungamus.

: XIII :

De dissonantiis

1 Diatessaron quam vulgo quartam dicimus a voce in vocem per tonos tres factam vel formatam tritonum musici vocitant [Ex. 2.12]; ea quoque tonis duobus et[23] semitonio fit, quam dixerunt antiqui consonantiam cum aliis vocibus consonis sociatam [Ex. 2.13]. Non tamen inter has neque perfectam neque imperfectam conproba-

the test of disputation by such learned men; above all, strings show that to be the case as they are stretched or relaxed.

However, since some people do not recognize them in the hand, I therefore decided I ought to say something about them. 3
It is established that the semitone *mi–fa* is sung everywhere, but yet it is sometimes greater, sometimes smaller; few have grasped where it is [one or the other]. For it makes a great difference whether *mi–fa* is ♮ C or E F, as stands to reason.[63] The notes are not equal in the case of ♮ and ♭ as they are in that of E, even though they are on the same line or in the same space; therefore the higher semitone [♮ C] [see Ex. 2.15] there naturally makes less of an interval to *fa* than elsewhere, but the latter [E F] is lower, from which a greater interval must follow [see Ex. 2.16].

There also those who say there is a semitone between ♭ and ♮, 4
but much smaller in extent.[64] Which we rightly believe, for we often recognize this quite clearly in the strings of the lyre or cithara. I have touched briefly on the semitone because some less skillful singers think that Boethius did not understand music, a manifestly false notion that the ignorant have taken on trust from them. But now let us append a few remarks about dissonance.

: XIII :

On dissonances

The diatessaron, which we commonly call the fourth, when it is 1
made or formed from pitch to pitch across three tones, musicians call a tritone [see Ex. 2.12]; it is also made of two tones and a semitone, which the ancients said was a consonance when associated with other consonant pitches [see Ex. 2.13]. But we do not accept it as one either perfect or imperfect, but count it with the dis-

mus, verum cum dissonis eam connumeramus. Hanc diapentes gratia minus discrepare cum discantu videmus.

2 [59v] Dissonantias autem semitonium, tonum, diatessaron vel tritonum, et eptaden vel septimam musici dicunt. Hactenus de his. Nunc de contrapuncti ordine regulas notemus.

: XIIII :

De contrapuncti regulis

1 Ars ipsa contrapunctum ita ordine proprio expostulat. Principio namque canendi perfectarum locus praeberi debet finique; non enim per imperfectas initium nancisci finemque quiescere noverimus. Cum deinde musica plana per tonos aut semitonia scandit, vel per segregatas notulas, discantus, id est contrapunctans, descendat.[24]

2 Eodem quoque modo contra cum alter ipsorum descendit, alter ascendat, vel aliquando contrapunctans in quibusdam gradum sistat ascendendo vel descendendo, hoc iuxta secundum normam animadvertatur.

3 Tertia [60r] vult regula non binas vel plures perfectarum solius speciei, secus diversae, per amborum sive ascensum sive descensum committi. Imperfectarum vero plurimarum continuationem ad sex usque per ascensum descensumque posse fieri concedit.

4 Quarta norma hoc notat. Nunquam fa et mi aliquibus consonantiis poni e contrario debere, nam tritonum perfectis imperfectisque id reddet effectum, turpem sonum et minus plenum.[25]

5 Quintus locus est notatione dignus. Semper singulas perfectas neumarum principio, medio, et fine conserere possumus, imperfec-

sonant intervals. We observe that it clashes less with the discant because of the diapente.[65]

Musicians call dissonances the semitone, tone, diatessaron or tritone, and heptad or seventh. So much for them. Now let us mark the rules for the ordering of counterpoint. 2

: XIV :

On the rules of counterpoint

The art itself requires counterpoint to be properly ordered. For at the outset of singing a place of perfect [consonances] should be provided, and at the end. For by imperfects we shall not know how to acquire a beginning or rest at the end.[66] Then, when the plainchant rises by tones or semitones, or non-adjacent notes, let the discant, that is, the contrapuntal voice, descend. 1

And conversely, in the same way, when one of them descends let the other ascend, or let the contrapuntal voice stand still at times in some places in its ascent or descent; let this be observed according to the second rule. 2

The third rule requires that when two or more of the perfect intervals are juxtaposed as the two parts ascend or descend, they should not be of only one species, but different; however, it allows that a succession of up to six imperfect consonances ascending and descending may be made. 3

The fourth rule is as follows: that *fa* and *mi* should never be placed opposite each other in any consonances, for that will produce, for perfect and imperfect [alike], a tritone, an ugly and less full sound.[67] 4

A fifth point is worthy of note. We can always combine all the perfect consonances at the beginning, middle, and end of *neumae*, 5

tas vero medio earum cum suis perfectis aptissime digeremus. Unde has singularum imperfectarum regulas notabimus hoc modo. Post unicam vel plures imperfectas sua perfecta dari debet, nam post tertiam (ut de hac primo loquar) plana musica scan[60v]dente unisonus sequatur, descendente vero quinta postponatur. Post vero sextam diapason sequatur, reliquis compositis illud idem observetur, ut decimae octavam vel duodecimam ad tertiae similitudinem aptabimus. Tertiae decimae vero quintam decimam ad sextae instar dabimus, et ita deinceps in reliquis hoc ordine procedatur.

6 Sexto notatu digno non semper post imperfectas suas dari perfectas posse, sed his factis alius[26] speciei imperfecta sequi posse aut non sua perfecta, utpote post tertiam vel plures sexta vel decima sequatur.[27] Hoc non arti repugnabit, nam multi compositores optimique musici observant.

7 Postremo notandum est nunquam gradum in discordantiis firmandum, nisi in diatessaron, hisque ab ea deductis, ars ipsa fert.

8 Novissime quoque animadvertendum videtur: paenulti[61r]ma notula cadentiae sive conclusionis syllaba, in neumis terminandi thematis per imperfectam fieri, quae ut plurimum per diapenten cum tono inter alterutrum, id est a tenore ad discantum, effici debet, quamvis eandem paenultimam et in reliquis imperfectis collocare queamus.

9 Hucusque de normarum serie. De contrapuncti experimento pergamus.

but we shall always most aptly arrange imperfect consonances together with their [associated] perfect ones[68] in the middle of them. Whence we shall record the following rules for each imperfect consonance in this manner. After one or more imperfect consonances, the appropriate perfect consonance should be put, for after a third, to speak of this first, when the plainchant is rising, let a unison follow, when it is falling, let a fifth be placed after it. After a sixth let the octave follow, and in the remaining compound intervals let the same principle be observed, so that we shall fit the octave or the twelfth to the tenth in the manner we dealt with the third; to the thirteenth we shall give the fifteenth on the model of the sixth, and thereafter let the same procedure be adopted in the remaining cases.

Sixthly it is worth noting that imperfect consonances cannot al- 6
ways be succeeded by the appropriate perfect ones, but in this case an imperfect consonance of another species may follow, or a perfect one other than its correlative, for instance after one or more thirds a sixth or tenth may follow. This will not be repugnant to the art, for many composers and excellent musicians observe this practice.

Lastly it should be noted: the art itself requires that one should 7
never come to rest on discords except the fourth and those derived from it.[69]

And finally it seems necessary to bear in mind that the penulti- 8
mate note of a cadence or syllable of a conclusion should, in the *neumae* for ending a theme, be produced on an imperfect consonance, which for the most part should be achieved by a sixth between the two, that is, from the tenor to the discant, although we may place the same penultimate on the other imperfect consonances too.

So much for the list of rules. Let us continue with counterpoint 9
in practice.

: XV :

De experiundo contrapuncto per regulas notissimas

1 Incohata quadam perfectarum singularis nota vel plures sequentur, quae absque lineae vel spatii medio procedent, aut per lineas et spatia inter se separatae sequentur a prima ceterae. Hanc enim ab invicem separationem per ternam vocem, quaternam, quinam, vel deinceps accidere posse perspeximus. Quibus nimirum rebus quo ordine simus usu[61^{v}]ri, breviter suo loco regulas aperiemus.

2 Primo igitur duarum notularum absque medio scandentium, deinde descendentium et separatarum item normam edemus.

3 *Regula prima.* Prima regula de perfectis consonantiis hoc instituet. Contrapunctans quacumque perfectarum consonantia se viderit unicam descendat vocem. Quod si in imperfectis id acciderit, tunc et ipse pariter scandat; si autem et in sexta id esset, gradum tunc sistat, nam post ipsam quinta sequetur.

4 Eodem pacto de notulis descendentibus in hoc quoque praecipit. Si quis in voce aequisona fuit, ascendere unicam, vel quartam vel quintam vel septimam vocem potest. Sin autem in quinta, ibidem quiescat, vel tertiam vel quintam scandat. Verum si in tertia [62^{r}] fuerit, pariter descendat, vel unam vel ternam vel quinam vocem in altum tendat. Sin autem in sexta, vel pariter descendat vel unam vel quartam inde vocem extollat.

5 *Regula secunda.* De notulis in ternam vocem scandentibus hoc secunda regula nobis aperiet. In unisono autem vel voce consistemus vel tertiam, vel quartam vocem descendemus.[28] In quinta vero vel

: XV :

On practicing counterpoint through very well-known rules

When some one of the perfect [consonances] has been begun, a single note or several will follow, which will proceed without the intermediation of a line or space, or the rest will follow from the first, separated among themselves by lines and spaces. For we have seen that this mutual separation may happen by[70] three pitches, four, five, and so on. Naturally, as to the order in which we shall use these things,[71] we shall reveal the rules briefly in the proper place.[72] 1

First, we shall state the rule of two successive notes ascending, then descending and at a distance. 2

First rule [tenor rising or descending a step]. The first rule concerning perfect consonances will establish the following: let the singer of the contrapuntal voice, in whichever of the perfect consonances he observes himself, descend a tone. But if that happens in the imperfect consonances, then let him rise by the same interval. But should it be in the sixth, let him stand still, for after it a fifth will follow.[73] 3

It [the rule] teaches the same thing about descending notes in the following case too. If one has been in a unison, he may rise a tone, or a fourth, or a fifth, or a seventh. But if in a fifth, let him rest there, or rise either a third or a fifth. But if he is in a third, let him likewise descend or move a tone, a third, or a fifth upwards. But if he is on a sixth, let him either descend likewise, or raise his voice a tone or a fourth thence. 4

Second rule. On notes rising to a third, the second rule will reveal to us the following. On a unison we shall either stand still with our voice or descend a third or a fourth, whereas on a fifth we 5

unicam sursum vel eandem deorsum vel quartam movebimus vocem. Verumtamen in tertia vocem ibidem firmabimus vel per unam vel quartam descendemus. Sed in sexta vel ibi mora<m> faciemus, vel per ternam vel quinam vocem descendemus. Descendentibus hisdem hoc nos quoque eadem docebit. Unisonus ibidem supersedebit vel ternam vel quartam vel sextam [62v] vel octavam vocem efferet. Quinta vero unicam vel quartam vocem subibit. Sed tertia quoque vel ibidem morabitur, vel unicam vel quartam vocem sublimabit. Sexta vel morabitur vel tertiam vel quintam poterit ascendere.

6 *Regula tertia.* Tertia regula notularum per diatessaron scandentium haec nos commonebit. In unisono unicam ascendemus vocem, vel descendemus eandem vel tertiam vel quintam. In quinta vero vel gradum sistet, vel tertiam vel quintam vocem descendet. Verum in tertia firmat se contrapunctans, vel tertiam vel quintam descendet. Sed in sexta unicam vel quartam deprimit. Earundem descensus sic se habet: cum in unisono quis fuerit unicam descendat, vel eandem vel tertiam vel quinta scan[63r]dat; sin autem in sexta, vocem sub vel super ferat vel quartam extollat.

7 *Regula quarta.* De notulis per diapenten scandentibus regula quarta hoc nobis instituet. Si in unisono quispiam se deprehensum viderit, vocem solam descendat, vel ibidem moretur, vel quartam vel sextam infra vocem deponat. In quinta vero solam vel quartam descendat. Sin autem in tertia, vel unicam sursum vel deorsum, <vel deorsum> quartam vel sextam attingat. Sin vero in sexta, in eodem loco vel moretur, vel inde per tertiam descendat. Verum cum eaedem inferiora petent hoc eadem regula nobis suadebit, id est ex unisono per unicam vel quartam vel sextam vel octavam scandi posse; e quinta vocem vel unam vel quartam ascendi, vel ibidem morari; e tertia vero [63v] per unicam vel quartam vel sex-

shall move our voice either a tone up or the same down or a fourth.[74] But in a third we shall stay our voice there or descend by a tone or a fourth. But on a sixth we shall either dwell there, or descend by a third or a fifth. And when they [the notes] descend, the same rule will teach us this too. The unison will remain there or utter the third or fourth or sixth or octave. But the fifth will climb[75] a step or a fourth; the third too will either stay there or elevate a step or a fourth. The sixth will either stay or be able to rise a third or fifth.

Third rule. The third rule, of notes rising by a fourth, will remind us of the following. On a unison we shall rise one tone, or descend the same, or a third, or a fifth. On the fifth it will either stand still or descend a third or a fifth. But on a third the contrapuntal voice stops, or will descend a third or fifth. But on a sixth it presses down a tone or a fourth. The descending fourth is treated as follows.[76] When one is on a unison, one should descend a tone, or rise by the same, or a third, or a fifth. But if on a sixth, one should go down, or up, a tone,[77] or rise by a fourth. 6

Fourth rule. On notes rising by a fifth, the fourth rule will teach us this: If one finds himself caught on a unison, he should go down one tone only, or stay in the same place, or lower the voice by a fourth or a sixth. On a fifth, however, he should go down a single tone or a fourth. But if one is on a third, he should reach either the tone above or below or the fourth or sixth below. If on a sixth, he should either stay in the same place, or descend thence by a third. But when they [the tenor notes] are making for the lower regions, the same rule will urge us as follows, namely that from a unison, ascent is possible by a tone, a fourth, a sixth, or an octave.[78] From a fifth, one may rise a tone or a fourth, or remain in the same place.[79] But from a third one may test his voice by a tone, 7

tam vel octavam experiri vocem. Sed e sexta vel inde non vocem moveat vel per ternam sursum vel deorsum eandem agitet. Et deinceps in ceteris segregationibus experimento ipso reliqua indagemus. Haec de consonantiis in contrapuncto temptandis dicta sufficiant.

8 Iam quid ut potero brevius de compositione subiungam.

: XVI :

De compositione

1 Compositio, id est contrapuncti per plurimas voces institutio, longe praedicta reddens meliora, post ipsum contrapunctum reperta fuit, quam hoc in loco existimavi ponendam esse, quoniam et contrapuncti figuratique cum speculativo fundamento rem suam perficit. Dicitur autem ordinatio plurimarum vocum sive notularum ad harmoniam per tonos ac semitonia con[64^{r}]ficiendam servatis planae musices et contrapuncti cum ratione terminis.

2 Nam ut diximus contrapunctum super planam musicam inter duos inventum veteres habebant. Moderni deinde ad tres, vel quattuor, vel quinque, vel sex, vel plures voces eundem in compositione cantuum iucundiorem reddiderunt. Haec enim tenorem, discantum, contratenorem et altum et imum, plures quoque tenores vel discantus vel etiam diversos contratenores instituet, servatis tamen contrapuncti terminis, quoad id fieri potest.

3 Sunt autem quattuor genera compositionis. Unum ad placitum habebit eventum. Cuius ad faulx bourdum (ut Gallici dicunt) prima species erit vel tenore et contratenore alto vel basso altera componetur. Secundum genus ad fugam, id est earundem neumarum per tem[64^{v}]poris intervallum resumptarum voces alterutro-

a fourth, a sixth, or an octave.[80] But from a sixth one should either not move the voice away or drive it by a third upwards or downwards. And from here on, in the other intervals, let us track down the rest by experiment. Let these remarks suffice on attempting consonances in counterpoint.

Now I shall add something on composition as briefly as I can. 8

: XVI :

On composition

Composition, that is, the establishment of counterpoint through several voices, rendering the aforesaid things far better, was invented after counterpoint itself; I have judged it appropriate to be placed here, since it achieves its purpose with a theoretical foundation of both counterpoint and polyphony. It is defined as the arrangement of several pitches or notes according to a harmony to be achieved by tones and semitones, with rational observation of bounds of the plainchant[81] and counterpoint. 1

For as we have said, the ancients had discovered counterpoint over a plainchant in two voices.[82] The moderns then made it pleasanter with three, or four, or five, or six or more voices in the composition of vocal music. For this [composition] will create tenor, discant, contratenor both altus and bassus, and several tenors or discants too, or even different contratenors, but maintaining the limits of counterpoint, so far as is possible. 2

Now there are four genera of composition. The first will produce an effect at will. Its first species will be in fauxbourdon (as the French say), and the second will be composed with a tenor and contratenor altus or bassus. The second genus is *ad fugam,* that is, it has brought together the pitches of the same notes reprised at a 3

rum compulit. Tertium difficillimos verborum canones investigat. Quartum imitativum per diversas neumas tamen ab his tribus cursus similitudinem auferet. Unumquodque brevibus verbis aperiemus.

: XVII :

De prima compositionis specie

1 Prima igitur species id est ad faulx bourdum hoc pacto componitur. Completo discantu tenor nil praeter sextas cum octavis in eo sonet, in quo diapente super eodem incepta discantus notulae contratenori inservient. Secunda vero specie tenorem vel contratenorem altero altiorem vel bassiorem, componere poterimus vel unum<quem>que per easdem deductiones reductionesque coaequare.

2 *De secunda specie*. Secundi generis species, quam [65^{r}] fugatam dicimus, ita componetur. Possumus a quocumque easdem neumas reiterare intervenientibus inter hosdem aliquibus pausis: id est, prius et discantus et tenor et contratenor incipere potest, deinde alterum alter sequatur. Eodem modo uterque horum vel prius vel posterius pausarum interventu alternatim, ut ita dixerim, inire vel imitari debebit.

3 *Tertia species compositionis, hoc est de canone et speciebus suis*. Illud autem tertium genus, hoc est cum canone compositio diversis temptandum modis perspiciemus. Namque vel per deductionem vel reductionem secrete notulas aptatas in contrapuncto comperiemus. Hoc quamplurimis neumis per diversas deductiones erit nobis in-

temporal interval from each other. The third surveys the most difficult verbal canons. The fourth is imitative using different notes, but will derive a similarity in its course from these three. We shall briefly explain each of them.

: XVII :

On the first species[83] of composition

The first species, then, that is, in fauxbourdon, is composed in the 1
following way. When [composition of] the discant has been completed, let the tenor sound nothing but sixths and octaves with it, while the notes of the discant [sung at the fourth below and] beginning a fifth above [the tenor] will serve for the contratenor. In the second species, we shall be able to compose a tenor or contratenor higher or lower than the other, or make each equal by the same ascending and descending sequences.[84]

Of the second species. The species of the second genus, which we call 2
in *fuga*, will be composed thus. We can from any voice part repeat the same notes with some rests between the same voices: that is, first the discant or tenor or contratenor may begin, then let one follow another. In the same way each of them will have to enter or imitate the first or the later with intervening rests in alternation, so to speak.

The third species of composition, that is, of the canon and its species. But 3
that third genus, namely composition with a canon [i.e., a rule], we shall see being attempted in various ways. For we shall find notes secretly fitted together in either ascending or descending sequences in counterpoint. We shall need to study this with some care, using very many notes in various sequences.[85] Sometimes we

vestigandum diligentia quadam. Quandoque quasdam [66r] planae musicae notulas a quovis cantu ablatas inveniemus, id contrapuncto nobis indicante. Aliquando verborum canonis vocales litteras vel syllabas vel dictiones notabimus, in quibus diversas figuras collocando cui ipsorum competant eae experiemur.

4 Sunt autem qui notulas uno loco positas alibi pronuntiandas volunt, hoc est transferri de proprietate ad proprietatem vel in altum vel imum; sunt autem qui quasdam notulas in aliquo locorum, id est vel discantus vel tenoris vel contratenoris, sub aut supra spatii vel lineae terminum praeterire non permittunt. Vel quasdam notulas tacendas et quasdam ibidem pronuntiandas quadrare videbimus. Multotiens finem loco principii et e contrario praeponendum videbimus. Vel finito versu per hasdem notulas retrogradiemur. [65v] Saepe quoque notulas deprimemus extollendas vel deprimendas efferemus.

5 Aliquando non eandem mensuram uni et eidem versui in hisdem notulis observabimus, id est diminutas vel auctas in uno eodemque versu protulerimus. Vel easdem notulas in circulo vel semicirculo perficiendas vel imperficiendas primo vel secundo vel tertio aut pluries inveniemus.

6 Sunt item qui notas alicuius rei imaginibus comparant. Hocque multis eventis scrutari potest, ut per lineas et spatia notulae crescant vel descrescant ascendendo vel descendendo quemadmodum crescit vel decrescit imaginis forma ipsius rei. Huius enim compositionis species reliquas item diversis ita modis quis investiget, ut diversa sunt compositorum ingenia. Etsi difficillima cognitu nobis canon offert, tamen recta contrapuncti indagatio [66v] facillima reddet.

shall find that some notes of plainchant have been removed from a composition, this being indicated to us by the counterpoint.[86] Sometimes we shall note the vowel letters or syllables or words of the canon, place various notes against them, and test[87] which one they fit.[88]

There are [composers] who wish notes written in one place to 4
be performed in another, that is, to be transferred from hexachord (*proprietas*) to hexachord either upwards or downwards.[89] There are others who do not allow certain notes in one of the places, that is, the discant, tenor, or countertenor, to pass below or above the limit of a space or line.[90] Or we shall see it to be appropriate that some notes be suppressed and some sung in the same place. Many times we shall see the end must be put first in the place of the beginning and vice versa.[91] Or when the [line of] verse is complete, we shall return in retrograde through the same notes.[92] Often too we shall go down on notes that should go up, or up on those that should go down.[93]

Sometimes we shall not observe the same measure for one and 5
the same verse in the same notes, that is, we shall perform them in diminution or augmentation in one and the same line.[94] Or we shall find that the same notes in circle or semicircle must be perfected or imperfected, the first or second or third time,[95] or several times.

There are also canons that compare notes to images of some 6
thing. And this may be observed in many instances, that the notes grow larger or smaller over the lines and spaces, rising or descending as the shape of the image of the thing itself increases or decreases.[96] And the other species of this [kind of] composition may be pursued in different ways, just as composers' casts of mind are different. Although the canon presents us with things that are very hard to understand, nevertheless the proper study of counterpoint will render them very easy.

7 *De quarta compositionis specie.* Quartum genus quod imitativum dicitur omnes has species et genera mutatis neumis ipsorum et cadentiis quam saepissime compositionem longe eorundem trium generum meliorem reddet. Quod recte quis per se ipsum quaerens inveniet, praesertim cum optime contrapunctus ei inserviat.[29]

8 In omni compositionis genere troporum modullos observandos ars ipsa censet. Et quoniam in plana musica et contrapuncto et hic neuma sive cadentia utimur, idcirco quid sit breviter videamus.

: XVIII :

De neuma et cadentia

1 Neumam multi cantilenae partem vel cantus esse dicunt quae pthongorum[30] geminatione fit. Aliqui cantus dulcedinem vel cantum dul[67ʳ]cem definiunt. Nos autem quas in cantuum coaptatione notulas ut alter ab altero tono differatur institutas novimus, hasdem per aggregationem vel segregationem contentas hisdem modis neumam dicemus. Eandem vernacula lingua cadentiam vocitarunt, quam finita verborum sententia ut plurimum compositores veluti clausula utuntur. Exemplum posuimus harum; et primo neumae, deinde cadentiae [Exx. 2.1, 2.2].

Of the fourth species of composition. The fourth kind, which is called imitative, <employing?> all these species and genera, having changed their *neumae* and cadences,[97] will very often render a composition of the same three genera much better. A person will find the correct way by seeking it out for himself, especially since the counterpoint renders[98] him excellent service. 7

In every kind of composition the art itself holds that the melodies of the modes [*troporum*] should be observed.[99] And since in plainchant and in counterpoint and here[100] we use a *neuma* or cadence, let us briefly see what it is. 8

: XVIII :

On the neuma and cadence

Many people say that the *neuma* is a part of the song or chant that is made by the doubling of notes.[101] Some say that it is the sweetness of the song, or a sweet song.[102] But to those notes that we know were devised in assembling songs in order that one tone[103] should differ from another, and which are contained by aggregation or segregation in the same modes, we shall apply the name of *neuma*. In the vernacular it has been called a cadence.[104] Composers use it mostly like a clausula when the verbal sentence is finished. We have given examples of these, first of a *neuma*, then of a cadence [see Ex. 2.1 and Ex. 2.2]. 1

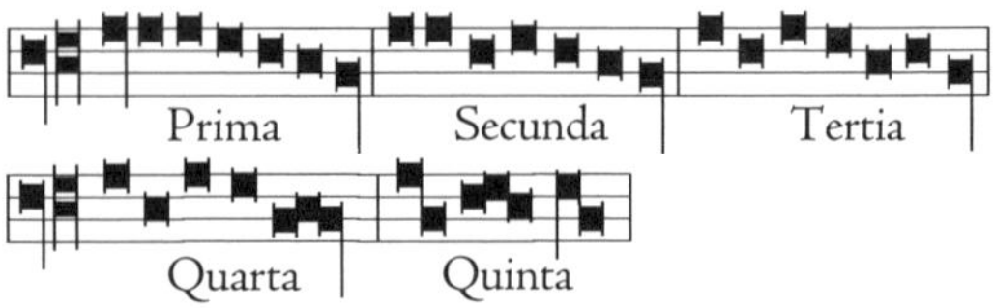

EX. 2.1

2 Omnes autem hae proficiscuntur ab hac prima, quae est modi primi. Multas quoque et diversas quaereremus hoc or[67v]dine, et item modis omnibus vel tonis, quod nimis nunc longum foret. Cadentiae iam describamus exemplum.

EX. 2.2 *Cadentiae in circulo*

EX. 2.3 *Cadentiae in semicirculo*

3 Semper enim cadentiam in sua dimensione, hoc est in circulo aut semicirculo finitam cum thematis sententia desinere decebit compositorem. Nam possumus duas aut plures alteram post alteram neumas iungere. Sed tamen hoc facto conclusionis loco cadentiam postponemus.

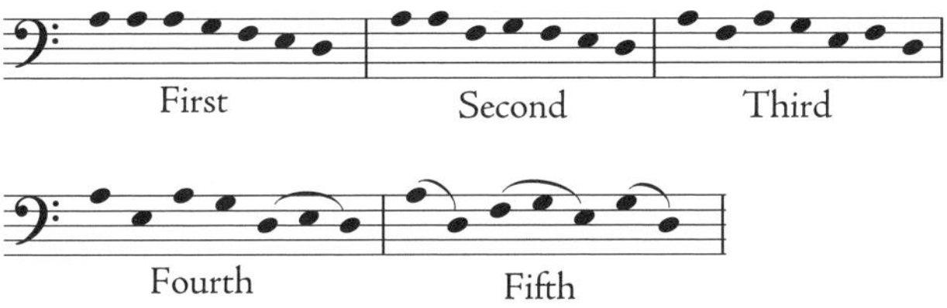

EX. 2.1

Now all these start from this first one, which is in the first 2
mode. And we could seek many different ones in this set, and the same in all the modes or tones, which would take too long now. Let us write out an example of a cadence.

EX. 2.2 *Cadences in circle [perfect mensuration]*

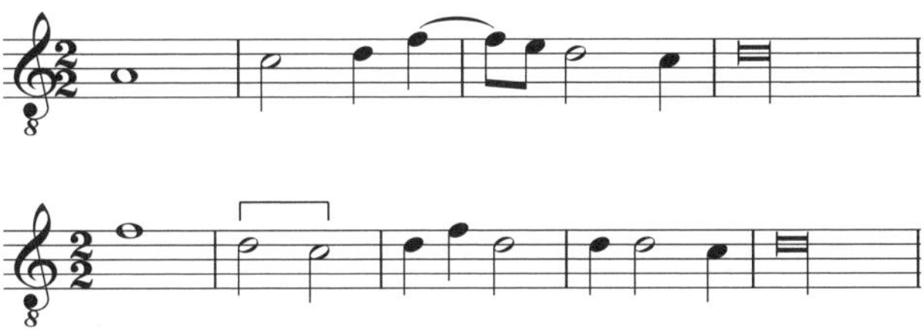

EX. 2.3 *Cadences in semicircle [imperfect mensuration]*

For it will always be appropriate for the composer to end a ca- 3
dence complete in its mensuration,[105] that is, in a circle or semicircle, with a sentence of the text. For we can join two or more *neumae* one after the other; but having done so in place of a conclusion we shall place the cadence last.

4 Iam quorundam praemissorum exempla scribamus.

[68r]

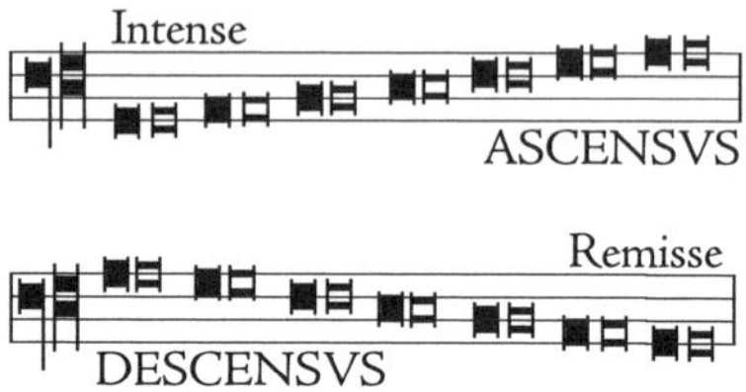

EX. 2.4 *Aequisonae vel unisoni duarum notularum exemplum Haec autem est origo et initium consonantiarum*

EX. 2.5 *Ditonus vel tertia maior*

EX. 2.6 *Semiditonus vel tertia minor*

EX. 2.7 *Diapente vel quinta perfecta consonantia*

EX. 2.8 *Diapente non plena nec resonans*

EX. 2.9 *Sexta maior vel exaden*

Now let us write out examples of some of the foregoing. 4

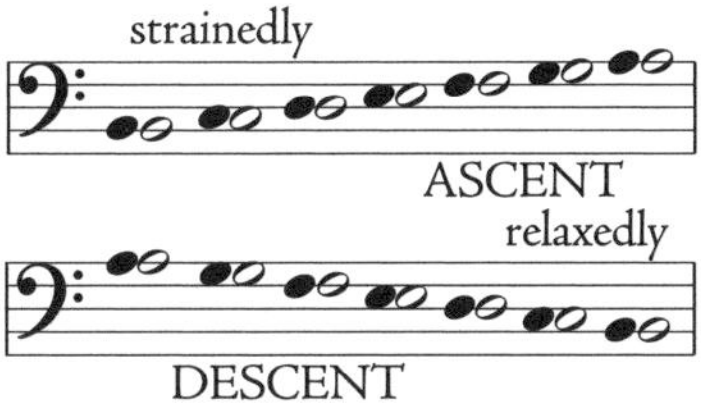

EX. 2.4 *Example of the equal-sounding [voice], or the unison of two notes*
This is the origin and beginning of the consonances.

EX. 2.5 *Ditone or major third*

EX. 2.6 *Semiditone or minor third*

EX. 2.7 *Diapente or perfect fifth*

EX. 2.8 *Imperfect, non-resonant fifth*

EX. 2.9 *Major sixth or hexad*

EX. 2.10 *Sexta minor*

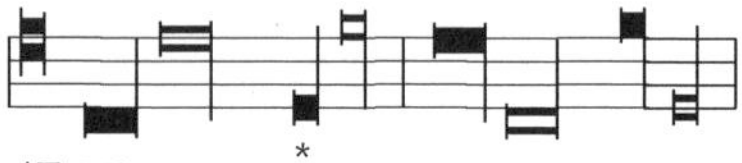

*E *MS*

EX. 2.11 *Diapason perfectissima consonantia*

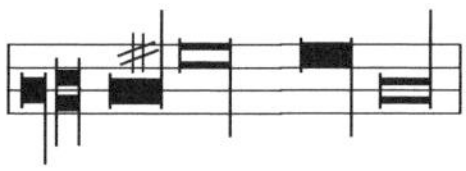

EX. 2.12 *Tritonus vel quarta maior*

EX. 2.13 *Diatessaron consonantia cum aliis diapentes virtute*

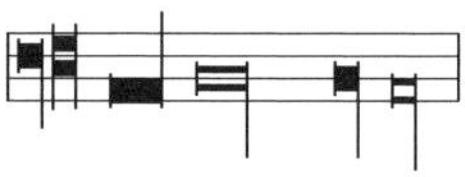

EX. 2.14 *Tonus vel sesquioctavus*

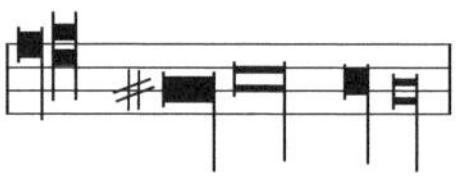

EX. 2.15 *Semitonium minus vel diesis*

EX. 2.16 *Semitonium maius vel apotome*

EX. 2.10 *Minor sixth*

EX. 2.11 *Diapason, the most perfect consonance*

EX. 2.12 *Tritone or major fourth*

EX. 2.13 *Diatessaron, a consonance with the others by virtue of the diapente*

EX. 2.14 *Tone or sesquioctave*

EX. 2.15 *Minor semitone or diesis*

EX. 2.16 *Major semitone or apotome*

[68v] Et quoniam nimis esset prolixum genera speciesque compositionis hac figuratione demonstrare, idcirco alias id concinne aggrediemur. Quare ad figurativam nos hinc musicam conferamus.

EXPLICIT LIBER SECUNDUS

And since it would take too long to illustrate the genera and species of compositions by means of this notation, we shall therefore elegantly attack the question in another way. For which reason, let us betake ourselves hence to figurative music.

END OF BOOK TWO

• [LIBER III] •

[69R] INCIPIT EIUSDEM FIGURATIVAE MUSICES LIBER TERTIUS AD EUMDEM ILLUSTRISSIMUM AC REVERENDISSIMUM DOMINUM ET D. ASCANIUM CARDINALEM DIGNISSIMUM

: I :

Interpretatio quorundam figurativi cantus terminorum Caput primum incipit

1 Figurativum cantum,[1] vel organicam musicam tertio in loco iam locandam dixeramus, quoniam ab ipso contrapuncto compositioneque profectam novimus. Sed antequam hinc alio progrediamur, aliqua de huiusmodi arte utillima breviter prius conquiramus: quid figura, quid circulus, quid semicirculus, quid linea, quid cauda.

2 Et primo figura, ut in geometria Boethius [69v] inquit:

> 3 est quod sub aliquo vel sub aliquibus terminis continetur. Terminus quod cuiusque est finis. Circulus vero est figura quaedam plana et circumducta et sub una linea contenta. Semicirculus autem est plana figura, quae sub diametro, et ea quam diametrus apprehendit, circumferentia continetur. Haec ille.

4 Linea vero ut Sanctius geometra dicit est longitudo absque latitudine in cuius extremitate duo puncta sunt.

· [BOOK III] ·

HERE BEGINS THE SAME AUTHOR'S THIRD BOOK, ON FIGURATIVE MUSIC, TO THE SAME MOST ILLUSTRIOUS AND REVEREND LORD AND MASTER ASCANIO, MOST WORTHY CARDINAL

: I :

The interpretation of certain terms of figurative song. Chapter 1 begins

We had already said that figurative song, or organic music, was to be placed in third position, because we know that it came out of counterpoint proper and composition. But before we progress from here to elsewhere, let us first briefly assemble some very useful matter concerning this art: what is a figure, what is a circle, what is a semicircle, what is a line, what is a tail. 1

First of all, "a figure," as Boethius says in his *Geometry*, 2

> is that which is bounded by a limit or limits. A limit is that which is the boundary of anything. A circle is a certain plane figure drawn all round and bounded within one line. A semicircle is a plane figure that is bounded by a diameter and the circumference that the diameter cuts off.[1] 3

But a line, as Sánchez the geometer says,[2] is a length without breadth with two points at its extremity.[3] 4

5 Cauda vero est linea aliquibus figuris contigua quae diversas in earum valore notulas, hoc est maiores minoresve reddit. Punctum apud geometras dicitur centrum, et aliquando lineae initium finemque. Centron dicit Censorinus est nota circuli medii. Diametron est recta linea per centron immissa et in utramque partem secans circulum. Haec ille.

6 Haec de his dicta sufficiant. Iam [70r] nos ad ipsam artis materiem conferamus.

: II :

Unde figurativus cantus dicitur, et de figuris eiusdem

1 Figurativus igitur cantus a suis figuris, id est maxima, longa, et similibus, item a circulo, <et> semicirculo dicitur. Hunc enim compositionis ornatum vocitare possumus et contrapuncti florem vel fructum. Sunt enim figurae iuxta Johannem de Muris ceterosque seniores quinque, id est maxima, longa, brevis, semibrevis, et minima. Illi vero a duobus extremis hoc est a maximo minimoque principium et finem sumpserunt, cum medio eorundem, id est longitudine, brevitate, et semis.

2 Sed nos animadvertentes minimum non illud esse de quo Philosophus inquit, id est ultra minimum non esse divisionem—nam corpus minimale etiam in minores figuras [70v] divisivum discretam quantitatem habet, ipse quoque Philosophus omnem divisibilem quantitatem dicit iterum divisibilem fore—et ideo nos[2] ultra minimam has humanae voci pronuntiatu possibiles adiunximus, scilicet semim<i>nimam, semisemim<i>nimam, crossutam, semicrossutam, fugielam, et semifugielam. Et quoniam

A tail is a line attached to some figures that makes notes 5
different in their value, that is, larger or smaller. A point among geometers means the center and sometimes the beginning or end of a line. "The center," says Censorinus, "is the point in the middle of the circle. The diameter is the straight line drawn through the center and cutting the circle in half."[4]

Let these remarks suffice on these matters. Now let us betake 6
ourselves to the actual matter of the art.

: II :

Why figurative song is so called, and on its figures

Figurative song, then, is so called from its own figures, that is, 1
maxima, longa, and the like, and also from the circle and semicircle.[5] We may call it the ennoblement[6] of composition and the flower or fruit of counterpoint. The figures, according to Johannes de Muris[7] and the other elders, are five (in number), namely the maxima, long, breve, semibreve, and minim. But they have taken their beginning and end from the two extremes, that is, from the greatest and least, together with their middle, that is, length, brevity, and the half.

But, since we have observed that the smallest is not that to 2
which the Philosopher's words apply, namely, that beyond the smallest there is no division[8]—for the minimal body, even when divided into smaller shapes, has a discrete quantity, and the Philosopher himself says that every divisible quantity is divisible again[9]—we have therefore added beyond the minim the following notes, which the human voice is capable of uttering, namely the semiminim, the semisemiminim, the *crossuta*, the *semicrossuta*, the *fugiela*, and the *semifugiela*.[10] And since all these are mea-

hae omnes modo, tempore, prolatione metiuntur, ideo quod illud sit brevi sermone animadvertamus.

: III :

De dimensionibus notularum, id est modo, tempore, et prolatione

1 Modum non hic ut in plana musica accipimus, sed is et tempus et prolatio figurarum valor est. Nam in maxima et longa modi dimensionem reperiemus, breve tempus, semibreve prolationem, ceteris vero indifferenter haec tria communiter et [71r] non proprie cognoscemus. De his autem Goschalcus Parisiensis:

> 2 Duplex est modus scilicet perfectus et imperfectus, et quilibet ipsorum est duplex, scilicet maior et minor. Maior modus accipitur respectu maximarum in habitudinem ad longas; minor vero modus accipitur respectu longarum in habitudinem ad breves. Maior modus perfectus est quando maxima valet tres longas. Maior quoque modus imperfectus est quando maxima valet tantum duas longas, minor vero modus perfectus est quando longa de se valet tres breves, imperfectus quando longa tantum valet duas breves. Et potest esse maior modus <perfectus> minore existente imperfecto et e contrario.
>
> 3 Item tempus capitur et attenditur respectu brevium penes earum habitudinem ad semibreves, et est duplex, scilicet per[71v]fectum et imperfectum: perfectum quando brevis de se tres valet semibreves, imperfectum quando valet duas semibreves.

sured by mode, tempus, and prolation, therefore let us in a few words take note of what that is.

: III :

On the dimensions of notes, that is, mode, tempus, and prolation

We do not understand "mode" here as in plainchant, but it, and tempus, and prolation are values of figures. For in the maxima and the longa we shall find the measurement of mode, in the breve tempus, in the semibreve prolation; in the others we shall recognize these three things without distinction, in common and not peculiarly.[11] On them Goschalcus of Paris says: 1

> Mode is twofold, namely perfect and imperfect, and each of them is twofold, namely major and minor. Major mode is understood in respect of maximas in relation to longs; minor mode is understood in respect of longs in relation to breves. Perfect major mode is when the maxima is worth three longs. Imperfect major mode is when the maxima is worth only two longs; perfect minor mode is when the long in itself is worth three breves, imperfect when the long is worth two breves. And there can be perfect major mode when there is imperfect minor mode and vice versa. 2
>
> Likewise tempus is understood and observed in respect of breves in relation to semibreves, and is twofold, namely perfect and imperfect: perfect when the breve in itself is worth three semibreves, imperfect when it is worth two semibreves. 3

4 Item prolatio attenditur respectu semibrevium penes earum habitudines ad minimas. Et est duplex, scilicet perfecta, id est maior et imperfecta, id est minor. Perfecta sive maior est quando semibrevis valet tres minimas, imperfecta quando valet solum duas minimas.

5 E quibus patet quod triplex est perfectio, id est modi, temporis, et prolationis, et omnis perfectio consistit in tribus, imperfectio vero in duobus. Vel perfectio in ternario numero, imperfectio vero binario consistit. Haec ille.

6 Haec autem circuli semicirculique in cantuum initio positi demonstrant. Qui tali sunt figura scripti.

Circulus ○⃛ ○̈ ⊙ ○ ⌀ O_3 O_2
Semicirculus C⃛ C̈ Ċ Ȼ C C_3 C_2

7 [72r] Et quoniam hi diversis figuris dominantur, ideo singulatim quomodo sese habent causam reddiderimus. Et primo de circulis ipsis, deinde semicirculis.

: IIII :

Quid circuli quadranguli que in figuris ostendant[3]

1 Non enim moderni his omnibus ut iam maiores utebantur initio[4] cantuum eos suorum praeponunt, sed eorundem loco proportiones usurpant, praesertim maioris mensurae. Tamen ut eorum natura sit nota aliqua breviter eloquamur. Circulus autem tribus in medio punctis modum maiorem perfectum in maxima nobis ostendit [Ex. 3.1], cum duobus eundem in longa modum signabit [Ex. 3.2]; item cum unico, tempus perfectum maioris prolationis

Likewise prolation is observed in respect of semibreves in their relation to minims, and is twofold, namely perfect, that is, major, and imperfect, that is, minor. Perfect or major is when the semibreve is worth three minims, imperfect when it is worth only two minims. 4

From which it is clear that perfection is threefold, that is, of mode, tempus, and prolation, and all perfection consists in three, imperfection in two. Or perfection consists in the number three, imperfection in the number two.[12] 5

These are shown by circles and semicircles placed at the beginning of songs. They are written with the following shapes: 6

Circle ⊙ ⊙ ⊙ ○ ⌀ O_3 O_2
Semicircle ⋵ ⋵ ⋵ ₵ C C_3 C_2

And since these govern different note shapes, we shall discuss them each in turn. And first about circles, then semicircles. 7

: IV :

What circles and rectangles will show in note shapes

The moderns do not put all these signs at the beginning of their vocal music in the way that the ancients used them, but in their place they employ proportions, especially of greater measure. But in order that their nature may be known, let us make some brief remarks. The circle with three points in the middle indicates to us perfect major mode in the maxima [see Ex. 3.1];[13] with two points it will mark the same [major] mode in the long [Ex. 3.2].[14] Likewise, with a single point, perfect tempus of major prolation in the 1

in breve solum [Ex. 3.5]. Sine aliquo puncto, tempus perfectum minoris prolationis in eadem monstrabit [Ex. 3.6].

2 [72^{v}] Circulus cum virgula per medium dividente suum vel cito notulas cucurrerit vel loco prolationis semibreves habebit, id est has minimarum trium loco dividendas vel pro sesqualtera proportione eaedem pronuntiabuntur [Exx. 3.5, 3.6]. Circulus vero paenultimus aliquando ut per dimidium modum demonstret ponitur vel proportionem quandam maioris mensurae exprimet. Extremus autem imperfectum modum per medium in maxima tenet et imperfectum tempus in breve. Consueverunt quoque maiores loco primi et secundi circuli his quadrangulis cum virgulis tribus in medio vel punctis etiam duobus uti, quorum figuram hoc pacto perscripserunt ⊏|||⊐ ⊏||⊐ ⊏···⊐ ⊏··⊐ [Exx. 3.1, 3.2]; hi modum perfectum in maxima et longa praebebant. Iam semicirculorum proprietatem naturamque dicamus.

: V :

[73^{r}] Quomodo differant a circulis semicirculi

1 Sunt autem qui dicunt primis duobus semicirculis maiores usos esse, ut hi modum minorem perfectum in maxima et longa significarint, sed non alterationem longae vel brevi, ut circuli dederint. Nos vero cantus multorum praesertim antiquorum vidimus, non tamen in hos ipsos incidimus; sed ut opinio horum extat, et nos quoque quaedam de his sicut digna commemorabimus.

2 Semicirculus igitur cum tribus in medio punctis modum minorem perfectum in maxima, cum duobus vero in longa eundem figurat [Exx. 3.3, 3.4]. Semicirculus cum unico puncto prolationem perfectam in semibreve dabit, id est tres minimas loco no-

breve alone [Ex. 3.5]. Without any points, it will show perfect tempus of minor prolation in the same [Ex. 3.6].[15]

The circle with a stroke dividing it in half [ø] will either run quickly through the notes,[16] or have semibreves in place of prolation, that is, [have] them needing to be divided [in half] in place of three minims [Exx. 3.5, 3.6],[17] or else they will be performed in sesquialtera proportion.[18] Sometimes the penultimate circle [O3] is put in order to show the mode is halved, or will express some proportion of a major mensuration. The last one [O2] will show the imperfect mode halved in the maxima and imperfect tempus in the breve.[19] Our forefathers were also accustomed, in place of the first and second circle [⊙ ⊙], to use the following rectangles with three strokes or dots in the middle, and also to use two points, whose shapes they wrote in the following manner ▥ ▥ ⊡ ⊡ [Exx. 3.1, 3.2].[20] These used to provide perfect mode in the maxima and long. Now let us state the property and nature of semicircles. 2

: V :

How semicircles differ from circles

There are those who say that our forefathers used the first two semicircles [Ͼ Ͼ] to show perfect minor mode in the maxima and long, but not to grant alteration to the long and breve like circles. But despite having seen the vocal music of many composers, especially the ancients, we have not come across these semicircles. But since they are believed in, we too shall mention some things about them as meriting discussion. 1

The semicircle, then, with three points in the middle marks perfect minor mode in the maxima, with two the same [minor mode] in the long [Exx. 3.3, 3.4].[21] The semicircle with a single point will yield perfect prolation in the semibreve, that is, three 2

tulae plani cantus, quas sub perfecta mensura cecinerimus [Ex. 3.7]. Sine puncto prola[73v]tionem imperfectam ibidem continebit semicirculus. Cum virgula ipsum transversante tempus imperfectum minoris prolationis per medium, hoc est, duae breves loco duarum semibrevium computabuntur [Ex. 3.8]. Paenultimus vero semicirculus aut prolationem perfectam, sesqualteram, vel triplam signabit. Sed extremus semper tempus imperfectum per medium, hoc est pro duabus semibrevibus breves duas praebebit.

3 His quoque quidam compositores aversis cornibus usi fuerunt, ut in hac figura Ↄ⁝ Ↄ∴ Ↄ· Ↄ Ↄ̸, qui nihil ab his differebant. Fuerunt item qui circulum et semicirculum ut hi modum et perfectum et imperfectum in eorum cantibus tribuerent, hoc est per augmentum in brevibus et semibrevibus, praeposuerunt, quoniam tunc pro maxima longa, et pro longa brevis, et pro breve semibrevis figuratur. Hac [74r] enim comparatione nostra quoque aetate utimur.

4 Hucusque de circuli semicirculique proprietate. De eorundem officio sequamur.

: VI :

Quomodo circuli semicirculique tribuerunt perfectionem aut alterationem figuris

1 Circulus quem maiorem modum maximae dare diximus, longae quoque eundem dabit, brevi perfectum tempus, semibrevi perfectam prolationem [Ex. 3.1]. Item longae alterationem, brevique et semibrevi[5] et minimae. Secundus vero longae perfectionem, ceterisque non secus atque antecedens officium suum exercebit [Ex.

minims instead of the note of plainchant, which [minims] we shall sing under perfect mensuration [Ex. 3.7]. Without a point the semicircle will contain imperfect prolation in the same place; with a stroke crossing it, imperfect tempus of minor prolation is halved, that is, two breves will be counted instead of two semibreves [Ex. 3.8].[22] The penultimate semicircle [C3] will mark either perfect prolation, sesquialtera, or tripla; but the last one [C2] always imperfect tempus halved, that is, instead of two semibreves it will yield two breves.

Some composers also used them with their horns facing the op- 3
posite way, as in this shape Ↄ⋅ Ↄ⋅ Ↄ Ↄ Ↄ̸, but they were no different.[23] There were also those who prefixed circle and semicircle so that these should confer perfect and imperfect mode in their vocal compositions, that is, by augmentation in breves and semibreves, because then the long is written for the maxima, the breve for the long, and the semibreve for the breve. We use this equivalence in our age too.[24]

So much for the properties of circle and semicircle; let us con- 4
tinue with their function.

: VI :

How circles and semicircles conferred perfection or alteration on notes

The circle that we said gives major mode to the maxima [⊙] will 1
also give it to the long, perfect tempus to the breve, perfect prolation to the semibreve [Ex. 3.1]. It will also give alteration to the long, and the breve, and the semibreve and minim. The second (circle) [⊙] will give perfection to the long, and will exercise its function on the rest no otherwise than the preceding [Ex. 3.2].

3.2]. Tertius autem brevi perfectionem semibrevi et alterationem et perfectionem, minimae quoque alterationem impertietur [Ex. 3.5]. Quartus quoque brevi perfectionem et semibrevi alterationem solum distribuit [Ex. 3.6]. Hoc idem et quintus observabit [Ex. 3.6].

2 Duos ex[74v]tremos diverse posuerunt compositores: per primum ut per medium in maxima modum indicaverint vel proportionem; per secundum vero eundem modum in longa sine brevis perfectione et semibrevis alteratione indicarunt.

3 Sed duo primi semicirculi modum minorem perfectum quo in loco et circuli absque aliarum alteratione[6] nisi in semibreve perfectionem et minima alterationem retinentibus concedunt [Exx. 3.3, 3.4]. Tertius vero et sextus in semibreve perfectionem et minima alterationem solum conservat [Exx. 3.7, 3.9]. Quartus in omnibus tam maioribus quam minoribus figuris imperfectionem tenebit [Exx. 3.8, 3.10]. Quintus et septimus in longa tempus imperfectum designabunt [Ex. 3.8].

4 Hactenus de his. De mensuris eorundem sequamur.

: VII :

De modi temporisque et prolationis partitione

1 [75r] Modus maior perfectus quem in maxima diximus per tres longas dividi debet, maior vero imperfectus qui in longa est per tres breves. Eodem modo minor perfectus minorque imperfectus in his divisionem patietur.

2 Tempus perfectum maioris prolationis per tres semibreves tres minimas in unaquaque habentes segregationem habebit. Perfec-

The third [⊙] will impart perfection to the breve, both alteration and perfection to the semibreve, and also alteration to the minim [Ex. 3.5]. The fourth too [O] only allots perfection to the breve and alteration to the semibreve [Ex. 3.6]. The fifth [Ø] will do the latter too [Ex. 3.6].

Composers have placed the last two in different ways: by the 2
first [O_3], to indicate halving of the mode in the maxima, or a proportion; by the second [O_2], they marked the same mode in the long without perfection of the breve and alteration of the semibreve.

The first two semicircles [Ͼ Ͼ] allow perfect minor mode where 3
circles do, without alteration of the other (notes) except in the semibreve and minim, which retain perfection and alteration respectively [Exx. 3.3, 3.4]. The third [Ͼ] and sixth [C_3] preserve only perfection in the semibreve and alteration in the minim [Exx. 3.7, 3.9]. The fourth [C] will hold imperfection in all notes, both larger and smaller [Exx. 3.8, 3.10]. The fifth [¢] and seventh [C_2] will record imperfect tempus in the long [Ex. 3.8].[25]

So much for these. Let us continue with their mensuration. 4

: VII :

On the division of mode and tempus and prolation

Major perfect mode, which we have mentioned in the case of the 1
maxima, ought to be divided by three longs; major imperfect mode, which is in the long, by three breves. In the same way[26] perfect minor and imperfect minor mode will undergo division in these [notes].

Perfect tempus of major prolation will be broken into groups of 2
three semibreves, containing three minims in each. Perfect [tem-

tum vero minoris prolationis per hasdem semibreves duas solum minimas habentes segregabitur. Tempus autem imperfectum maioris prolationis per duas semibreves minimas tres habentes quaelibet[7] harum dividemus, imperfectum vero <minoris prolationis> per duas hasdem solum minimas binas habentes. Sed per medium per binas breves loco semibrevium receptas illud idem tempus dividemus. Hoc idem et in modo per medium dividundo eveniet.

3 Prolatio [75v] perfecta in semibreve existens per tres minimas patietur divisionem, imperfecta vero per duas solum.

4 Quod si secus atque diximus quis invenerit, aut libri depravationem inveniet, aut inscitiam compositoris cognoscet.

5 Hucusque de mensuris.[8] De ligaturis figurarum normam sequamur.

: VIII :

De notularum sive figurarum colligatione

1 Ligatio est plurium notularum sed adminus duarum ad invicem connodatio. Hanc enim tribus modis noveris: aut caudae vel lineae in parte dextra erunt sursum vel deorsum, aut in sinistra vel laeva, aut sine his notulae descendent vel ascendent. Caudae igitur vel lineae in dextra parte sursum vel deorsum terminatae solum maximarum aut lo<n>garum sunt, ut in hac figura 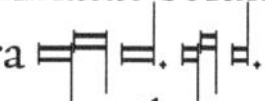. Si vero [76r] haec in laeva parte ascenderit, duae primae semibreves erunt, ut hac figuratione ; sin autem ea ipsa descenderit prima figura brevis erit vel simul plures esse possunt, ut hic .

pus] of minor prolation will be broken into groups of these same [three] semibreves containing only two minims. Imperfect tempus of major prolation we shall divide by two semibreves, each of them having three minims, but imperfect tempus <of minor prolation> by these same two [semibreves] having only two minims each. But we shall divide the same tempus by half by two breves taken in place of semibreves. The same thing will happen in dividing the mode by half.[27]

Perfect prolation in the semibreve will undergo division by 3
three minims, imperfect by only two.

But if anyone finds (things done) otherwise than we have said, 4
either he will find a corruption in the book, or he will recognize the composer's ignorance.

So much for mensurations. Let us continue the rule for liga- 5
tures of notes.

: VIII :

On the ligation of notes or figures

Ligation is the knitting together of several notes, but at least two. 1
This you will recognize in three ways: either there will be tails or lines on the right, upward or downward, or on the left, or the notes will descend or ascend without these. Tails, then, or lines on the right ending upward or downward belong only to maximas or longs, as in this figure 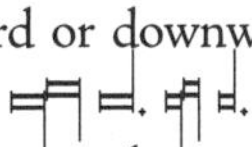. But if this tail rises up on the left, the first two will be semibreves, as in this illustration 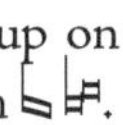. But if it descends, the first figure will be a breve, or there may be several together, as here .[28]

2 Sed cum nullam terminationem aliqua in parte ligatura habebit, mox singularum notularum proprium suo loco dicemus. At nunc de duabus his ligaturis quasdam figurationes ponamus, et primo maximae cum longa , longae cum breve , brevis cum longa , semibrevium cum breve , plurium brevium simul , plurium brevium cum maxima vel longa, ut hic , et sic in pluribus vel his paucioribus.

3 Earum vero sine cauda existentium has regulas praebemus. Quotiescumque duae vel plures ascendent, semper breves erunt una figuratione, excepta quam post has ponemus, sic . Sunt [76v] hae ascendentes quas dixi. Descendentibus solum duabus quadratis longae semper erunt, ut in hac figura . Si enim inter has una vel plures quadratae erunt breves efficientur, id est mediae illae, nam ipsae extremae longae perseverabunt, ut hac figuratione . Semper enim ultima deorsum quadrata longa erit. Inter has etiam maximam cum longa vel duas maximas simul in descensum vel longam cum breve saepe reperiemus. Exemplum earum hoc est   .

4 Earum figurationem quas diximus postponendarum in hac figura perspiciemus. Nam breves erunt omnes praeter extremam, quae longa est, ut hic   , quandoque etiam duae ascendentes longae erunt , et deinceps ceterae ligaturae.

5 Quidam quoque quasdam notulas suo more perver[77r]terunt, quas ligaturas non solum reprehendimus, sed etiam penitus reprobamus et abicimus, quarum forma haec est   . Quasdam quoque Marchetti notulas, id est semibreves cum cauda ascendenti vel descendenti figuratas non comprobamus, quoniam in Parisiensi studio (ut Goschalchus inquit) doctores abiecerunt. Ideo talium figurationem non conseram.

6 Iam de figurarum perfectione imperfectioneque sequamur.

But when the ligature has no ending on either side, we shall in 2
due course state what is proper to each note. But for the moment let us present some illustrations of these two ligatures: first of maxima with long , long with breve , breve with long 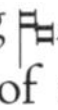, semibreves with breve 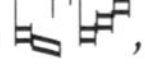, of several breves together , of several breves with maxima or long, as here 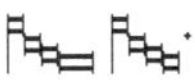. And so in the case of more or fewer than these.

But for those that have no tail we provide these rules. When- 3
ever two or more ascend, they will always be breves in a single figure, except for the one we shall put after them, thus .[29] These are the ascending notes we mentioned. When only two square notes descend, they will always be longs, as in this figure . If between them there are one or two squares, they will be made breves, that is, those in the middle, for the outer ones will remain longs, as in this illustration . The last square, going downward, will always be a long. Between them we shall often find a maxima with a long or two descending maximas together or a long with a breve. This is an example of them 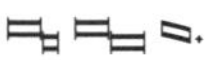.

We shall observe an illustration of those we said should be put 4
at the end in the following figure, for they will all be breves except for the last one, which is a long, as here 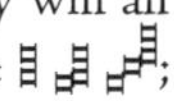; sometimes, too, the two ascending notes will be longs , and so on for the other ligatures.[30]

Some persons, too, have perverted the notes in their own way, 5
which ligatures we not only reprehend but utterly reprove and cast out;[31] they look like this .[32] And some of Marchetto's notes, that is, semibreves represented with ascending or descending tail,[33] we do not approve, because in the school of Paris, as Goschalcus says, the doctors have rejected them.[34] Therefore I shall not include a representation of such things.

Now let us continue with the perfection and imperfection of 6
notes.

: IX :

Quot modis figurae perficiuntur aut imperficiuntur

1 Perfectio semper in tribus, imperfectio duobus a musicis consideratur. Diximus autem circulos quosdamque semicirculos perfectionem in quibusdam notis vel figuris ostendere. Quo igitur ordine perficiantur aut imperficiantur singulas regulas no[77v]tabimus.

2 Et primo notulae vel figurae circulis aut semicirculis sibi perfectionem praebentibus sex de causis perficientur: hoc est, maiore succedente, simili, ligatura, completione perfectionis minorum,[9] puncto additionis vel valoris, et duabus pausis minoribus postpositis [Ex. 3.11]. Tribus modis demptionem patientur: hoc est, minore praecedente, minore sequente vel earum comparatione [Ex. 3.12], et colore ipsas figuras implente [Ex. 3.13]. Hoc maiores observavere, minores quoque et praesertim compositores optimi hos secuntur. Verum similem ante similem praecedente minore non unquam imperficiunt.

3 Erit longae maior maxima, brevis ipsa longa, semibrevis ipsa brevis, et deinceps, ut supra sunt ordinatim perscriptae; eodem quoque modo maximae minor longa, longae brevis, et ita de sin[78r]gulis. Similis maximae eadem, longae longa, et sic ceterarum. De ligatura in minoribus illud accipimus, non autem aut maioribus aut similibus. Perfectionis completio est in tribus, sex, novem, et deinceps.

4 Et quoniam de puncto nil adhuc diximus et pausis, idcirco quid ex his est dicendum advertamus.

: IX :

In how many manners notes are perfected, or imperfected

Perfection is always understood by musicians in three, imperfection in two. Now we have said that certain circles and semicircles indicate perfection in certain notes or figures; we shall therefore list all the rules on the procedure for perfecting or imperfecting them.[35] 1

First, notes or figures will be perfected[36] under circles or semicircles providing them with perfection from six causes: that is, by a larger note following, by a similar note, by a ligature, by the completion of a perfection of smaller notes,[37] by a point of addition or value,[38] and by two smaller rests after them [Ex. 3.11].[39] They will undergo docking in three ways:[40] that is, by a smaller note preceding, by a smaller note following, or by their pairing[41] [Ex. 3.12][42] and by color filling them [Ex. 3.13].[43] This is what our forefathers practiced; their successors too and especially the best composers follow them. But they never imperfect a similar note before a similar note when a smaller one precedes. 2

The larger (note) of the long[44] will be the maxima, of the breve the long, of the semibreve the breve, and so on, as they were set out in order above. And in the same way too, the smaller (note) of the maxima will be the long, of the long the breve, and so for each. The similar (note) of the maxima is the same, of the long the long, and so too for the rest. Concerning the ligature, we apply the rule to smaller, not either larger or similar notes. The completion of a perfection is in three, six, nine, and so on. 3

And since we have said nothing yet about the point and rests, therefore let us note what is to be said of them. 4

: X :

De puncti officio

1 Punctum non ut in geometria accipimus, ut sit lineae initium, sed pro figurarum additamento vel quarundam segregatione; nam semper cui figurae postponitur, illi perfectionem auget, quoniam non <im>perficiendis figuris daretur ipse punctus. Si maximae dabitur longam adiciet, similiter longae brevem, et deinde in ceteris [Exx. 3.11, 3.12].

2 Punctus vero divisionis alterandas figuras ab ipso actu alterationis ipsas extorquet [Ex. 3.12]. Quid alteratio suo loco dicemus. Igitur punc[78v]torum alterum figuris augmentum praebere dicimus, alterum vero divisionem facere.

3 Et quoniam colorem contrarium huic officium habere novimus, idcirco quid breviter videamus.

: XI :

De colore et eius auctoritate

1 Colorem vel figuras lituratas quadrifariam reperiemus; namque aut notulis <im>perficiendis aut alterandis, aut imperfectis aut quibusdam cum aliis adiungendis, is condonabitur [Ex. 3.16]. Primo igitur tertiam partem aufert, secundo mediam, tertio quartam; quarto nil praeter societatem exercebit. Maiores nostri notulas nigras vel alio colore plenas habebant pro nostris albis; verum pro coloratis vacuas dimiserant; et in ipsis proportionibus color

: X :

On the function of the point

We do not understand "point" as in geometry, making it the beginning of a line, but as an addition to notes, or the separation of them. For always it increases perfection for the figure after which it is placed, since the point would not be put in order to imperfect notes.[45] If it is put with a maxima it will add a long; similarly to a long (it will add) a breve, and so on with the rest [see Exx. 3.11, 3.12]. 1

On the other hand, the point of division wrenches notes due to be altered from the very act of alteration [see Ex. 3.12]. What alteration is we shall say in due course. Therefore we say that one of the points confers increase on notes, the other divides them. 2

And since we know that color has the contrary function, let us therefore see briefly what it is. 3

: XI :

On color and its authority

We shall find color or inked-in figures of four kinds, for it will be assigned for imperfecting, for altering notes,[46] for joining imperfect notes, or for joining some to others [Ex. 3.16]. Firstly, then, it takes away a third part; secondly a half; thirdly a quarter;[47] fourthly it will have no effect except companionship.[48] Our ancestors had black notes, or notes filled in with another color, for our white notes, but where we color them, they had left them empty; and in those proportions the color does not take away from notes 1

ipse non eo modo ut supra diximus figuris aufert, sed pro ve[79r]terum notulis positum noverimus.

: XII :

Quomodo alteratio fiat

1 Alteratio dicitur notulae sive figurae duplicatio; hanc nunquam boni compositores nisi sequatur sua propria maior effici volunt, nam si maior suae maioris, aut similis, aut minor sequatur, non eam recte fieri dicimus. Non enim omnes circuli vel semicirculi omnes figuras alterandas compellunt; sed cum quis ipsorum in aliqua figurarum perfectionem dederit, tunc in minore earundem fiet alteratio, quam hoc modo cognoscemus. Computato in propria mensura aliquo numero vel inter duas maiores manentibus duabus minoribus aut quinque aut octo <vel undecim>[10] vel deinceps, semper extremam duplicabimus, hoc est, secundam, quintam, octavam, undecimam, etc. [Ex. 3.14].

: XIII :

De pausis

1 [79v] Pausa recreandi spiritus causa vel contrapuncti vitia evitandi instituta est. Haec quot spatia linearum occupat, tot tempora conticescit [Ex. 3.17]. De modo tria spatia habebit ad summum, nam si his plura occupasset finalis vel terminalis diceretur, et absque mensura relinqueretur. Loco maximarum duae[11] longae

in the same way as we said above, but we shall know it is put instead of the ancients' notes.

: XII :

How alteration takes place

Alteration is the name for doubling of a note or figure; good composers never wish it to be carried out unless the note's own proper larger note follows, for if the next larger note, or a similar note, or a smaller note follows, we say it does not rightly occur.[49] Not all circles or semicircles compel all notes to be altered, but when one of them has conferred perfection on one of the notes, then alteration will take place in the next smaller one. We shall recognize it in the following way. Having counted some number in its own mensuration,[50] when either two smaller notes remain between two larger notes, or five, or eight, or so on, we shall always double the last, that is, the second, fifth, the eighth, the eleventh, etc. [Ex. 3.14].[51] 1

: XIII :

On rests

The rest was devised for regaining breath or avoiding faults of counterpoint. It is silent for as many tempora as it occupies spaces between lines [Ex. 3.17]. It will usually have three spaces at most, for if it occupied more, it would be called final or terminal and left without mensuration. Instead of maximas, two longs are usually 1

poni consueverunt, minor quarum duo tenet spatia; illa vero quae unum habet spatium, id est contingens duas lineas, brevis est. Sed ea quae a linea ad spatij medium inferiora petens, et quae ad altiora tendit, altera semibrevis, altera vero minimae semper erit. Ea quoque minimae, cum caput paulisper uncum habebit, semiminimae erit. Quare neque his maiores minoresve vetustiores et posteri in quantitate instituere.

2 Ipsa quoque pausa, cum sua similis figura natu[80r]raliter ob circulum semicirculumque perfecta vel imperfecta est, eandem retinet proprietatem, nec unquam signo aliquo augeri diminuique potest nec alterari. Quae harum notularum sit mensura videamus.

: XIIII :

De duplici cantuum mensura

1 In omni genere cantuum sive specie proportionum tantum duplicem mensuram meminimus: alteram semibrevem tris minimas habentem, alteram vero duas. In his autem notulas cantando pausasque conticendo non secus in humana voce atque in musicis instrumentis pro una cantus plani notula proferemus.

2 Eadem mensura uti poterimus multis modis; nam in diminutionibus semibrevibus aut brevibus utemur pro minimis, et sic deinceps ceteris. Diminutionem enim dicimus quando maxima loco longae vel brevis [80v] uteremur. Hoc quoque pacto augmentum in figuris vocitamus, quando minorem pro maiore per suas minores partes augemus.

3 Et quoniam saepe proportiones illud clarius ostendunt, idcirco de his iam quaedam manifestemus.

placed, the smaller of which[52] takes up two spaces. The one that occupies one space, that is, touching two lines, belongs to the breve. But the one that strains from a line to mid-space going downward, and the one that strains upward, will always belong to the semibreve and minim respectively. And that of the minim, when it has a slightly hooked head, will be that of the semiminim.[53] Wherefore older and later composers never devised (rests) larger or smaller than these in quantity.[54]

And when the corresponding note is naturally perfect or imper- 2
fect owing to a circle or semicircle, the rest too retains the same property, nor can it ever be increased or diminished by any sign. Let us see what these notes' mensuration is.

: XIV :

On the twofold mensuration of vocal music

In every genus of vocal music or species of proportions we recall 1
only two kinds of mensuration: one semibreve containing three minims, the other two.[55] In these, we shall perform the notes by singing, and the rests by being silent, no otherwise with the human voice than on musical instruments, to match one note of the plainchant.[56]

We shall be able to use the same mensuration in many ways; 2
for in diminutions we shall use semibreves or breves instead of minims,[57] and so on for the rest. We also speak of diminution when we use a maxima for a long or a breve. In this way too we call it augmentation in figures when we increase a smaller note by its smaller parts in place of a larger note.

And since proportions will often demonstrate that more clearly, 3
let us therefore now set out some things about them.

: XV :

Quid sit proportio quomodoque accipiatur

1 Proportionem Boethius dicit esse duorum ad se terminorum comparationem; terminos autem numerorum summas vocitat. Hanc enim vel proprie vel communiter accipiemus. Illa quae est dicta communiter reperitur in omnibus quae aequale vel maius vel minus seu etiam simile suscipiunt. Et ideo in quibuscumque potest aliqua comparatio fieri proportio invenitur, quam sic definiemus: Proportio est duorum quorumcumque[12] eiusdem generis vel speciei [81r] unius ad alterum habitudo.

2 Sed illam proprie dictam hoc pacto definiemus: Proportio est duarum quantitatum eiusdem generis vel speciei communis unius ad alteram habitudo; quam in solis quantitatibus reperimus. Ea duplex est, scilicet coniuncta et disiuncta.

3 Disiuncta semper est inter quattuor terminos formaliter. Exemplum: qualis est proportio 16 ad 8, talis est 4 ad 2. Proportio vero coniuncta semper est inter iii terminos formaliter, licet sint quattuor termini virtualiter. Exemplum: qualis est proportio 8 ad 4, talis est 4 ad 2. Et sic sunt tres termini formaliter, licet sint 4 virtualiter, quia unum sumitur bis, scilicet quattuor.

4 Item quaedam est proportio aequalitatis, quaedam inaequalitatis. Proportio aequalitatis (ut diximus) est duarum [81v] quantitatum aequalium unius ad alteram habitudo. Proportio inaequalitatis est duplex, aut est maioris aut minoris: maioris inaequalitatis, quando maior numerus comparatur minori, ut iii ad ii, vi ad iiii; minoris vero inaequalitatis, quando minor numerus comparatur maiori, ut ii ad iii, iiii ad vi.

: XV :

What proportion is and how it is understood

Proportion, says Boethius, is the comparison of two terms with each other;[58] by "terms" he means the values of numbers. This we shall understand in either its proper or its common sense. That which is commonly so called is found in all things that allow of equal or greater or less or even similar. And therefore, in all things in which any comparison can be made, proportion is found, which we shall define as follows: Proportion is the relation to each other of any two things[59] of the same genus or species. 1

But proportion properly so called we shall define thus: Proportion is the relation to each other of two quantities of the same kind or a common species. We find it only in quantities. It is twofold, namely conjunct and disjunct.[60] 2

Disjunct proportion is always formally between four terms. Example: as is the proportion 16 : 8, so is 4 : 2. But conjunct proportion is always formally between three terms, even though there are four terms virtually. Example: as is the proportion 8 : 4, so is 4 : 2. And thus there are three terms formally, although there are four virtually, since one of them is taken twice, namely 4. 3

Furthermore there is a proportion of equality and one of inequality. The proportion of equality (as we have said) is the relation to each other of two equal quantities. The proportion of inequality is twofold: it is either of the greater or the lesser (inequality). Of the greater inequality, when the greater number is compared with the smaller, as 3 : 2, 6 : 4. Of the lesser inequality, when the smaller number is compared with the greater, as 2 : 3 and 4 : 6. 4

5 Proportionis inaequalitatis maioris quinque sunt genera, totidemque possunt poni minoris inaequalitatis, ut postea videbimus.

6 De his haec Boethius in Arithmetica:

> 7 Omne enim aut aequale est aut inaequale quicquid alterius comparatione metimur. Et aequale quidem est quod ad aliquid comparatum neque minore summa infra est, neque maiore transgreditur ut denarius denario vel ternarius ternario vel cubitum cubito vel pes pedi.

8 Et pau[82r]lo post: 'Omnis enim aequalitas unam servat in propria moderatione mensuram.' Deinde subiungit:

> 9 Inaequalis quantitatis vero gemina divisio est. Secatur enim quod inaequale est in maius aut minus, quae contraria sibimet denominatione funguntur. Namque maius minore maius est, et minus maiore minus est, et quae ipse pergit.

10 Et paulo post:

> 11 Maioris inaequalitatis v partes sunt: est enim una quae vocatur multiplex, alia superparticularis, tertia superpartiens, quarta multiplex superparticularis, quinta multiplex superpartiens. His igitur quinque inaequalitatis maioris partibus oppositae sunt aliae quinque partes minoris, quemadmodum ipsum maius minori[13] semper opponitur. Quae minoris species ita singillatim speciebus quinque maioris his [82v] quae supradictae sunt opponuntur ut eisdem nominibus nuncupentur, sola tantum 'sub' praepositione distantes: dicitur enim submultiplex, subsuperparticularis, subsuperpartiens, multiplex subsuperparticularis, et multiplex subsuperpartiens.

12 Hoc idem in sua musica diffuse demonstrat. Haec eadem et Enchiriadis libro inveniemus. Johannes quoque de Muris in Proportionibus suis hoc inquit:

Of the proportion of the greater inequality there are five kinds, 5
and as many can be posited of the lesser inequality, as we shall see later.

Of these Boethius says the following in his *Arithmetic*: 6

> For everything that we measure by comparison with some- 7
> thing else is either equal or unequal. And equal is what when compared with another neither falls short of it with a smaller value nor surpasses it with a larger, as the number 10 to 10,[61] or 3 to 3, or a cubit to a cubit, or a foot to a foot.[62]

And a little later: "For every equality preserves a single standard in 8
its own measurement."[63] Then he adds:

> Of unequal quantity there is a twofold division. For what is 9
> unequal is cut into greater or smaller, which employ opposite names to each other, for the greater is greater than the smaller, and the smaller is larger than smaller, etc.[64]

And a little later: 10

> Of the greater inequality there are five parts, one called mul- 11
> tiple, another superparticular, a third superpartient, a fourth multiple superparticular, a fifth multiple superpartient. To these five parts of the greater inequality stand opposed another five parts of the lesser, even as the greater is always opposed to the lesser. These species of the lesser are individually opposite to the five species of the greater stated above in such a way that they are called by the same names, differing only in the prefix "sub." For they are called submultiple, subsuperparticular, subsuperpartient, multiple subsuperparticular, and multiple subsuperpartient.[65]

This same thing he demonstrates in his *Music* at length.[66] 12
These same things we shall also find in the book of Enchiriades.[67] Johannes de Muris, too, in his *Proportions* says the following:[68]

13 Omnis autem numerus ad alium comparatus aut est aequalis aut inaequalis. Nam haec competunt cuilibet quantitati. Si aequalis unum sunt et idem in quantitate, ideo non variantur et ex aequalibus non fit consonantia;[14] si autem inaequalis, aut maior aut minor. Dicitur autem unum maius altero quinque modis, ut multiplex, superparticularis, et superpartiens, [83r] multiplex superparticularis, et multiplex superpartiens. Appositaque ista dictione 'sub' dividitur tot modis, quot supra divisum est,[15] et quae ipse pergit.

14 Unumquodque genus harum proportionum speciesque singulas perscribamus.

: XVI :

De primo proportionum genere speciebusque suis

1 Multiplex genus est quando maior numerus minorem multipliciter continet, scilicet bis, ter, quater, quinquies, et deinceps in infinitum. Eius species sunt dupla, tripla, quadrupla, quinquipla,[16] et sic de ceteris.

2 Proportio dupla est quando maior numerus continet minorem bis praecise vel quasi minorem, ut ii ad i, iiii ad ii, vi ad iii, et sic de ceteris. Proportio tripla est quando maior numerus minorem [83v] continet ter, seu quasi minorem, ut iii ad i, vi ad ii, viiii ad iii, xv ad v, et de reliquis. Proportio quadrupla est quando maior numerus minorem continet quater seu quasi minorem. Species talis generis hae sunt iiii ad i, viii ad ii, xii ad iii, et deinceps.

3 Proportio quinquipla est quando maior numerus minorem continet quinquies vel quasi minorem, ut x[17] <ad> ii, xx ad iiii, xxv ad v, xxx ad vi, et in ceteris. Proportio sextupla est quando

Now every number, compared with another, is either equal or unequal. For these pertain to every quantity. They are one and the same in quantity, and therefore do not vary, and out of equal [sounds] consonance is not made. But if it is unequal, it is either greater or smaller. Now one thing is said to be greater than another in five ways, namely multiple, superparticular, superpartient, multiple superparticular, and multiple superpartient. And by adding the word "sub" the division is made in as many ways as it was made above, etc. 13

Let us write out each genus of these proportions and all its species. 14

: XVI :

On the first genus of proportions and its species

The multiple genus is when the greater number contains the smaller many-fold, that is, twice, thrice, four times, five times, and so on to infinity. Its species are duple, triple, quadruple, quintuple, and so on. 1

Duple proportion is when the greater number contains the smaller, or as it were smaller,[69] twice exactly, as 2 : 1, 4 : 2, 6 : 3, and so on. Triple proportion is when the greater number contains the smaller, or as it were smaller, thrice, as 3 : 1, 6 : 2, 9 : 3, 15 : 5, and so on. Fourfold proportion is when the greater number contains the smaller, or as it were smaller, four times. The species of this genus are 4 : 1, 8 : 2, 12 : 3, and so forth. 2

Fivefold proportion is when the greater number contains the smaller, or as it were smaller, five times, as 10: 2, 20 : 4, 25 : 5, 30 : 6, and so on. Sixfold proportion is when the greater number 3

maior numerus minorem continet sexies[18] vel quasi minorem, ut vi ad i, xii, ad ii, xviii ad iii, xxiiii ad iiii, et deinceps. Proportio septupla est quando maior numerus minorem continet septies, ut vii ad i, xiiii ad ii, xxi ad iii, etc.

4 Proportio octupla est quando maior minorem continet octies, ut viii [84^{r}] ad i, xvi ad ii, xxiiii ad iii, xxxii ad iiii, etc. Proportio nonupla est quando maior numerus minorem continet novies, ut viiii ad i, xviii ad ii, xxvii ad iii, etc. Proportio decupla est quando maior numerus minorem decies continet, ut x ad i, xx ad ii, xxx ad iii. Et sic in infinitum omnes formaremus.

: XVII :

De secundo proportionum genere speciebusque suis

1 Superparticulare est quando maior numerus minorem continet cum eius[19] parte aliquota minoris numeri, ut sunt isti numeri iii ad ii, vi ad iiii, etc. Pars aliquota est illa quae aliquotiens sumpta reddit suum totum numerum praecise, <ut sunt .ii. de .iiii., bis enim sumpta reddunt totum quaternarium. Pars non aliquota est illa quae aliquotiens sumpta suum totum numerum non reddit praecise,>[20] sed reddit maius vel minus, ut iii sunt pars non aliquota de v vel iiii de vii, et sic de aliis. Generis istius hae [84^{v}] sunt species: sesqualtera, sesquitertia, sesquiquarta, sesquiquinta, et deinceps.

2 Proportio sesqualtera est quando maior numerus minorem continet semel cum medietate minoris, ut iii ad ii, vi ad iiii, xii ad viii, xv ad x, et in ceteris. Dicitur autem a sesqui, quod est totum et altera idem pars, quasi totum minorem numerum et eius medietatem continens. Graece autem emiolia dicitur ab emis quod est semis et olon quod est totum, quasi continens totum numerum

contains the smaller, or as it were smaller, six times, as 6 : 1, 12 : 2, 18 : 3, 24 : 4, and so on. Sevenfold proportion is when the greater number contains the smaller seven times, as 7 : 1, 14 : 2, 21 : 3, etc.

Eightfold proportion is when the greater number contains the 4
smaller eight times, as 8 : 1, 16 : 2, 24 : 3, 32 : 4, etc. Ninefold proportion is when the greater number contains the smaller nine times, as 9 : 1, 18 : 2, 27 : 3, etc. Tenfold proportion is when the greater number contains the smaller ten times, as 10 : 1, 20 : 2, 30 : 3. And so we should form them all ad infinitum.

: XVII :

On the second genus of proportions and its species

The superparticular is when the greater number contains the 1
smaller with an aliquot part of the smaller number, as are the following numbers: 3 : 2, 6 : 4, etc. An aliquot part is that which, taken several times (*aliquotiens*), yields its complete number precisely, <as 2 is of 4, for taken twice it yields the complete number 4. A non-aliquot part is one that taken several times does not yield its complete number precisely,> but yields something larger or smaller, as 3 is a non-aliquot part of 5, or 4 of 7, and so forth. Of that genus, the following are the species: sesquialter, sesquitertian, sesquiquartan, sesquiquintan, and so on.

Sesquialter proportion is when the greater number contains the 2
smaller once with half the smaller, as 3 : 2, 6 : 4, 12 : 8, 15 : 10, and so forth. It is so called from *sesqui,*[70] which is the whole and also the second half,[71] as if containing the smaller number and its half. In Greek it is called *hemiolia*[72] from *hemis,*[73] which is a half, and *holon,*[74] which is the whole, as if containing the whole of the

minorem <et eius medietatem>. In codicibus autem vetustis non sesquialteram, sed sesqualteram scriptum comperii.

3 Proportio sesquitertia est quando maior numerus minorem semel et tertiam partem minoris numeri continet, ut iiii ad iii, viiii ad vi, xii ad viiii, xvi ad xii, etc. Graece [85r] autem epitritam dicimus, ab epi, quod est supra, et triti tertia, quasi minorem numerum <continens> et tertiam partem supra. Proportio sesquiquarta quando maior numerus minorem et cum hoc quartam partem continet, <ut> v ad iiii, x ad viii, xv ad xii, xx ad xvi.

4 Proportio sesquiquinta est quando maior numerus minorem et cum <hoc> quintam partem minoris continet semel, ut vi ad v, xii ad x, xviii ad xv. Proportio sesquisexta est quando maior numerus minorem et cum hoc sextam partem minoris continet, ut vii ad vi, xiiii ad xii, xx ad xviii. Proportio sesquiseptima est quando maior numerus minorem et septimam <partem> huius continet, ut viii ad vii, xvi ad xiiii, xxiiii ad xxi.

5 Proportio sesquioctava est quando maior numerus minorem [85v] semel et octavam partem minoris continet, <ut> viiii ad viii, xviii ad xvi, xxvii ad xxiiii. Proportio sesquinona est quando maior numerus minorem et nonam partem eius continet, ut x ad viiii, xx ad xviii, xxx ad xxvii, xl[21] ad xxxvi. Proportio sesquidecima est quando maior numerus minorem semel et decimam partem <eius continet>, ut xi[22] ad x, xxii ad xx, xxxiii ad xxx, xliiii ad xl.

: XVIII :

De tertio proportionum genere speciebusque suis

1 Superpartiens est quando maior numerus minorem semel et partem non aliquotam minoris numeri continet, ut v ad iii, vii ad iiii, x ad vi<i>. Hoc enim genus tripliciter reperitur: uno modo ex

smaller number <and its half>. In old manuscripts I have found it spelled not *sexquialtera* but *sexqualtera*.[75]

Sesquitertian proportion is when the greater number contains 3
the smaller once and the third part of the smaller number, as 4 : 3, 8 : 6, 12 : 9, 16 : 12, etc. In Greek we call it *epitrita*,[76] from *epi*,[77] which is "over," and *triti*[78] "third," as if "<containing> the smaller number and its third part (left) over." Sesquiquartan proportion is when the greater number contains the smaller and with it the fourth part, 5 : 4, 10 : 8, 15 : 12, 20 : 16.

Sesquiquintan proportion is when the greater number contains 4
the smaller once and with it the fifth part, as 6 : 5, 12 : 10, 18 : 15. Sesquisextan proportion is when the greater number contains the smaller and with it the sixth part, as 7 : 6, 14 : 12, 20 : 18. Sesquiseptiman proportion is when the greater number contains the smaller and its seventh part, as 8 : 7, 16 : 14, 24 : 21.

Sesquioctave proportion is when the greater number contains 5
the smaller once and the eighth part of the smaller number, as 9 : 8, 18 : 16, 27 : 24. Sesquinone proportion is when the greater number contains the smaller and its ninth part, as 10 : 9, 20 : 18, 30 : 27, 40 : 36.[79] Sesquideciman proportion is when the greater number contains the smaller once and its tenth part, as 11 : 10, 22 : 20, 33 : 30, 44 : 40.

: XVIII :

On the third genus of proportions and its species

The superpartient is when the greater number contains the 1
smaller once and a non-aliquot part of the smaller number, as 5 : 3, 7 : 4, 10 : 7. This genus is found threefold: in one mode

parte numeri <maioris>[23] superpartiens, altero modo ex parte denominationis partium numeri [86r] minoris, tertio mixtim ex ambobus.

2 Primi generis species sunt superbipartiens, supertripartiens, superquadripartiens,[24] superquinquepartiens,[25] etc. Superbipartiens proportio est quando maior numerus minorem semel et cum hoc duas partes minoris continet, quae simul iunctae faciunt partem non aliquotam minoris numeri, ut v ad iii, x ad vi,[26] viiii ad vii.

3 Proportio supertripartiens est quando maior numerus minorem semel et cum hoc tres[27] partes minoris continet, quae simul iunctae non sunt pars aliquota illius minoris numeri, ut vii ad iiii. Nam vii continet iiii semel et cum hoc iii unitates, quae simul iunctae sunt pars non aliquota illius minoris numeri, scilicet de iiii. Istae sunt eius species: x ad vii, xi ad viii, xiii ad x, xiiii ad xi, et [86v] sic de ceteris.

4 Proportio superquadripartiens est quando maior numerus minorem et cum hoc quattuor partes minoris numeri continet, quae simul iunctae non sunt pars aliquota illius numeri minoris, ut viiii ad v, x ad vi, xi ad vii, xv ad xi. Proportio superquinquepartiens[28] est quando maior numerus minorem continet et cum hoc v partes minoris numeri, quae simul iunctae pars non aliquota[29] numeri minoris sunt, ut xi ad vi, xii ad vii, xiii ad viii. Et sic ceteras multas poteris per te invenire.

5 Secundi modi species sunt iste: superpartiens tertias, superpartiens quartas, superpartiens quintas, et sic deinceps. Superpartiens tertias est quando maior <numerus>[30] minorem semel continet et cum hoc duas tertias mi[87r]noris numeri, ut v ad iii, nam v continet iii et cum hoc duas partes, <id est> unitates, quarum quaelibet est tertia pars iii. Superpartiens quartas est quando

superpartient by a part of the <greater> number, in the other by a part of the name of the parts of the smaller number, in the third by a blend of the two.[80]

The species of the first genus[81] are superbipartient,[82] supertripartient, superquadripartient, superquinquepartient, etc. Superbipartient proportion is when the greater number contains the smaller number once and with it two parts[83] of the smaller, which added together make a non-aliquot part of the smaller number, as 5 : 3, 10 : 6,[84] 9 : 7. 2

Supertripartient proportion is when the greater number contains the smaller number once and with it three parts (that is, units) of the smaller, which added together are not an aliquot part of the smaller number, as 7 : 4. For 7 contains 4 once and with it three units, which added together make a non-aliquot part of the smaller number, namely 4. These are its species: 10 : 7, 11 : 8, 13 : 10, 14 : 11, and so on. 3

Superquadripartient proportion is when the greater number contains the smaller and with it four parts of the smaller number, which added together are a non-aliquot part of that smaller number, as 9 : 5, 10 : 6,[85] 11 : 7, 15 : 11. Superquinquepartient proportion is when the greater number contains the smaller and with it five parts of the smaller number, which added together are a non-aliquot part of the smaller number, as 11 : 6, 12 : 7, 13 : 8. And thus you will be able to find many others for yourself. 4

The species of the second mode are these: *superpartiens tertias,*[86] *superpartiens quartas, superpartiens quintas,* and so forth. *Superpartiens tertias* is when the greater contains the smaller once and with it two-thirds of the smaller number,[87] as 5 : 3, for 5 contains 3 and with it two parts, that is, units of which each is the third part of 3. *Superpartiens quartas* is when the greater number contains the 5

maior numerus minorem semel continet et cum hoc iii partes numeri minoris quae simul iunctae sunt pars non aliquota minoris numeri, ut vii ad iiii. Nam septem continet iiii et cum hoc iii partes de vii quarum quaelibet est una quarta pars de iiii seu minoris numeri. Proportio superpartiens quintas est quando maior numerus minorem semel continet et cum hoc iiii[31] partes minoris numeri, quae simul iunctae sunt pars non aliquota minoris quarum quaelibet est una quinta <pars> minoris, ut vii ad v, viii ad vi, viiii ad vii,[32] et sic de singulis.

6 Tertii modi, id est mixtim, hae sunt species: superbipartiens tertias, supertripar[87^{v}]tiens[33] quartas, superquadripartiens quintas,[34] superquinquepartiens[35] sextas etc. Proportio superbipartiens tertias est quando maior numerus minorem semel continet et cum hoc duas unitates quae sunt non aliquota minoris quae duae unitates sunt duae tertiae minoris, ut v ad iii, nam v continet iii et ii^{as} unitates, quarum quaelibet est una iii^{a} minoris, scilicet iii, nam duae unitates sunt duae tertiae. Proportio supertripartiens[36] quartas est quando maior numerus minorem semel continet et cum hoc iii partes minoris, quarum quaelibet est iiii pars minoris numeri, ut vii ad iiii. Nam vii continet iiii et iii quae sunt tres partes de iiii et quaelibet illarum partium est quarta pars de quattuor.

7 Superquadripartiens quintas proportio[37] est quando maior numerus minorem semel [88^{r}] continet et cum hoc <iiii> unitates et sic est quadripartiens, quarum quaelibet est una quinta, ut viiii ad v, nam viiii continet v et cum hoc quattuor partes, quarum quaelibet est una quinta minoris numeri. Proportio superquinquepartiens sextas est quando maior numerus minorem continet et quinque partes desuper, quarum quaelibet est una vi^{a}, ut xi ad vi, xii ad vii, et sic de reliquis.

smaller once and with it three parts of the smaller numbers, which added together are a non-aliquot part of the smaller number, as 7 : 4. For 7 contains 4 and with it three parts of 7, of which each is a quarter of 4, or the smaller number. *Superpartiens quintas* proportion is when the greater number contains the smaller once and with it four parts of the smaller number, which taken together are a non-aliquot part of the smaller number, of which each is a fifth of the smaller, as 7 : 5, 8 : 6, 9 : 7,[88] and so on.

Of the third mode, that is, by mixture, the species are these: 6
superbipartiens tertias, supertripartiens quartas, superquadripartiens quintas,[89] *superquinquepartiens sextas*, etc. *Superbipartiens tertias* proportion is when the greater number contains the smaller once and with it two units that are a non-aliquot part of the smaller, which two units are two-thirds of the smaller, as 5 : 3. For 5 contains 3 and two units, of which each is one-third of the smaller, namely 3. For the two units are two-thirds. *Supertripartiens quartas* proportion is when the greater number contains the smaller once and with it three parts of the smaller, of which each is a quarter of the smaller number, as 7 : 4. For 7 contains 4 and 3, which is three parts of 4 and each of those is a quarter of 4.

Superquadripartiens quintas proportion is when the greater num- 7
ber contains the smaller number once and with it four units (and is thus quadripartient) of which each is a fifth, as 9 : 5. For 9 contains 5 and with it four parts, of which each is a fifth of the smaller number. *Superquinquepartiens sextas* proportion is when the greater number contains the smaller and five parts in addition, of which each is one-sixth, as 11 : 6, 12 : 7,[90] and so on for the rest.

: XIX :

De quarto proportionum genere speciebusque suis

1 Genus multiplex superparticulare est quando maior numerus minorem multipliciter continet, scilicet bis, ter, quater, etc., et cum hoc partem aliquotam minoris numeri, ut v ad ii, vii ad iii, cuius species sunt istae: dupla ad sesqualteram, dupla ad sesquitertiam, dupla ad sesquiquar[88v]tam, dupla ad sesquiquintam, et deinceps.

2 Dupla ad sesqualteram est quando maior numerus minorem <bis> continet et cum hoc medietatem[38] minoris numeri ut v ad ii, xx ad viii,[39] xv ad vi, etc. Dupla ad sesquitertiam est quando maior numerus minorem continet bis et <cum hoc> tertiam partem minoris numeri ut vii ad iii, xiiii ad vi, xxi ad viiii. Dupla ad sesquiquartam est quando maior numerus minorem <bis> continet et cum hoc quartam partem minoris numeri ut viiii ad iiii, xviii ad viii, xxvii[40] ad xii. Dupla ad sesquiquintam est quando maior numerus minorem continet bis et <cum hoc> quintam partem minoris numeri, ut xi ad v, xxii ad x, xxxiii ad xv, et deinceps.

3 Vel alio modo ponuntur species huius generis, id est multipli[89r]ci<s> superparticularis, tripla ad sesqualteram, tripla ad sesquitertiam, tripla ad sesquiquartam, tripla ad sesquiquintam, et sic de singulis. Tripla ad sesquialteram est quando maior numerus minorem ter continet et cum hoc medietatem illius numeri minoris ut vii ad ii, xiiii ad iiii, xxi ad vi. Tripla ad sesquitertiam est quando maior numerus minorem ter continet et cum hoc tertiam partem minoris numeri, ut x ad iii, xx ad vi, xxx ad viiii.

4 Tripla ad sesquiquartam est quando maior numerus minorem ter continet et cum hoc quartam partem minoris numeri, ut xiii ad iiii, xxvi[41] ad viii, xxxviiii ad xii. Proportio tripla ad sesquiquinta<m> est quando maior numerus minorem ter continet

: XIX :

On the fourth genus of proportions and its species

The multiple superparticular genus is when the greater number contains the smaller several times, that is, twice, thrice, four times, etc., and with it an aliquot part of the smaller number, as 5 : 2, 7 : 3. Its species are the following: *dupla ad sesquialteram,*[91] *dupla ad sesquitertiam, dupla ad sesquiquartam, dupla ad sesquiquintam,* and so on. 1

Dupla ad sesquialteram is when the greater number contains the smaller twice and in addition half the smaller number, as 5 : 2, 20 : 8,[92] 15 : 6, etc. *Dupla ad sesquitertiam* is when the greater number contains the smaller twice and in addition one-third of the smaller number, as 7 : 3, 14 : 6, 21 : 9. *Dupla ad sesquiquartam* is when the greater number contains the smaller twice and in addition a quarter of the smaller number, as 9 : 4, 18 : 8, 27 : 12. *Dupla ad sesquiquintam* is when the greater number contains the smaller twice and one-fifth of the smaller number, as 11 : 5, 22 : 10, 33 : 15 and so on. 2

Alternatively, species of this genus, that is, the multiple superparticular, are stated in another mode:[93] *tripla ad sesquialteram, tripla ad sesquitertiam, tripla ad sesquiquartam, tripla ad sesquiquintam,* and so on. *Tripla ad sesquialteram* is when the greater number contains the smaller thrice and in addition half the smaller number, as 7 : 2, 14 : 4, 21 : 6. *Tripla ad sesquitertiam* is when the greater number contains the smaller thrice and in addition one-third of the smaller number, as 10 : 3, 20 : 6, 30 : 9. 3

Tripla ad sesquiquartam is when the greater number contains the smaller thrice and in addition one-quarter of the smaller number, as 13 : 4, 26 : 8, 39 : 12. *Tripla ad sesquiquintam* is when the greater 4

et cum hoc quintam [89v] partem minoris numeri, ut xvi ad v, <x>xxii[42] ad x, xlviii[43] ad xv.

: XX :

De quinto proportionum genere speciebusque suis

1 Genus multiplex superpartiens est quando maior numerus minorem multipliciter continet, scilicet bis, ter, quater, etc., et cum <hoc> partem non aliquotam minoris numeri, ut viii ad iii, xxvii[44] ad iiii, cuius species sunt istae: dupla superbipartiens, dupla supertripartiens, dupla superquadripartiens, et sic deinceps.

2 Dupla superbipartiens est quando maior numerus minorem bis continet et cum hoc duas partes minoris numeri, quae simul iunctae sunt non pars aliquota illius numeri, ut viii ad iii, quia viii con<tinet> iii bis et cum eo duas partes, id est unitates, quae simul iunctae sunt pars [90r] non aliquota illius numeri minoris, scilicet ternarii, ut xii ad v,[45] xvi ad vii.

3 Dupla supertripartiens est quando maior numerus minorem bis continet et cum eo tres partes minoris numeri quae simul iunctae sunt pars non aliquota illius minoris numeri, ut xi ad iiii, nam xi[46] continebit bis iiii et cum hoc tres partes seu unitates ipsius quae faciunt partem non aliquotam ipsius quattuor, ut xiii ad v, xvii ad vii, xviiii ad viii.

4 Dupla superquadripartiens est quando numerus maior minorem bis continet et cum hoc quattuor partes <minoris numeri quae simul iunctae sunt pars non aliquota>[47] illius minoris numeri, ut .xiiii. ad .v., nam .xiiii. continet bis quinque et ultra quattuor unitates, et sic de aliis speciebus.

5 Vel aliter: quando prima species primi generis comparatur et unitur secundae speciei se[90v]cundi generis, ut tripla supertripar-

number contains the smaller thrice and in addition one-fifth of the smaller number, as 16 : 5, 32 : 10, 48 : 15.

: XX :

On the fifth genus of proportions and its species

The multiple superpartient genus is when the greater number con- 1
tains the smaller several times, namely twice, thrice, four times, etc. and with it a non-aliquot part of the smaller number, as 8 : 3, 27 : 4.[94] Its species are these: duple superbipartient, duple supertripartient, duple superquadripartient, and so forth.

Duple superbipartient is when the greater number contains the 2
smaller number twice and with it two parts of the smaller number, which added together are not an aliquot part of that number, as 8 : 3; for 8 contains twice 3, and with two parts, that is, units that added together are a non-aliquot part of that smaller number, namely 3, as 12 : 5, 16 : 7.

Duple supertripartient is when the greater number contains the 3
smaller number twice and with it three parts of the smaller number, which added together are a non-aliquot part of that smaller number, as 11 : 4. For 11 will contain twice 4 and with it three parts or units of it which make a non-aliquot part of the four, as 13 : 5, 17 : 7, 19 : 8.

Duple superquadripartient is when the greater number contains 4
the smaller number twice and with it four parts of the smaller number, <which added together are a non-aliquot part of that smaller number>, as 14 : 5, for 14 contains twice 5 and in addition four units, and so for the other species.

Another way is when the first species of the first genus is com- 5
pared and united with the second species of the second genus, as

tiens, aut quando tertia species primi generis, ut quadrupla superquadripartiens,[48] et sic de singulis.

6 Dupla superbipartiens est quando maior numerus minorem bis continet et cum hoc duas partes minoris numeri, quae simul iunctae sunt pars non aliquota illius minoris numeri, ut viii ad iii, nam viii continet bis iii et est dupla et continet duas partes minoris quae simul iunctae sunt pars non aliquota illius seu non sunt partes aliquotae. <Dupla supertripartiens est quando maior numerus minorem bis continet et cum hoc tres partes minoris numeri, quae simul iunctae sunt pars non aliquota illius minoris numeri;>[49] exemplum xiii ad v, xvii ad vii.

7 Tripla supertripartiens est quando maior numerus minorem ter continet et cum hoc tres partes minoris quae simul iunctae sunt pars non aliquota minoris, ut xv ad iiii, xviii ad v, xxiiii ad vii, etc.

8 Quadrupla su[91r]perquadripartiens[50] est quando maior numerus minorem quater continet et cum hoc quattuor partes minoris, quae simul iunctae sunt pars non aliquota illius numeri minoris, ut xxiiii ad v, xxviii ad vi, xxxii ad vii. Quinquipla superquinquepartiens est quando maior numerus minorem quinquies continet et cum hoc quinque partes minoris numeri quae simul iunctae sunt partes non aliquotae illius numeri minoris, ut xxxv ad vi, xl ad vii.

9 Et fiat denominatio respectu minoris numeri: quaelibet unitatum illarum superantium erit tertia si minor est iii, aut quarta si minor est iiii, aut quinta si minor est v, et sic erit superpartiens tertias, aut superpartiens quartas, aut superpartiens quintas, et sic de singulis. Has breviter perstrinxi quo[91v]niam per se legens infinitas quoquo genere et speciebus formare poterit.

triple supertripartient, or when the third species of the first genus (is so united), as quadruple superquadripartient, and so on for all cases.

Duple superbipartient is when the greater number contains the smaller number twice and with it two parts of the smaller number, which added together are a non-aliquot part of that number, as 8 : 3, for 8 contains twice 3 and is duple and contains two parts of the smaller (number), which added together are a non-aliquot part of it or are not aliquot parts.[95] <Duple supertripartient is when the greater number contains the smaller number twice and with it three parts of the smaller number, which added together are a non-aliquot part of that number>, for example 13 : 5, 17 : 7. 6

Triple supertripartient is when the greater number contains the smaller number thrice and with it three parts of the smaller number, which added together are a non-aliquot part of the smaller (number), as 15 : 4, 18 : 5, 24 : 7. etc. 7

Quadruple superquadripartient is when the greater number contains the smaller number four times and with it four parts of the smaller number, which added together are a non-aliquot part of that number, as 24 : 5, 28 : 6,[96] 32 : 7. Quintuple superquinquepartient is when the greater number contains the smaller number five times and with it five parts of the smaller number, which added together are non-aliquot parts of that smaller number, as 35 : 6, 40 : 7. 8

And let the name be given with respect to the smaller number: each of those units that exceed it will be a 'third' if the smaller number is 3, or 'fourth' if it is 4, or 'fifth' if it is 5, and thus it will be *superpartiens tertias* or *superpartiens quartas*, or *superpartiens quintas*, and so on for each.[97] I have touched on these briefly because the reader will be able to form an infinite number of them of any kind and species by himself. 9

: XXI :

De quibusdam proportionum indicibus

1 Musici persaepe compositoresque boni consueverunt has proportiones suis in cantibus usurpare quas circulis aut semicirculis ostendere conantur. Item arithmeticis characteribus vel litteris vel (ut lingua vernacula utar) cifris hasdem patefaciundas edunt. Quandoque notulae lituratae sive coloris plenae ad albas proportionem faciunt. Aliquando varia signa diversas reddunt proportiones.

2 Etsi diversae tantorum generum proportiones tamque diversarum reperiantur specierum, tamen non mensurae vel maioris vel minoris diversitate formantur, quoniam quemadmodum circuli semicirculique, non secus atque vidimus, nullam mensuram praeter [92r] has duas ostendunt, ita quoque characteres eo pacto proportiones ipsas mensas vel maiore vel minore mensura disponunt.

3 Quare contrapuncti potius ars id indicabit, quam certam veritatis normam sine verborum prolixitate aperire queamus. Igitur positis prius quorundam praemissorum exemplis, harum postea quaedam figurata perscribemus [Exx. 3.18–22].

EX. 3.1 *Partitio modi maioris perfecti per tris longas*

: XXI :

On certain indicators of proportions

Good musicians and composers have very often been wont to use 1
these proportions in their vocal pieces, which they attempt to show by means of circles or semicircles. They also declare that they are to be revealed by arithmetical characters or letters, or (to use the vernacular) ciphers.[98] Sometimes notes inked in or full of color create a proportion with respect to the white ones.[99] Sometimes various signs render different proportions.

Although different proportions of so many genera and such 2
different species are found, yet they are not formed by difference of mensuration, whether major or minor, because as the circles and semicircles, just as we have seen, demonstrate no mensuration besides these two, so too the characters arrange in the same way the proportions measured either by a major or a minor mensuration.

For this reason, it is rather the art of counterpoint that will in- 3
dicate it, which sure rule of truth we should be able to reveal without prolixity of words. Therefore, we shall first set out examples of some of the foregoing, and then write out some (examples) of these (proportions) in notation [see Exx. 3.18–22].

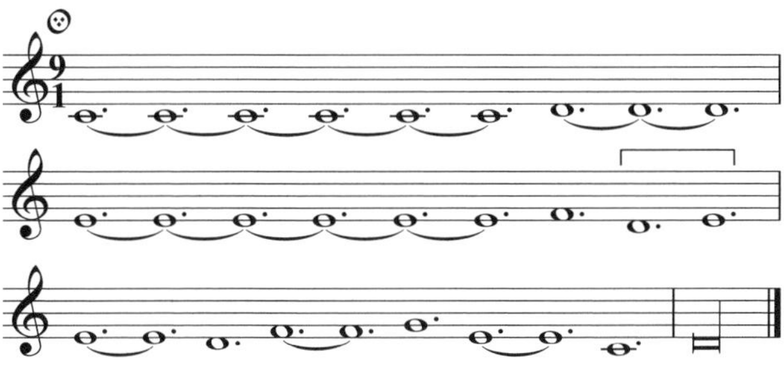

EX. 3.1 *Division of perfect major mode by three longs*

EX. 3.2 *Partitio modi maioris imperfecti per tris breves*

[92^{v}]

EX. 3.3 *Partitio modi minoris perfecti per longas*

EX. 3.4 *Partitio modi <minoris> imperfecti per breves*

EX. 3.2 *Division of imperfect major mode by three breves*

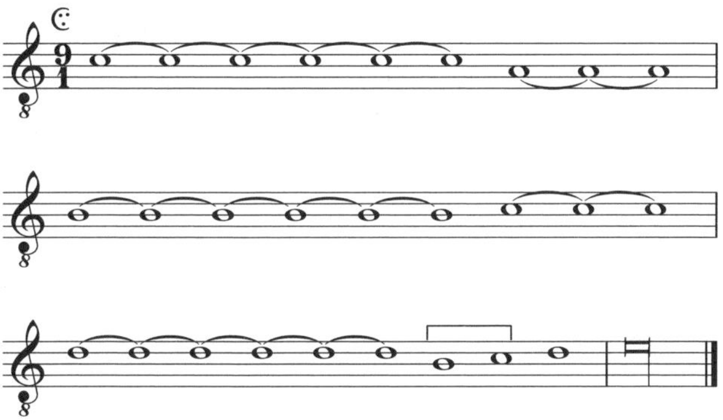

EX. 3.3 *Division of perfect minor mode by longs*

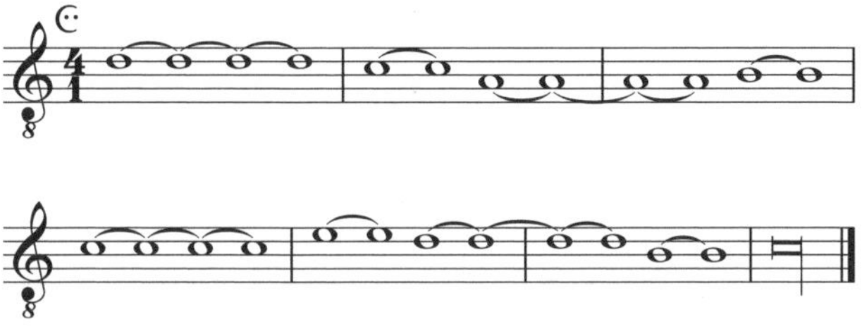

EX. 3.4 *Division of imperfect minor mode by breves*

EX. 3.5 *Partitio temporis perfecti maioris prolationis*

EX. 3.6 *Partitio temporis perfecti minoris prolationis*

EX. 3.7 *Partitio temporis imperfecti maioris prolationis*

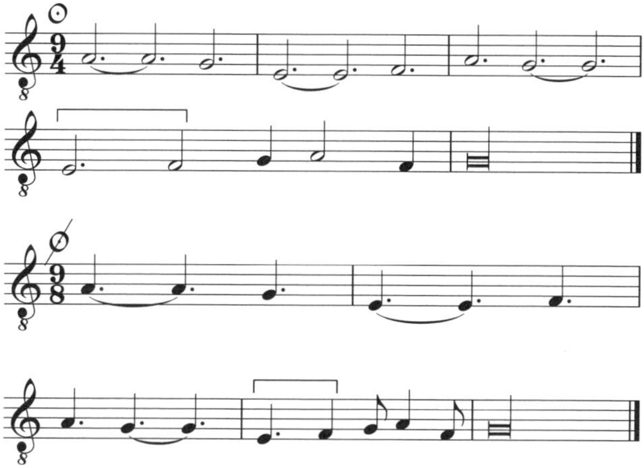

EX. 3.5 *Division of perfect tempus of major prolation*

EX. 3.6 *Division of perfect tempus of minor prolation*

EX. 3.7 *Division of imperfect tempus of major prolation*

[93r] 

EX. 3.8 *Partitio temporis imperfecti minoris prolationis*

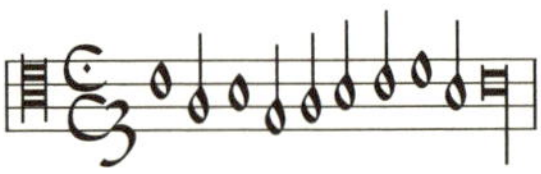

EX. 3.9 *Prolatio maior sive perfecta in semibrevi*

EX. 3.10 *Prolatio minor sive imperfecta in semibreve*

EX. 3.8 *Division of imperfect tempus of minor prolation*

EX. 3.9 *Major or perfect prolation in the semibreve*

EX. 3.10 *Minor or imperfect prolation in the semibreve*

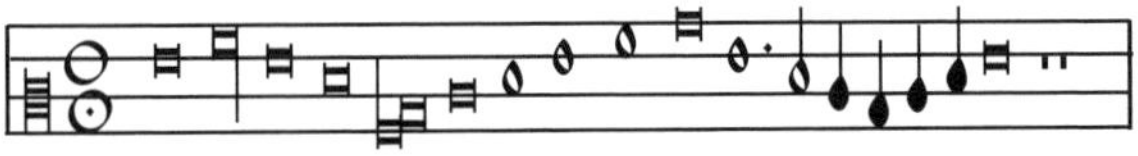

EX. 3.11 *Quot modis potest perfici brevis signis, idem ceteris evenire figuris. Quod in aliis quoque.*

EX. 3.12 *Quo pacto breves imperficiantur*

EX. 3.11 *That in as many ways as a breve may be perfected by signs, the same comes about for the other figures. Which is true in other cases too.*[100]

EX. 3.12 *How breves are imperfected*

[93^{v}]

EX. 3.13 *Notulae coloratae vel lituratae dictae*

EX. 3.14 *Alteratio in semibreve .i. quinta sive secunda*

EX. 3.15 *Exceptio ob colorem alterandae*

EX. 3.13 *Notes called colored or inked in*

EX. 3.14 *Alteration in the semibreve, that is, the fifth or second*

EX. 3.15 *Exception of the note needing alteration due to color*

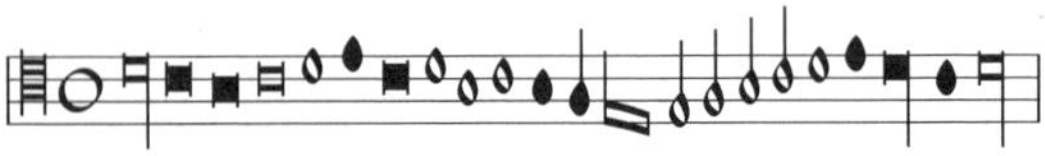

EX. 3.16 *Quot modis color figuris tribuitur, totidem*[51] *modis ceteris hac comparatione praeberi potest.*

[94r]

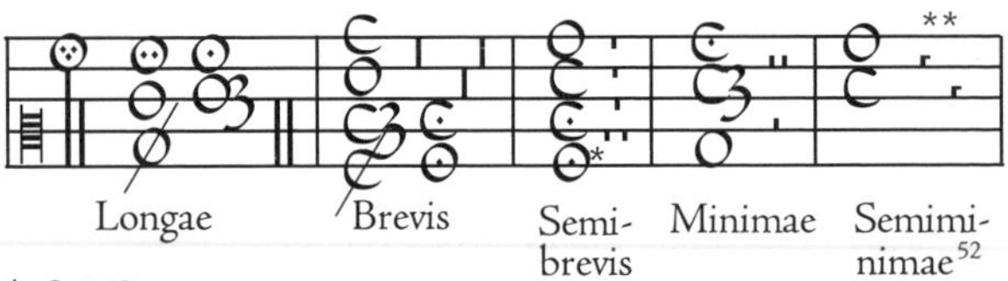

* *O MS*

** semibreves *in MS*

EX. 3.17 *Pausarum secundum usum figuratio*

* ■ *MS*

EX. 3.16 *In as many manners as color is bestowed on notes, in so many manners it may be furnished to the rest by this analogy.*

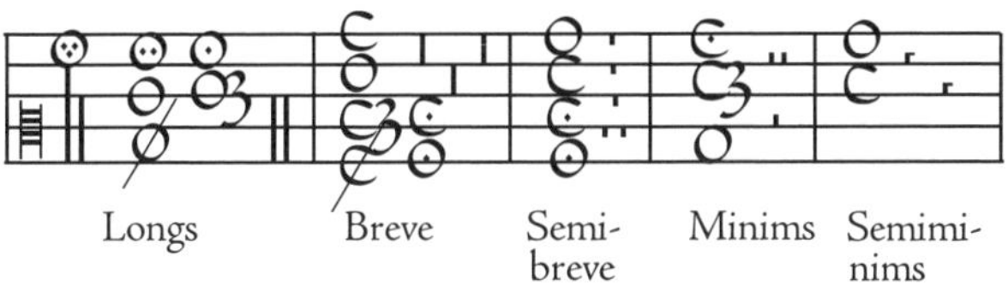

EX. 3.17 *The formation of rests according to custom*

4 Proportionum exempla quarundam

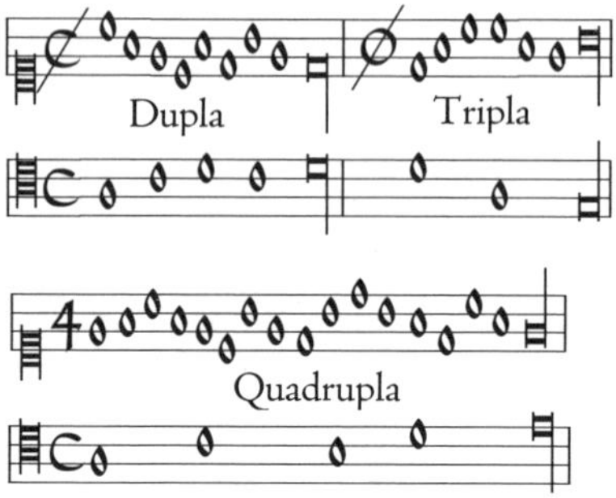

EX. 3.18 *Proportiones primi generis.*[53] *Multiplex*

Examples of some proportions 4

EX. 3.18 *Proportions of the first genus, multiple*

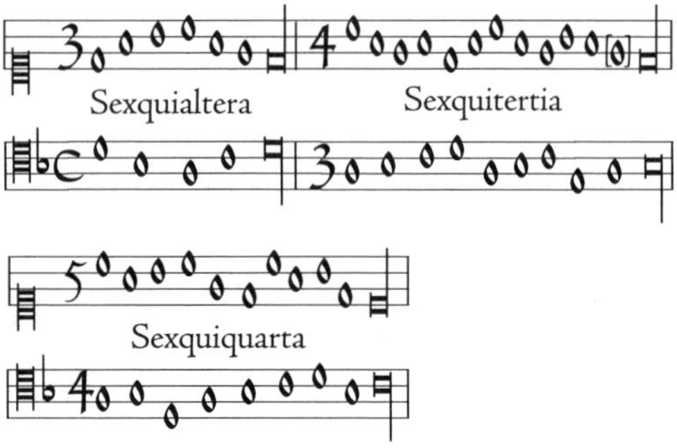

EX. 3.19 *Proportiones secundi generis. Superparticulare*

EX. 3.19 *Proportions of the second genus, superparticular*

[94v]

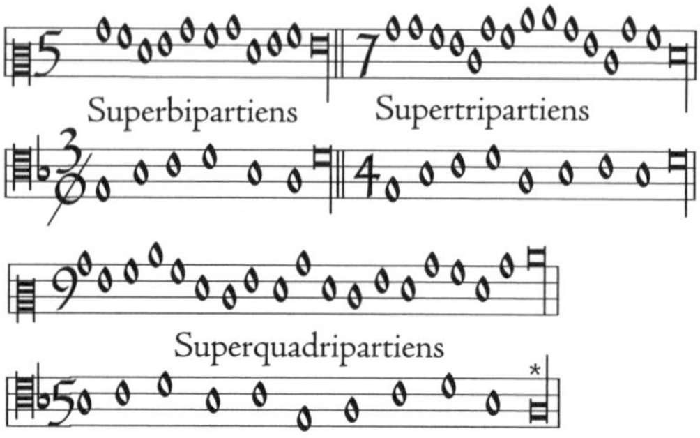

* B♭ *MS*

EX. 3.20 *Proportiones tertii generis. Superpartiens*

EX. 3.20 *Proportions of the third genus, superpartient*

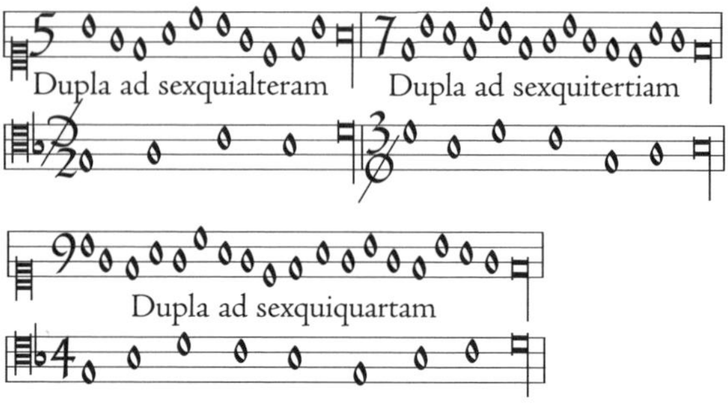

EX. 3.21 *Proportiones quarti generis. Multiplex superparticulare*

EX. 3.21 *Proportions of the fourth genus, multiple superparticular*

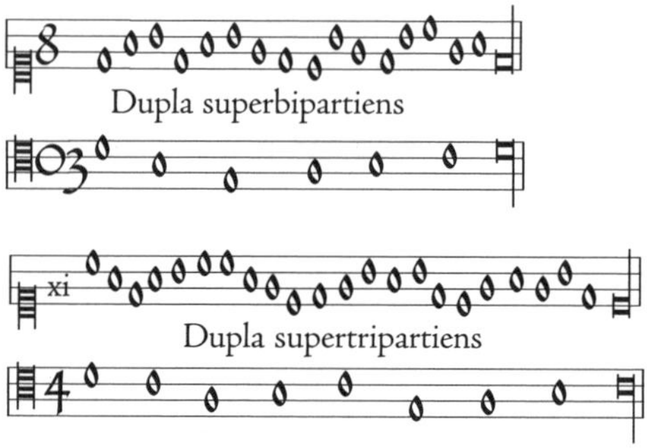

EX. 3.22 *Proportiones quinti generis. Multiplex superpartiens*

EX. 3.22 *Proportions of the fifth genus, multiple superpartient*

[95] EPIGRAMMA IN CONTINENTIAM LIBRI

Discere cui libeat varios distinguere cantus,
  Instruet hic mira qui valet arte liber;
Sive figuratas quid sit suspendere voces
  Sive cupis quid sit Musica scire, docet.
Quod modulis tempus, quot sint in voce figurae,
  Circulus in rhythmis, linea, cauda quid est;
Quid centron, quid pausa, color, clavisque modusque
  Et mensura suo quid parit artifici;
Quid sit inaequales pariles vel promere voces,
  Quid gracili interdum quidve tonare gravi,
Denique cuncta manu redigit modulamina laeva,
  Vt sua quaeque suo sint bene ducta tono.

Per Franciscum Tranchedinum

EPIGRAM ON THE CONTENT OF THE BOOK

Whoever would gladly learn how to distinguish the various kinds of song,
This book, which is possessed of wondrous skill,[1] will instruct;
Whether you wish to know what it is to suspend mensural *voces*[2]
Or to know what music is, it teaches you.
What tempus there is in melodies,[3] how many figures there are in the *vox*,[4]
What the circle, line, and tail are in rhythms,
What the point, the rest, color, and clef, and mode
And mensuration create for their maker;
What it is to produce unequal or equal voices,
What to sound at times in a thin, what in a heavy one.
Finally it records all melodies on the left[5] hand,
So that they may be well performed, each in its own tone.

By Francesco Tranchedini

Note on the Text and Translation

THE MANUSCRIPT

The *Liber Musices* exists in a single manuscript,[1] a luxurious presentation copy made for Cardinal Ascanio Sforza. Formerly belonging to Don Carlo Trivulzio,[2] it is now in the Archivio Civico e Biblioteca Trivulziana in Milan under Trivulzio's shelfmark 2146 and includes his ex-libris, as well as his extensive notes bound in at the beginning and end. Trivulzio obtained the manuscript in March 1775 from the estate of the cultivated Count Paolo Monti, who had died on the previous 19 October;[3] it had already been in Monti's collection thirty years earlier, when Filippo Argelati mentioned it in his biographical notice of Ascanio.[4] Its previous history is unknown, but Trivulzio noted that "una barbara mano" had already excised a leaf containing the end of Book I and the beginning of Book II, probably for its "belle miniature."

The manuscript is bound in limp worn vellum, with two leather ties. On the front cover, at bottom left, is written "2146," on the spine "Florentius Musicus" followed by traces of other letters, which may read "CXV." The front pastedown has Trivulzio's ex-libris. There follow four paper leaves (paginated 1–8) of Trivulzio's notes, and a leaf of heavy parchment (fol. 0), whose corresponding stub appears between fols. 10 and 11. Folio 0^{r} is blank; on the verso is the illuminated title page (see Pl. I), set in a frame measuring 222 × 133 mm, not including the gold decorations across the top and gutter margins. At the top left the roundel shows a Roman coin with a female head and the legend ANTONIA AVGVST(A); it represents Antonia Minor (36 BC–AD 37), posthumously commemorated on coins struck by her son the Emperor Claudius (41–54). The other coins have no inscriptions. The illuminated dedica-

tion follows on fol. 1ʳ (see Pl. II), the first of 95 leaves of fine parchment, numbered by Trivulzio; the stub visible between fols. 48 and 49 confirms that only one folio is missing. The leaves measure 243 × 157–62 mm, with a text block of 145 × 78 mm and 21 lines per page. The gathering structure is in 10s except for gathering 6 (fols. 50–57ʳ), which has four bifolia, and the last gathering (fols. 88–96ᵛ), which has nine. All the edges of the pages were originally tipped in gold; on the bottom edge is written "Florentius musicus." Folio 95ᵛ is blank; it is followed by two more, unnumbered pages of Trivulzio's notes, glued onto the last parchment folio, which is pasted to the back cover.

The illuminations are very fine. Trivulzio, who assumed that the manuscript was copied in Milan, thought he discerned in the elderly musician depicted in the left-central roundel on fol. 0ᵛ the likeness of Leonardo da Vinci and hypothesized that the illuminator was a student of the latter, who was then in Milan (p. 3 of his notes). This of course will not do: for one thing Leonardo was not yet 40 when the treatise was written. Rather than attribute the illuminations to the workshop of the leading Florentine illuminator, Attavante degli Attavanti, as some scholars have done,[5] we follow Albinia de la Mare in ascribing them to the master himself;[6] she also identified the scribe as one of the most famous Florentine calligraphers of the end of the Quattrocento: Alessandro da Verrazzano. He signed 17 manuscripts copied between 1477 and 1508, and another 17 are attributable to him.[7] Toward the end of his career, she remarks, he worked extensively with Attavante, and she places the manuscript in the 1490s, suggesting a date of "ca. 1495–96?"; as we shall see, that would make for an appropriate interval after the composition of the text. She also identified the different handwriting of the Epigram on fol. 95ʳ as that of its author, Francesco Tranchedini.

Apart from the illuminated M on fol. 1ʳ, in which the author presents his book, the initials are decorated, those to Books I and

III (fols. 7ʳ, 69ʳ) having flowered borders. However, if Book II had an illuminated initial, the disappearance of this rather than any other leaf could be explained; the gap would be less noticeable than at the beginning of the text.

The cardinal's arms appear at the bottom center of fols. oᵛ and 1ʳ, accompanied by two of his devices: a rainbow partially hidden by clouds, and three tree-topped mountains with the motto IDEM.[8] Illuminated initials grace the chapter openings and major subdivisions, alternating gold on gold, red, and blue, and gold on gold, red, and green. The musical staves are in blue, the notes in thick gold ink.

SPELLING

The manuscript shows such characteristic medieval spellings as *augumentum* for *augmentum*, *diffinio* or *definio*, *iccirco* for *idcirco*, *loycus* for *logicus*, *rethorica* for *rhetorica*, *sigillatim* for *singillatim*, *spera* for *sphaera*, *tybia* for *tibia*, *Hysidorus* for *Isidorus*, *Epaminundas* for *Epaminondas*, *Virgilius* for *Vergilius*, and *Boetius* or even *Bœtius* for *Boethius*. Humanistic influence brings with it *ę* or *æ* frequently used for classical *ae* instead of medieval *e*, but also in places where simple *e* is correct; similarly, classical *auctor* has everywhere ousted medieval *author*, but *authenticus* has hypercorrectly become *auctenticus*. The prefix *sesqu(i)-* is regularly written *sexqu(i)-*; *quoad* is written as two words and *ac si* as one. There are also Italianisms such as *mictam* (pronounced *mittam*, cf. Philipoctus de Caserta = Filippotto), *legittimus* or *legiptimus* (also pronounced with *-tt-*) for *legitimus*, cf. Italian *legittimo*. In accordance with the norms of the I Tatti Renaissance Library, we have adjusted the scribal spelling to match that of the *Oxford Latin Dictionary*, but distinguished between vocalic *U u* and consonantal *V v*; however, we have not converted the irremediably barbarous *exaden* and *eptaden* into the appropriate case of *hexas* and *heptas*. We have preserved the legiti-

mate alternatives *secuntur* and *sequuntur*, *-iens* and *-ies*, along with the variant spellings *Goscalchus*, *Goschalcus*, *Goschalchus* while using only the second in English as the nearest to the Frankish etymon Godeschalk; we have corrected *Ubaldus* to *Hucbaldus* and *Ugo* to *Hugo* (Hugh of St. Victor), but left Florentius in the belief that *Enchiriades* (or *Enchyriades*) was a person, and allowed Pseudo-Odo to remain *Addo*.

Roman numerals have been left as written, except that preceding and following periods have been omitted; the fourth chapter of each book appears as IIII in Latin, though in the translation we write IV according to the modern convention that confines IIII to clockfaces in accordance with the medieval preference for that form.

Greek written in Greek letters has been respelled in accordance with modern conventions with the correct accentuation; however, we have not concealed the graver errors at 1.5.17. Greek written in Latin letters has been left as in the manuscript and minimally corrected in the translation, more exact transliteration being reserved where necessary for the notes.

We have not recorded places where Verrazzano has corrected his own errors. We have also modernized punctuation and regularized the paragraphing; so far was Verrazzano from understanding the text that he often began a new paragraph in mid-sentence.

EMENDATION

Although the MS is presumably at one remove from the fair copy, Verrazzano's obvious incomprehension of the subject matter and our own experience as copy-editors of authorial carelessness have led us to emend any errors that we deemed to be slips of the pen rather than the mind; we are conscious that in many places another judgment might be possible, but to edit is to choose. Changes and omissions are signaled in the following notes; addi-

tions are marked in the text, and where appropriate the translation, by angle brackets < >.

QUOTATIONS

We have, as a matter of principle, made our own translation of authors quoted by Florentius; no disrespect is thereby intended to the authors of existing English versions. The policy was also adopted because these quotations sometimes incorporate corruptions in manuscripts or early editions of the authors cited; they also show minor slips or reworkings apparently of his own. We do not normally comment unless they affect the sense, nor correct unless they destroy it; when we supply in the Latin text omitted matter taken from the original, we do not signal the fact in the translation.

PRINCIPLES OF TRANSLATION

Expressions such as *Haec ille,* "these things he said," used like the modern spoken "End quote," have been omitted, being replaced in print by closing quotation marks or reversion to flush left setting. Likewise, such phrases as *et quae ille pergit,* "and what he goes on (to say)," indicating that the passage cited continues to be relevant after the end of the quotation, have been rendered as ", etc." Brackets [ ] are used to mark words supplied for the sake of idiom or clarity.

We have tried to make Florentius's thought as clear as possible (sometimes it is not possible), while giving the reader a flavor of his style, in particular his straining after variety.

Since the freedom of Latin word-order is not easy to replicate in English, and the sequence in which ideas are presented is often more important than the grammatical construction, we have not hesitated to turn active verbs into passives when in the original the object preceded the subject.

The word "note" has been employed in its British sense, referring to the sounding pitch (U.S. "tone" from German *Ton*) as well as the written note, since that is closer to Latin *nota* or *notula*, which like "letter" in premodern usage covers name, shape, and sound.

NOTES

1. For a detailed paleographical description, see Rossi, "Un manuale," 1:2–17. It is also described in Christian Meyer, *The Theory of Music*, vol. 6: *Addenda, Corrigenda* (Répertoire international des sources musicales, B III[6]; Munich: G. Henle Verlag, 2003), 519–24.

2. On Trivulzio, see Giovanni Seregni, *Don Carlo Trivulzio e la cultura milanese dell'età sua MDCCXV–MDCCLXXXIX* (Milan: Ulrico Hoepli Editore, 1927); on our MS see pp. 124–26. He was descended from Gianfermo Trivulzio (d. 1491), brother of the condottiere Gian Giacomo, who commanded French forces in the invasion of Milan (d. 1518); never a priest, he is described as an *abate* in spirit as well as name.

3. *Famiglie notabili milanesi*, vol. 2 (Milan, 1881), Monti, tav. III, on Paolo Monti-Melzi; Trivulzio on p. 1.

4. *Philippi Argelati Bononiensis Bibliotheca scriptorum Mediolanensium*, 2 vols. (Milan: In aedibus palatiis, 1765), 2, col. 1375: "Ei dicatur à Flaminio [*sic*] Musico opus de Musica arte, eleganti Codice in Membrana MS, quod extat apud Co. Paulum Montium, Codex est auro, et picturis insignis."

5. Caterina Santoro, *I codici medioevali della biblioteca Trivulziana* (Milan: Biblioteca Trivulziana, 1965), 311–12 ("decorazione di scuola attavantesca"); Giulia Bologna, *Miniature italiane della biblioteca Trivulziana* (Milan: Castello Sforzesco, 1974), 82 ("bottega di Attavante degli Attavanti"), with colour plates on pp. 114 (title page), 115 (dedication), 116 (detail: the initial M).

6. In her description of the MS in *Biblioteca Trivulziana del Comune di Milano*, ed. Angela Dillon Bussi and Giovanni M. Piazza (Fiesole: Nardini Editore, 1993), 198. Three pages from the manuscript appear

as pls. CXLIX–CLI. Jonathan J. Alexander, whom we consulted, also agrees that Attavante was the illuminator.

7. See Albinia de la Mare, "New Research on Humanistic Scribes in Florence," in *Miniatura fiorentina del Rinascimento, 1440–1525, un primo censimento,* ed. Annarosa Garzelli, 2 vols. (Florence: Giunta Regionale Toscana, 1985), 1:295–600 at 472–73, 480–81 (the latter a list of the MSS copied by or attributed to him).

8. For other manuscripts belonging to Ascanio, see Élisabeth Pellegrin, *La Bibliothèque des Visconti et des Sforza ducs de Milan, au XVe siecle* (Paris, 1955), 484, and Bologna, "Un fratello del Moro," 325–27.

Notes to the Text

PREFACE

1. *i.e.,* qua me morem gerere concupivisti.

2. *Spelled* Armonia, *hence the alphabetization.*

3. *Since this and* instituerunt *§19 are the only indicatives against 31 subjunctives in the indirect questions of this index, it is tempting to write* habeat *and* instituerint, *but usage in the chapter titles and the text is inconsistent.*

4. ii . . . xi *MS, perhaps by confusion between arabic 1 and 2, corr. Rossi.*

5. *Sic; under* g *of* Gradus.

6. R *MS, corr. Rossi; under* n *of* Indicia.

7. notulare *MS.*

8. ii *MS, perhaps by misreading of arabic 1 as 2.*

9. *This is evidently a relative clause, though the following accusatives would better follow a question; but in an index entry one would then expect* viderimus *and no answers.*

10. iii *MS.*

BOOK I

1. indicaverint *MS.*

2. *Conflation between* περὶ μουσικῆς *with genitive and Latin* de musica *with ablative.*

3. arithmetricae *MS, cf. n. 65; the* r *has intruded either from* geometr- *or possibly under the influence of the common false etymology* ars metrica.

4. tollendos *MS, corrected from Isidore.*

5. studiis *MS.*

6. cognatione *MS.*

7. *Censorinus's MSS have* nec tamen annon, *but the entire passage is corrupt.*

8. rusticis *MS.*

9. delphinas *Isidore, but some MSS have* -nos; *so Peter Löslein's edition (Venice, 1483).*

10. *Late MSS and early editions have* Creditum hoc a plerisque est; *for* est, *absent from the older MSS, modern editors read* esse, *ending sentences at* inveni *and* tibiarum.

11. tybicen *MS. We follow the early editions of Gellius; the correct reading is* tibicinium.

12. *So the early editions, with Latin translation by Theodore Gaza; Gellius's MSS omit the title, which appears from other evidence to have been* περὶ ἐνθουσιασμοῦ.

13. intentiones *MS, which can be said of stringed instruments but not auloi.*

14. *Correctly* visere, *but* viseret *in early editions from 1485 on.*

15. *So Gellius' MSS, though modern editions emend to* eos.

16. disiliret *MS, as in editions from 1485 on.*

17. *So the early editions; correct is* tamen.

18. orchium *MS;* orthium *correctly in the Roman editions of 1469 and 1472, in subsequent incunables* orthrium, *cf. Greek* órthros *'daybreak, matins.' The spelling* orcius *in a different sense is cited from MSS of Martianus Capella 9.985, 988 and Eriugena's commentary.*

19. *So in several early editions, but Gellius wrote* iecit.

20. et quid *MS.*

21. combrobantes *MS.*

22. reservantur *MS.*

23. musicis *MS.*

24. demonstraris *MS, corrected by later hand.*

25. *Wrongly altered in MS to* aperierunt; *cf. n. 40.*

26. musicos modulos continentes *after* exemplis *MS.*

27. *Here Florentius corrects Isidore, who seems to have written* Amphion *as if from a nominative* Amphios.

28. pervenire *MS.*

29. *Added from Macrobius.*

30. peryothes *MS.*

31. Estieus *MS.*

32. genere *MS.*

33. imponemus *MS.*

34. musicis *MS.*

35. Possem autem *repeated MS.*

36. proficere *MS.*

37. disserendi *MS, corr. Rossi.*

38. distinctos 1.5.3 *as in Cicero.*

39. nodus est *Cicero; Florentius's omission is not ungrammatical, but is un-Ciceronian.*

40. aperierunt *MS, cf. n.* 25.

41. redditum *MS.*

42. *Added from Macrobius.*

43. ac *MS.*

44. tumultuarius *MS.*

45. cosinographia *MS.*

46. augmentis *and* et *added from Apuleius.*

47. *An uncomprehending reduction of* animus autem oculorum effugit obtutitum, est autem unus ex omnibus rationis concentionisque (*corrected from* contentionisque), quae ἁρμονία Graeca, sempiternarum rerum et sub intellegentiam cadentium compos et particeps.

48. quae *MS.*

49. *This, the best reading, recurs in a manuscript used by Lambinus; see [Cicero], Ad C. Herennium de ratione dicendi (Rhetorica ad Herennium), trans. Caplan,* 190 *n.* 1.

50. *The MS tradition of Ad Herennium has here* conparat natura, *but for* natura *modern editors have adopted the conjecture* cura.

51. irrationabilium animantium *Isidore; two early MSS from Bobbio, which constitute the 'Italian family' of the tradition, add* vel animalium.

52. fractosque *MS.*

53. formata *MS.*

54. *So some MSS of Lactantius: correct is* (cum) in obstantia.

55. illisum *MS, corr. Rossi.*

56. *So some MSS of Lactantius; correct is* radit.

57. et *Lactantius.*

58. et *Lactantius.*

59. *So the old editions of Gellius;* λόγων *has since been emended to* ἀτόμων.

60. impleant continuo *('at once') Isidore, but the easier reading* (impleant) continuum *is found in some MSS.*

61. vehemens *not in Isidore.*

62. et *not in Isidore.*

63. in cudis *MS.*

64. sublime *Isidore, but several MSS have* sublimi, *some* sublimis; *second-declension forms are known, but we need the accusative of motion toward.*

65. arithmetrae *MS; cf. n. 3.*

66. *We expect* ad, *but medieval Latin sometimes extends the sense of* per.

67. sexcu- *here and throughout MS, possibly by analogy with* quincuplus = quinquiplus *and/or confusion with* sescuplus = sesquiplus, *'one-and-a-half-fold.'*

68. vocis *MS.*

69. personans *MS.*

70. licebit *MS.*

71. lineas . . . confectas *MS.*

72. *Thus for* κλείς κλειδός; *the final sigma, not used here, appears at 2.3.8.*

73. dictum *repeated MS.*

74. *We apparently have to understand* eam, *i.e.* manus figurationem.

75. accipi *MS.*

76. *Florentius appears to mean* Denique id animadvertendum videtur, quod his rebus summa cura notatis, omnibusque proprietatibus optime cognitis et voce sua cuique notulae per ascensum et descensum experiendo tributa, ne tum quidem lineas et spatia dinoscemus.

77. *Corrected in later hand over erasure.*

78. *Very faint (erased?)* u *above* a *in MS.*

79. figuratio *MS, corrected in a later hand.*

80. ascensula *MS.*

81. *The reason for the subjunctives* augeat *and* retineat *is unclear.*

82. *The rare but* classical *genitive of* alius -a -ud, *used again at 3.14.6.*

83. *We expect* in locis duarum notularum.

84. nomine *MS, possibly an authorial error.*

85. *For* notandum *followed immediately by direct speech cf. 1.11.1, 2.14.7; contrast* notandum quod *1.6.8.*

86. est *MS.*

87. bmolle *MS, corr. Rossi.*

88. Coniunctas . . . ostensas *MS.*

89. deaerunt *MS.*

90. *This incoherent gibberish appears to mean* hoc enim praesertim non facile dinoscemus, si maxime mutandum erit, in utram ex reliquis duabus proprietatibus mutare debeamus.

91. transferat vel *is Florentius's own addition.*

92. impares *MS.*

93. In all four places a space has been left for a capital Y; so too 2.4.2.

94. *The stem is that of Greek* τέταρτος *'fourth,' not Latin* tetrardus.

95. Kyrieł' *with stroke through* l *MS.*

96. *Evidently singers' slang for* excelsis Deo.

97. *MS* cuiusmodi *as one word, 'of what kind,' 'what [it] is like.'*

98. *These verses are variously transmitted with* est, est fa, *or nothing in the place of this* fa.

99. *We must either understand or supply* solfales notae.

100. ipsorum *qualifies* versibus, Gloria Patri *is plural (cf.* Gloria Patri . . . proficiscentes *1.16.7);* patebunt, *properly 'will be manifest,' is misused for* patefacient.

101. nec *MS.*

102. Dyph[r]ongon *MS, cf. French* diphtongue. *The correct Latin rendering of Greek* $\phi\theta$ *is* pth *not* phth *(and likewise* cth *not* chth *for* $\chi\theta$*); see Wilhelm Schulze, Orthographica, Marburg: Elwert, 1894, pp. xxvii–lvii (repr. Rome: Edizioni di storia e letteratura, 1958, 39–85).*

103. *Wrongly changed to* deductionum *MS.*

104. deductio *MS.*

105. canenti *MS.*

106. sub *MS.*

107. sub *MS.*

108. quorundam *MS.*

BOOK II

1. *Beginning of Book II defective; title supplied from index, fol. 3*[r]*.*

2. *One expects something like* eundemque eam (= musicam).

3. scire *before* investiget *MS.*

4. *Added by Rossi.*

5. quaevis *Gerbert in Hucbald, but Florentius will have found* vis *in his text.*

6. repetantur *Hucbald,* repetamur *MS.*

7. pluralibus *MS.*

8. plurimorum *repeated MS.*

9. in voce . . . in flatu . . . in pulsu *Isidore, but* in pulsu *was misread as one word as in the first edition ([Augsburg]: Günther Zainer, 1472).*

10. The scribe *Verrazzano, possibly following Florentius himself, has written the chapter number as* III *instead of* IIII *and misnumbered subsequent chapters accordingly:* IIII *for* V, V *for* VI, *etc.; they are correctly numbered in the Preface. We have renumbered the chapters from this point on.*

11. *Without this emendation the nominative would be an inexcusable error for* fonte et origine. *Arnaldus uses the stock phrase again, at 2.8.1.*

12. *After this word Macrobius has* eius.

13. *Added from Macrobius.*

14. *Added from Macrobius. Verrazzano consistently writes* xl, *not* xxxx, *for 40.*

15. dithesim *MS.*

16. *Under the first* t *there is a large point; if meant as a mark of deletion it is wrong.*

17. noverunt *MS, perhaps an authorial error.*

18. totidem, *'as many,' is put for* totiens, *'so many times,' but this is at best a paraphrase.*

19. *We expect* ne poterimus quidem.

20. *Evidently Florentius could not decide between* vel . . . vel *and* sit . . . sit *(cf. Italian* sia maggiore sia minore*); better than either would have been* sive maiori sive minori, *or else* maiusne sit an minor *attached to the following clause.*

21. Hanc *MS.*

22. numerus . . . conficit *MS.*

23. ex *MS.*

24. descendit *MS; unusually, the* i *is dotted.*

25. turpem sonum *before* reddet *MS;* reddet effectum *is a periphrasis for* efficiet.

26. *See Book I, n. 82.*

27. *Florentius has lost control of his construction: he should have written* imperfectam, suam perfectam, sextam vel decimam sequi.

28. descendamus *MS.*

29. inserviet *MS.*

30. ptongorum *MS; cf. above, Book I, n. 102.*

BOOK III

1. cantus *MS.*

2. *After the long parenthesis Florentius has forgotten how he began the sentence.*

3. ostendent *MS.*

4. in itio *MS.*

5. semibreuique *MS.*

6. alterationem *MS.*

7. *This should be* quamlibet, *but emendation may be overcharitable.*

8. musicis *MS.*

9. minori cum *MS.*

10. *Added in view of following* undecimam.

11. duas *MS.*

12. duarum quantitatum *MS from* §2.

13. minoris *MS.*

14. *So two of Fast's MSS; her own text reads 'Nec ex sonis aequalibus fit consonancia.'*

15. *This is obviously the true text, which in the MSS known to Fast has been variously corrupted into nonsense.*

16. quincupla *MS, and so throughout, but see Tacitus, Annals 1.36.3, Martial, Epigrams 14.4.tit.*

17. vi *MS, from the next sentence; but Verrazzano had no head for figures.*

18. sexties *MS.*

19. *Before* minoris numeri, *this word is superfluous, but seems to have crept in from other discussions such as those in Boethius or the Tractatus de proportionibus.*

20. *Something on these lines is missing; the supplement supposes that Verrazzano's eye skipped from one* praecise *to the next.*

21. xxxviiii *MS; perhaps Florentius wrote* xxxx, *which Verrazzano, instead of converting to* xl *(see Book II, n. 14), misread as* xxxix *and respelled in the alternative form.*

22. ii *MS, and so throughout; evidently Florentius wrote arabic* 11, *which Verrazzano took as roman* II; *cf. Preface, n. 4.*

23. *Added by Rossi.*

24. -quatri- *MS, and so several times below; the editors have adopted Boethius's spelling, found at De inst. mus. 2.4 (p. 230, ll. 11–12 Friedlein) and regularly in De inst. arith.*

25. -quinqui- *MS.*

26. *We expect* vii ad v.

27. duas *MS.*

28. super quincupartiens *MS, and so at 3.18.7.*

29. aliquotam *MS.*

30. *Added by Rossi.*

31. v *MS. Emended to* iiii *rather than* iv, *which never appears as an independent numeral in this MS; Verrazzano may have misread either roman* iv *as* v *or arabic* 4 *as* 5, *since in Quattrocento scripts the latter pair sometimes looked quite similar.*

32. vi *with an extra space MS.*

33. superbipartiens *MS.*

34. superbipartiens *MS.*

35. -quincu- *MS, and so at 3.20.8.*

36. superbipartiens *MS.*

37. propositio *MS.*

38. medietati *MS.*

39. *We expect* x ad iiii.

40. xxvi *MS.*

41. xviii *MS.*

42. *Corrected by Rossi.*

43. ad xxlviii *MS.*

44. xxv *MS.*

45. xv *MS.*

46. ii *MS, preceded by a subpuncted* ƚ *(usually a line-filler but not here), suggesting once more a misinterpreted arabic* 1.

47. *Added by Rossi.*

48. seperquadripartiens *MS.*

49. *The explication of* dupla supertripartiens *has been supplied by the editors.*

50. -quadru- *MS.*

51. tot iisdem *MS.*

52. Semimīmę *MS.*

53. *Here and below* Proportiones *is written in the left margin,* primi–quinti generis *in the right margin.*

Notes to the Translation

PREFACE

1. Literally "when we were with you"; not, in this context, the first person plural put for the singular, even though that usage is far less majestic in Latin than in English, but "with X" constructed with plural verb as if it were "and X," found in both Latin (though not Cicero) and Italian (*Grande dizionario*, s.v. *con*, 3: 450, sense 1, penultimate quotation: *Con mia madre non ci parlammo . . . ella cominciò a rimproverarmi*).

2. Literally "the sharpness of your intellect and the wonderful training of your nature": i.e., Ascanio has the mental discipline by nature that others acquire only by training.

3. Literally, "those whom I have chosen for myself for speaking," i.e., the authorities I have chosen to quote.

4. *Humanus* and *humanitas* may refer to kindness, culture, or their combination.

5. We assure the recipient of our love (in the broadest sense); Latin letter-writers more honestly ask to be loved.

6. See above, Introduction.

7. Hugh of St. Victor (d. 1142), polymath and theologian.

8. I.e. Odo of Cluny, to whom the anonymous *Dialogus de musica* was ascribed.

9. Roman antiquary and polymath, author of the miscellany *Noctes Atticae* (2nd cent. AD).

10. Monk (*fl.* 1025), reformer of music teaching, inventor of the staff.

11. See above, Introduction.

12. See above, Introduction.

13. Florentius consistently writes as if the *Enchiriadis* were the work of a man called *Enchiriades*, genitive *Enchiriadis*. He is not alone in this error.

14. William Brito, 13th-cent. lexicographer, author of *Expositiones vocabulorum Bibliae*.

15. Italian lexicographer, author of *Vocabularium* (1053).

16. The reference is not to Censorinus's *De die natali*, written in AD 238, but to some brief notes on various arts appended to it and regarded as his till Ludovicus Carrio's edition of 1583; the latter text will be referred to henceforth as "Pseudo-Censorinus."

17. Died 636; author of *Etymologiae* and other learned works.

18. Christian apologist, 3rd–early 4th cent.

19. Author of *Facta et dicta memorabilia*, early 1st cent. AD.

20. Italian music theorist and composer (*fl.* 1305–19), author of the fundamental treatises *Lucidarium in arte musice plane* and *Pomerium in arte musice mensurate*.

21. Roman miscellanist and Neoplatonist (*fl.* 430).

22. French music theorist and mathematician (ca. 1290×95–after 1344), author of influential treatises on notation.

23. Latin show-orator and Platonist of the 2nd cent. AD, best known as the author of *Metamorphoses* (*The Golden Ass*).

24. We retain the Latin term since "neume" in English refers to notation.

25. *Natura, bmolle, and ♮quadrum* are Florentius's names for the natural, soft, and hard hexachords. He is technically incorrect in calling the hard hexachord "♮quadrum," because "quadrum" refers to the shape, not the quality, of the note; he should have said "♮durum," but this category mistake is found as early as the *Ars nova* attributed to Philippe de Vitry.

26. Whereas in Greek *tetrágōnon* means "square," its calque *quadr(i)angulum* may be extended to "rectangle," as at Martianus Capella, *De nuptiis Philologiae et Mercurii* 7.754.

BOOK I

1. The MS reading *non indicaverint* makes no sense ("did not point out").

2. That is to say, number theory (*arithmētikḗ*), not arithmetic as we understand it (*logistikḗ, ars calculatoria*).

3. Latin *tibiae* = Greek *auloí*, plural of *aulós*, the double-reed instrument normally played in treble and bass pairs, sometimes mistranslated "flute." The player was a *tibicen*, in Greek *aulētḗs*, which we have rendered "aulete" on the analogy of "athlete" for *athlētḗs*.

4. Aulus Gellius, *Noctes Atticae* 1.11.1–3.

5. Valerius Maximus 2.1.10.

6. The context requires some such insertion; the transmitted text might be translatable as "I have found heedless and ill informed those who," but this is stylistically awkward and fits less well with the quotation from Cicero, standard in praises of music and a useful riposte to courtiers who despised music-making as beneath their dignity.

7. Theban general (d. 362 BC) who broke the power of Sparta.

8. Athenian statesman (early 5th cent. BC) who defeated Persia and foresaw the Spartan threat.

9. Cicero, *Tusculan Disputations* 1.4. In the early editions the work was entitled *Tusculan Questions*.

10. This goes back to Plato, *Timaeus* 35 B–36 B, where the blend of the Same, the Other, and Being is divided into portions according to the generating ratios of musical intervals. The original sense of Greek *harmonía* as a music term is "tuning." The classic source for the concept of the music of the spheres in Latin sources is the *Somnium Scipionis* of Cicero with its commentary by Macrobius.

11. We restore Isidore's *tolerandos* for MS *tollendos*, "doing away with," which makes no sense.

12. Isidore of Seville, *Etym.* 3.17(16).1–3.

13. In classical Latin *fore* is future infinitive, in medieval Latin present; since elsewhere in Florentius (Pr. 3, 1.12.3, 3.3.2) it has the latter value, we have so translated it here too, though in direct speech the future *erit* would have been possible, even elegant.

14. That is, that sung poetry was the oldest form of literature. Timagenes was a Greek historian and rhetorician of the 1st cent. BC.

15. Quintilian's *ille* qualifying *Iopas* implies that we do not need reminding who he was; it can often be translated "the famous," as below at fol. 11r. Iopas sang at the banquet Dido gave for Aeneas in Vergil, *Aen.* 1.740 ff.

16. *Aen.* 1.742: the sun's toils are his eclipses.

17. Quintilian, *Inst.* 1.10.9–11. Lit. "and the other things he goes on [to say]": namely that although oratory has left that topic to philosophy, it cannot be complete without it; "as we have said" refers to the proem, §10, where, however, he speaks of ethics.

18. Boethius, *De inst. mus.* 1.1, p. 181.10–11 Friedlein.

19. Pseudo-Censorinus 9.

20. This conflicts with the opening of the section, which states in so many words that music preceded meter ("Prior est musica inventione metrica"). Before *putes* the manuscript tradition has *nec tamen annon;* most editors emend *annon* to *non:* "but be assured that there were songs before meter, but rustic and uncouth ones." Another proposal is to omit *annon* as a scribal note (*an non?* "or should *nec* be *non?*") and insert *sine* before *numeris,* "do not think that the older songs were without rhythm, but that they were rustic and uncouth."

21. This is nonsense, but is what the text appears to say; the *licentior* he found in his source is an error for *decentior,* a proposal made long ago and since neglected. The punctuation after *legitima* adopted by some editors is no improvement ("music is more licentious and more restrained"). What Florentius imagined the words to mean is impossible to determine.

22. Isidore, *Etym.* 3.17(16).3.

23. Augustine, *De musica* 1.4.5.

24. Macrobius, *Comm.* 2.3.10.

25. The title, thought to be *On Divine Possession,* has dropped out of Gellius' MSS.

26. The correct reading in Gellius is *tibicinium,* "aulos music"; *adhibitum* therefore means "employed." The skill and measure belong to the doctor, not the musician, brought in by persistence error from the previous sentence.

27. The incoherence is that of the older editions; the text properly runs: "Just now I found in Theophrastus' book . . . that it has been believed by many . . . abated. That aulos music . . . cures adders' bites is also reported in Democritus' book . . . in which . . . auloi."

28. The Greek title, absent from the MSS, remains unknown; Gellius' first editor, Giovanni Andrea Bussi (Rome: Pannartz and Sweynheim, 1469), concocted one, to which Theodore Gaza appended a Latin translation.

29. Gellius, *Noctes Atticae* 4.13.

30. Quotation marks indicate direct speech in Gellius, frequently marked in the original by *inquit* ("he says"). Matter not so enclosed represents indirect speech in accusative and infinitive. In Herodotus' Greek original (*Histories* 1.23–24) the entire tale is cast in that construction, as a story for whose truth he does not vouch.

31. Literally, Periander "had as friend and beloved," i.e., a personal friend as distinct from an official *amicus* valued for his services in government.

32. I.e., the Greek cities of Sicily and southern Italy (the original sense of *Italía*).

33. The better MSS of Gellius have not *tum* but *tamen*: "the sailors, beastly and brutal as they were, were yet overcome . . ." (active changed to passive for the sake of the word order).

34. That is, the *órthios nómos*, a complex sequence of melodies sung to the cithara, associated with lamentation.

35. *Pius*, in both pagan and Christian language, denotes conduct toward another that is such as it ought to be according to the relationship between the parties; although dolphins have no recognized duty to human beings, their affection for them is a theme of many stories (Gellius himself tells one at *Noctes Atticae* 6.8; and see Xavier Jacques, "Le dauphin d'Hippone," *Les Études classiques* 33 [1965]: 18–33), so that we may reasonably understand an act of love and loyalty resulting from this dolphin's sense that Arion's merits gave him a right to its affection and devotion.

36. Taínaron, Cape Matapan, the southernmost tip of mainland Greece.

37. Gellius meant "believed it too little," i.e. less than (since it was true) he ought to have done; but Florentius may have understood *parum* in its postclassical sense of "little," which here would be a meiosis for "not."

38. Gellius, *Noctes Atticae* 16.19.1–22.

39. I.e., one or more pairs of stanzas with identical metrical structures.

40. The single god with whom for the Neoplatonist Macrobius all individual deities may be identified; the "hymn" is the music of the spheres.

41. Macrobius, *Comm.* 2.3.4–6.

42. The bishop of Seville (d. 636), author of the *Etymologiae* and other works (who has already been cited), was distinguished by Sigebert of Gembloux (*De scriptoribus ecclesiasticis* 55, compare 51) as "Isidore Junior" from Isidore bishop of Córdoba (fl. ca. 412), author of a lost commentary on the books of Kings dedicated to Orosius. The epithet appears in early editions of the *Etymologiae*

43. As often, two of Cain's great-great-great-great-grandsons have been confused: Jubal the musician and his half-brother Tubalcain the blacksmith (Gen. 4:21–3). On the late medieval preference of Jubal/Tubal over Pythagoras see Judith Cohen, "Tubal in the Middle Ages," *Yuval* 3 (1974): 83–99; James W. McKinnon, "Jubal vel Pythagoras, quis sit inventor musicae?," *Musical Quarterly* 64 (1978): 1–28; id., *New Grove*², 13: 274.

44. Isidore, *Etym.* 3.16(15).1.

45. Hugh of St. Victor, *Didascalicon* 3.2, ed. Buttimer, 49.10–13 (*PL* 176. 765 D).

46. Boethius, *De inst. mus.* 1.20.

47. Since the smiths hammered in a set order, each pitch returned after a fixed interval of time; but Macrobius seems also to mean the ratio between consonant pitches, which sounding together blend into one. The ancients' discussions of consonance and dissonance imply simultaneity, even though the only instance we know of in their practical music is doubling at the octave.

48. Lit. "put together"; one might expect to translate "if a lyre [*fides* plural] were constructed," but the sequel indicates the reference must be to strings.

49. Macrobius, *Comm.* 2.1.8–13. The last sentence is not only awkward in structure, one result clause leading into another, but confused in sense, passing from the tuning of strings to different pitches according to consonant ratios, to the sympathetic vibration of strings tuned to the same pitch; the sense of "agreeing" thus switches from harmony to identity. As is evident elsewhere in his musical chapters, Macrobius was not fully at home in his subject.

50. The words "Fertur . . . narratur" appear in a gloss on Boethius, *De inst. mus.* 1.20, p. 206.7 Friedlein, of which a slightly fuller version appears in *Glossa maior in Institutionem musicam Boethii,* vol. 1, ed. Michael Bernhard and Calvin M. Bower (Munich: Verlag der Bayerischen Akademie der Wissenschaften, 1993), 256, no. 17a; Florentius's text matches that in the tractate "Beatus Augustinus dicit," in *Clavis Gerberti: Eine Revision von Martin Gerberts Scriptores ecclesiastici de musica sacra potissimum (St. Blasien 1784),* vol. 1, ed. Michael Bernhard (Munich: Verlag der Bayerischen Akademie der Wissenschaften, 1989), 33–35 at 34, §11; the words "per hanc . . . putrefactus erat" were not known to Gerbert (*Scriptores,* 1:151, col. ii). This contrasts with the traditional story that Hermes/Mercury invented the lyre by scooping out a tortoise and stretching strings across its shell (e.g. *Homeric Hymn to Hermes* 24–62, where there are already seven strings); Diodorus Siculus 1.16.1 makes Hermes/Thoth invent a three-stringed lyre, one string for each Egyptian season. In Isidore, *Etym.* 3.22(21).8 Mercury encounters a rotting tortoise by the Nile and, finding its tendons resonant, models the lyre on it.

51. "This tetrachord," as the original context makes clear, is that of the octave, fifth, fourth, and basic note.

52. From here to the end of the paragraph Florentius's source is Boethius, *De inst. mus.* 1.20.

53. Correctly *Torr(h)ebus:* see Carl Jan, *Musici scriptores Graeci* (Leipzig: B. G. Teubner, 1895), 225–26 n. 1, noting that King Torrhebos is a historical figure. Calvin Bower in his translation of Boethius, *Fundamentals of Music* (New Haven: Yale University Press, 1989), 31 n. 101 observes that Boethius's MS tradition points to *Toroebus,* but that some copies have C.

54. See Bower, ibid., 313 n. 107.

55. The assertion of Jan, *Musici scriptores Graeci*, loc. cit., that the correct name, in both Boethius and his source Nicomachus, was Theophrastus is implicitly taken back ibid. 274, app. crit. on *Excerpta Nicomachi* 4, line 3.

56. Boethius in the chapter cited lists the notes of the Greater and Lesser Perfect Systems, but names no more musicians.

57. *De inst. mus.*1.2; see below, ch. 3.

58. That is to say, polyphony; for *organicam* see below, p. 325.

59. The original offers as alternatives (in reverse order, and in the plural) the synonyms *caput*, properly "head," and its diminutive *capitulum*, whence English "chapter."

60. See Isidore, *Etym.* 1.15(14).1: "music" is derived from the Muses (*a Musis*), who are so called from a Greek verb (variously corrupted in the manuscripts) meaning "to seek," because melodies were sought out; Romerus's (not, we think, Florentius's) Greek informant translated *a Musis* as *apò tôn Mousôn* and restored (with an elegant change of preposition) the "seeking" etymology from Plato, *Cratylus* 406 A, *apò toû môsthai.*

61. Or, coming from a Christian's pen, "God," worshipped though not known.

62. Antioch. See Socrates Scholasticus, *Historia ecclesiastica* 6.8, with the remarks of J. B. Lightfoot (ed. and trans.), *The Apostolic Fathers, Part II: Ignatius, and Polycarp*, 1:30–1.

63. See Augustine, *Confessions* 9.6.15. From "Now singing" onwards the source is Aurelian of Réôme; see Introduction, n. 29.

64. The first sentence is quoted exactly from Augustine, *De musica* 1.2.2; the rest are excerpted from 1.2.3. The famous definition, already found at Censorinus, *De die natali* 10.3, probably derives from Varro; see similar formulas for rhetoric (Quintilian, *Institutio oratoria* 2.14.5, 7.3.12). See too *Martiani Capellae de nuptiis Philologiae et Mercurii liber IX*, ed. Lucio Cristante (Padua: Antenore, 1987), 36 n. 5.

65. Isidore, *Etym.* 3.15(14).1.

66. Papias, *Vocabularium* (Milan: per Dominicum de Vespolate, 12 Dec. 1476), sig. [Qq11]^{rb}.

67. *Didascalicon* 2.8, ed. Charles Henry Buttimer (Washington, DC: Catholic University Press, 1939), 30.23–24 (*PL* 176. 755 D).

68. See Noel Swerdlow, "Musica dicitur a moys, quod est aqua," *Journal of the American Musicological Society* 20 (1967): 3–9.

69. William Brito, *Expositiones uocabulorum Bibliae,* ed. Lloyd W. Daly and Bernardine W. Daly (Padua: Antenore, 1975), 1:454.

70. Uguccione da Pisa, *Derivationes,* M 126.4–5, ed. Enzo Cecchini *et al.* (Florence: Edizioni del Galluzzo, 2004), 2:785, copied almost verbatim by Brito and acknowledged by him in the edition cited (though not e.g. in British Library, MSS Add. 17730, fol. 110^{rba}, Burney 39, fol. 93^{v}, Sloane 3319, fol. 178^{r}).

71. Ps.-Censorinus 11.1.

72. A frequent meaning of *artificium* in Cicero.

73. The MS has "may make progress," which makes little sense.

74. The opening sentences of this chapter are taken from Boethius, *De inst. mus.* 1.2. p. 187, ll. 18–23 Friedlein.

75. The *Somnium Scipionis* or *Dream of Scipio* is the vision of the world that ended the sixth and last book of Cicero's *De re publica* as the Myth of Er had ended the tenth and last book of Plato's *Republic.* Until the nineteenth century it was almost the only part of the work to survive, having been attached to copies of Macrobius's copy of it. The passage concerned is *De re publica* 6.22 in J. G. F. Powell's edition, in previous editions 6.18, also known as *Somnium* 5.2. Part of the passage, with a more correct reading, is cited again at 1.5.6.

76. That is, they are at the octave to one another: see *Cicéron: La République,* trans. Esther Bréguet (Paris: Les Belles Lettres, 1980), 2:186–87 (= p. 111 n. 1).

77. Boethius, *De inst. mus.* 1.2, p. 187.23–26 Friedlein.

78. Ibid., p. 187.26–27 Friedlein.

79. Macrobius, *Comm.* 2.1.5–7.

80. Boethius here uses not the technical term *acutarum* (duly supplied by a glossator in Paris, BNF lat. 7200: *Glossa maior,* ed. cit. 102) but *levium,* "light," the antonym of *gravis* in its everyday sense of "heavy."

81. As Bower, *Fundamentals of Music,* 10 n. 21 points out, Boethius is following *Nicomachean Ethics* 1.13 (esp. $1102^{a}25$–7), ignoring the doubts expressed at *De anima* 3, 9, esp. $432^{a}22$–26.

82. Boethius, *De inst. mus.* 1.2, pp. 188. 26–189.4 Friedlein.

83. Correctly "augmentations and increases derived through itself and from outside."

84. Apuleius, *De Platone* 1.9.199; not *Cosmographia,* another name for *De mundo* (a paraphrase of the Pseudo-Aristotelian *Perì kósmou*). Apuleius's authorship of both works has been disputed, though current opinion favors acceptance.

85. In the Latin of the Roman Republic, *animus* denotes not only the intellect and the emotions, but our consciousness as a whole, *anima* only the principle of life as such; in Imperial Latin *anima* was used in the broader sense of Greek *psychḗ* and English *soul.* (Hence, in discussing the immortality of the soul Cicero uses *animus,* Seneca and Christian authors *anima.*) In medieval scholastic Latin *anima* is used for the complete bundle of vital principles Aristotle associated with the soul, while *animus* is used strictly for the intellective soul, the powers of cognition.

86. So Florentius's garbled text; Cicero wrote: "But the soul escapes the sight of the eyes, but is alone of all beings seized and partaking of the reason and concord (which in Greek is *harmonia*) of things eternal and falling within our understanding" (*Timaeus* 27), expanding Plato's "itself is invisible but partakes of reason and attunement" (*Timaeus* 36 E–37 A).

87. *Didascalicon* 2.12, ed. Buttimer 33. 710 (*PL* 176. 756 D), quoting Ephes. 5:29.

88. I.e., water organs; for this reason *spiritus* is here translated "blown air" not "breath."

89. Literally "and," but this, while grammatical in Latin, yields poor syntax in English.

90. Boethius, *De inst. mus.* 1.2. p. 189.5–11 Friedlein.

91. Isidore, *Etym.* 3.18(17).1–2; from Cassiodorus, *Inst.* 2.5.5. For the translation see Guillaumin's note on *Etym.* 3.10.2; he translates "en usant de démonstrations."

92. As opposed to their meaning, which is their form.

93. Ed. cit., sig. [aa8]^{ra}.

94. The palate is missing here from the conventional list; see e.g. Peter of Spain, *Tractatus* 1.2, p. 1 De Rijk; Marchetto, *Lucidarium* 1.9.3, p. 90 Herlinger.

95. Not Cicero, but the *Rhetorica ad Herennium* 3.19–20, ascribed in the Middle Ages and early Renaissance to him.

96. Literally "softness," but as we call lead a soft metal; in English a soft voice is quiet and gentle, which is not the sense here.

97. Meaning "I shout": *boáō* is the original uncontracted form cited by grammarians to show the stem-vowel, *boô* the form found in most actual usage. See Papias, ed. cit., sig. [aa8]^{ra}.

98. Also meaning "I call." See ibid.

99. *De compendiosa doctrina*, 2 *ad fin.*, ed. W. M. Lindsay (Leipzig: B. G. Teubner, 1903), 1:277 (188.25).

100. *Moralia in Iob* 5.18.37, ed. Marc Adriaen, CSEL 143 (Turnhout: Brepols, 1979), 244.52–54.

101. Papias, ed. cit., sig. [aa8]^{rb}.

102. A spurious sermon on the Nativity of St John the Baptist, Appendix, no. 196, §4 (*PL* 39.2115).

103. Isidore, *Etym.* 3.20(19).2.

104. For this formulation, which we shall see repudiated by the far earlier Lactantius, see Quintilian, *Inst.* 1.6.34; see Robert Maltby, *A Lexicon of Ancient Latin Etymologies* (Leeds: Francis Cairns (Publications) Ltd, 1991), 636.

105. "or living beings" is a medieval interpolation.

106. Isidore's *abusive* represents Greek *katachrēstikôs*, "by catachresis," denoting a less than strict usage, whether a recognized extension or a slipshod misuse.

107. "Proper(ly)," in this sentence and the next, refers to regular diction, without catachresis, figure of speech, or other deviation.

108. From Joshua 6:5 "cumque insonuerit vox tubae longior atque concisior," with "infremuit" from Vergil, *Aeneid* 10.711, said of a cornered boar.

109. Vergil, *Aeneid* 3.556 "fractasque ad litora voces," "and voices (of waves) broken on the shore"; *ab lit(t)ore* is an ancient corruption, which may also be translated "broken voices from the shore"; but Isidore's next words suggest that he understood it as rendered above, the shore being personified and "fractas" imitating the Greek idiom "break voice" = "burst into speech."

110. The poetic word-order recalls "litorei clamant scopuli" (the rocks of the shore cry out), itself a metaphor, in Ausonius, *Epist.* 21.11, *The Works of Ausonius*, ed. R. P. H. Green (Oxford: Clarendon Press, 1991), 222 (the numbering of the *Epistulae* varies from edition to edition)

111. Vergil, *Aen.* 9.503; the next word, omitted by Isidore, is *increpuit*.

112. *De institutione grammatica* 1.1.1–2, ed. Martin Hertz, in *Grammatici Latini*, ed. Heinrich Keil (Leipzig: B. G. Teubner, 1855), 2:5–6.

113. The true reference is to *De opificio Dei* 15.1–4; the form of citation comes from misunderstanding of Jerome's statement that Lactantius "also wrote two books about the wrath and craftsmanship of God" ("de ira quoque dei et opificio Dei uolumina condidit": *Epist.* 70.5.2).

114. This reading, though nonsensical, is found in some MSS of Lactantius; correct is *radit*, "(while it) scrapes," successively corrupted to *redit*, "comes back," and *reddit* "gives back."

115. Lactantius wrote *et ore clauso*, "even when the mouth is closed."

116. Florentius's *ex* is otiose; the true reading is *et*, parallel to the *et* following: "(it is the case) both (that) . . . and (that)."

117. Although we have paragraphed the text as if the quotation from Lactantius were Florentius's own, the close connection between Romerus's and Lactantius's expositions makes it probable that the latter are cited through the former. See Introduction, p. xiv.

118. Vergil, *Aen.* 1.371.

119. There is a play on *quaestio perpetua,* "standing court."

120. Aulus Gellius 5.15.1.

121. Ibid. §§6–7. Despite "he says," this is not a verbatim quotation, though at *Timaeus* 67 B Plato does state that sound is "the blow transmitted by the air and the brain and the blood through the ear as far as the soul."

122. Immediately afterwards, in Gellius's MSS and modern editions; but until 1853 editors inserted here a sentence from Dexippus's commentary on Aristotle's *Categories:* see Adolf Busse, *Commentaria in Aristotelem Graeci* 4/2 (Berlin: Deutsche Akademie der Wissenschaften, 1888), 70.9 ff.

123. The true text is *atómōn,* "of atoms" (i.e. indivisible bodies). If *lógōn* were correct, it would refer to words combined into sentences, not individual vocables.

124. The Latin word includes the notion of "clearly audible."

125. See Vergil, *Aen.* 2.313, 11.192.

126. In Latin *altus,* used of a sound, may be either loud or high-pitched, but in antiquity the latter sense is confined to lay authors, the technical term being *acutus.*

127. The true text is *in sublime,* hence "reach the peak."

128. Isidore, *Etym.* 3.20(19).10–14.

129. *Inflexio vocis,* quoted by many writers, comes from Isidore, *Etym.* 3.20(19).8, who goes on to discuss arsis and thesis; note too *Liber Argumentorum,* no. VI, "musica est motus vocum, id est arsis et thesis," in *Expositiones in Micrologum Guidonis Aretini,* ed. Joseph Smits van Waesberghe (Amsterdam: North-Holland Publishing Company, 1957), 19, §7.

130. *Etym.* 3.20(19).9.

131. *Micrologus* 16.9.

132. In Greek *ársis*, "raising," and *thésis*, "placing, putting down," referred to the raising or lowering of the foot, and hence to the up- and downbeat respectively. In Latin they came to be misunderstood of the voice, so that *arsis* became the transition to a higher pitch and *thesis* to a lower. (By a further misunderstanding, modern writers on poetics use these terms for respectively the strong and the weak part of a foot, which is the wrong way round with respect to classical usage.)

133. That is, Boethius's discussion of pitches in *De inst. mus.* 4.5 relates them to the monochord, not the human voice; at 4.1 (p. 301.20–2 Friedlein) *vocula* means "sound," representing *phthóngos* in his source, Euclid, *Sectio canonis*, ed. André Barbera, *The Euclidean Division of the Canon: Greek and Latin Sources* (Lincoln, NE, and London: University of Nebraska Press, 1991), 114.11–13. (Note that Boethius uses *intentio*, not *intensio*.) By contrast, it is in a discussion of the human voice that Bartolomé Ramos de Pareja writes of "vocis elevatio sive intensio et depressio sive remissio" ("raising or tautening of the voice and lowering or loosening"): *Musica Practica*, ed. Johannes Wolf (Leipzig: Breitkopf & Härtel, 1901), 26.

134. That is, the letter names and syllables used for teaching plainchant, and all terms used in treatises on *musica plana*, i.e., the fundamentals of music.

135. Literally "head"; compare our "head motive."

136. For the diagram of the hand, see p. 66.

137. See n. 75; note the slight difference in text. The present quotation is correct.

138. Just above *voces* were clearly pitches; here the sense is that the ancients established the hexachord for the sake of the number six.

139. That is, 6 is a perfect number, meaning that it is equal to the sum of its factors, including unity (1 + 2 + 3). For the geometrical approach to the problem see Euclid, *Elements* 9.36.

140. That is to say, the circumference of a circle is six times its radius; in fact 2π is a little over 6.283 185 3. Naturally this has nothing to do with

Euclid. The Latin is as awkward as the English; perhaps Florentius imagined that he had used an absolute construction, "a circle having been drawn, etc.," and that *experitur* was a passive like *reperitur*, "is found."

141. *Intensio* denotes an increase of tension (as when the pitch of a string, or the voice, is raised) or of effort; here the sense seems to be that people worked harder at singing, and therefore increased its range. This is evidently the passage referred to at 1.6.3. Elsewhere Florentius uses *intensio* for "ascent"; see the music example on p. 160, where the rising notes are labeled *intense* (which we take as the adverb, rather than the nominative plural *intensae*).

142. I.e., the use of the same name for different things: as, *ut* is a conjunction in grammar, and also the name of a musical pitch.

143. It is by no means certain that the quotation ends here.

144. The hand is not normally drawn with strings, though Florentius's hand has staves superimposed (fol. 31). He is probably thinking of the diagrams in Boethius and Hucbald (see fol. 42^{r-v}).

145. See above, Preface, n. 25, on Florentius's mistaken use of ♮*quadrum* for ♮*durum*.

146. I.e., as long as they remain in that property?

147. *Optimas* is hypercorrect for *meliores*.

148. Florentius here uses *satis* in the sense of Italian *assai*, without implying (in)sufficiency.

149. In §9 of the preface to his son Eustachius; but the passage is lifted from Seneca, *Epistulae morales* 84.9.

150. Not so: Guido indicates *superacutae* by doubling the letters (*Micrologus* 2.8 *et passim*).

151. *De inst. mus.* 1.20.

152. A confused allusion to Boethius, *De inst. mus.* 1.20, p. 209.2–5 Friedlein, where the plural *hypatae hypaton*, used for both *hypate* and *parhypate hypaton*, is rendered "maximae maximarum aut grauissimae grauium aut excellentes excellentium," referring respectively to their length, pitch, and physical position (see Bower, *Fundamentals*, 36 n. 113).

153. Durán, *Lux bella*, sig. a3^v, lists eight: four general and four special clefs (four forms of b). For most theorists, every letter is a *clavis*. Florentius, in his historical mode, begins with Guido's invention of the staff.

154. MS "allowable," which seems pointless.

155. Florentius's F clef consists of a long followed by two breves contained within extended verticals (his C clef).

156. Correctly *kleís kleidós;* nominative and genitive singular respectively, the normal citation forms for a Greek or Latin substantive.

157. That is, the knuckle and the base.

158. See 2.7.2.

159. The expression is slightly compressed: the sense is that we shall complete our assignation of the hexachords by placing (the root of) third ♮*quadrum* on second Gsolreut, whence it will run up to Ela.

160. This is what the Latin says; Florentius not only needs an expression for later than "lastly," but seems to have sought a way of combining "worthy of note" and "needful to remark."

161. The sense is almost as obscure as the construction is confused; Florentius appears to mean that even when we understand relative pitch, we still need a marking for absolute pitch.

162. This implies that Florentius intended these clefs to be made up of black notes, but they are white in the MS.

163. I.e., on a line or in a space; Latin *in* does duty for both senses.

164. I.e., fear of sight-reading.

165. I.e., by way of a pitch common to both hexachords.

166. Romerus's subjunctives make no sense either as conditionals or as jussives.

167. In Latin, at first sight this conflicts with §4: in places with two or three *voces* the *vox* is not changed. However, in §4 *vox* meant "syllable," here it means "pitch."

168. Loosely put for "in places with two note names"; see §7.

169. The only possible referent of the masculines *uno ipsorum, idemque,* and *caeteros* is *loci;* the sense seems to be "to the pair of notes in any one of the places."

170. "Color" in this context reflects a rhetorical concept applied to music: the use of accidentals to ornament a song. Most theorists make a distinction between flats and sharps: the former are used *causa necessitatis,* to avoid a tritone or diminished fifth; the latter are added *causa pulchritudinis,* to beautify the song. See Marchetto, *Pomerium* 4.3: "quia in musica fiunt interdum colores ad pulchritudinem consonantiarum, sicut in grammatica fiunt colores rhetorici ad pulchritudinem sententiarum." The following chapter discusses the sharp sign. For Cristóbal de Escobar, however, the flat belongs to the chromatic genus (according to the modern understanding, not the Boethian one), and one gives "color" to the fourth diapente (F–C) by changing B♮ to B♭. (*Esta es una introduccion,* sig. a2[v]). This passage is discussed in Bonnie J. Blackburn, "Music Theory and Musical Thinking after 1450," in *Music as Concept and Practice in the Late Middle Ages,* ed. Reinhard Strohm and Bonnie J. Blackburn (The New Oxford History of Music, rev. edn., vol. 3, pt. 1; Oxford: Oxford University Press, 2001), 301–45 at 312.

171. Here the abbot mistakenly combines two concepts. The definition of *coniuncta* is similar to Goschalcus's first definition: "Est enim coniuncta quedam acquisita canendi actualis attribucio in qua licet facere de tono semitonum, et e converso" (*The Berkeley Treatise,* 50–51; translated by Ellsworth as "For a *coniuncta* is the attribute, realized in actual singing, of permitting one to make a semitone out of a tone and conversely"). Permutation, a term invented by Marchetto, concerns only the mutation between *fa* and *mi* (*Lucidarium* 8.1.1): "Permutation is a change in the name of a syllable or note lying in the same space or on the same line but with a different pitch" (*The Lucidarium of Marchetto of Padua: A Critical Edition, Translation, and Commentary,* ed. and trans. Jan W. Herlinger [Chicago: University of Chicago Press, 1985], 271). Florentius contrasts it with ordinary mutation (or *commutatio*) in the next chapter.

172. That is to say: the flat can be used in place of a clef. Florentius seems to be referring to clefless compositions, in which the location of *fa* is shown only by flats.

173. The abbot's terminology is unusual, for a *disiuncta* comes about when one is forced to jump to another hexachord without any notes in common.

174. See Guillermus de Podio, *Enchiridion*, ed. in Karl-Werner Gümpel, "Das *Enchiridion de principiis musice discipline* des Guillermus de Podio," *Gesammelte Aufsätze zur Kulturgeschichte Spaniens* 27 (1973): 359–96, at 386, where he rails against certain unnamed Spaniards for using the term "bfami." *Bfami* also occurs in treatises of the Hollandrinus tradition.

175. Reading *admittunt* (or possibly *ammittunt*, Italian *ammettono*); MS *amittunt*, "lose," does not fit the context.

176. The exposition may appear self-contradictory, but Florentius is switching from bfa♮mi, the single position on the hand, to bfa and ♮mi, its different sounding realizations distinguished by different forms of the letter B.

177. The intended sense appears to be as given, but the original syntax is beyond repair.

178. In Latin *inferiora petentibus* (see 2.17.7, 3.1.1); literally "seek(ing) lower things." The phrase, first attested at Manilius, *Astronomica* 3.371, had long since become a cliché.

179. Florentius ungrammatically construes *cantantes* with the logical subject of the impersonal passive *ventum fuerit* as if he had written *pervenerimus*.

180. See the Commentary.

181. Literally "not the least," but in Latin this means "considerably more than the least," in English (in this context) "not even the least."

182. *Modus* here has its classical meaning.

183. Guido speaks only of transformation.

184. *Micrologus* 10.2–4.

185. Florentius repeats two widespread word-plays: Greek *authentikós* is derived from *authéntēs* (classically "murderer" or "perpetrator") in its later sense of "master, lord" (whence Turkish *efendi*); *magistri* has then been

understood as "schoolmasters," whose pupils suffer beatings (*plagae*). The true etymology of *plagalis* is Greek *plágios*, "transverse."

186. *Micrologus* 13.

187. Marchetto, *Lucidarium* 11.4.49, for the beginnings of the first mode, and so for the others.

188. Summary of Pseudo-Odo, *Dialogus* 11–18 (*Scriptores*, ed. Gerbert, 1:259–63). The ranges are often more extensive than those in Gerbert's text, but we still await a modern edition.

189. So explicitly Pseudo-Odo, who also specifies that in the seventh mode the 9th pitch is *b*♮.

190. These verses are widespread in medieval treatises; naturally St. Gregory had nothing to do with them.

191. That is to say, we ought not so to assign them because, although the melody is the same, the ligature pattern is different; the bad habit consists in doing so none the less.

192. See 1.16.7.

193. See Commentary.

194. Literally "first"; the maxima.

195. Literally "shortened"; the semibreve.

196. For this term, denoting a two-note oblique ligature, see *Lexicon musicum Latinum*, 1:75–6; it is treated at length by Guillermus de Podio, but also mentioned by earlier authors. See also Book III, n. 32.

197. Italian for "touched"; a descending plica. Guillermus de Podio calls it "tocus" (and "uncus") (*Ars musicorum*, fol. 45^{v}) but explains its etymology as follows: "prius usurpare invenitur tocus non improprie vocata fuit. Tocus enim grece teste papia: usura dicitur" (i.e. *tókos* "interest").

198. Literally "hooked"; an ascending plica.

199. This is probably the sense, but *illud* has no construction.

200. Syntax again breaks down; taking *ubique* as "and where" would not help even if we then understood an indirect question with *potest* wrongly written for *possit*, "and (shall state) where . . ."

201. Florentius or Verrazzano has written *deductio* by error, mentally switching the two terms at issue. For the definition, compare that of Goschalcus, above, n. 170, followed immediately by the same second definition.

202. Odd but right; B in the lower octave in the medieval system is only B♮.

203. Rossi points out that this should be Csolfaut.

204. Florentius shows the intonation of the first, second, fourth, and eighth tones.

205. There are some differences from the doxologies of the responsories given in *New Grove II*, 20:461, especially in the eighth mode, which begins on *c′* rather than *g–c′* and ends on *c′* rather than *g*; it also irregularly includes *b♭*.

206. There is a blank space in the manuscript where the heading should have been added. The end of the doxology in the sixth mode and those for modes 7 and 8 would have appeared on the recto of the missing folio 49. Here too there are some differences from the standard Vatican sources; the first doxology, for example, should end on *d* and the fourth on *e*.

BOOK II

1. One folio at the end of Book I and the beginning of Book II had been removed before the manuscript was foliated; the chapter title is taken from the table of contents.

2. The translation of this incomplete sentence must be tentative, but the sense may be that although the practitioners of the *ars antiqua* wrote their music in "points" (i.e., mere noteheads without tails), which gave their name to counterpoint, the principles of the latter apply no less to music written in the notation of Florentius's own day.

3. See 1.1.35, 43–4; Boethius, *De inst. mus.* 1.20.

4. That is, each inner string makes a fifth with the more distant of the outer string and a fourth with the nearer.

5. Interpretation tentative.

6. Hucbald has "which are equal pitches, and uniformly similar to each other, and which again are unequal, and at certain distances from each other."

7. There may be a hint at the use of *elementa* for letters of the alphabet, letters, syllables, and words being the analogues of pitches, intervals, and phrases.

8. The expression is awkward; Gerbert's emendation *quaevis*, "any one," makes better sense, but cannot be what Florentius read or wrote.

9. *Musica* 2–4, ed. Chartier, 136–38 = *Scriptores*, ed. Gerbert, 1:104.

10. In a definition, *et* links the general to the particular, so that *modulatio* is the control of pitch by tuning (the broadest ancient sense of *harmonia*). *Modulatio* is not "modulation," in its modern sense of change of key, but is derived from *modulus*, "measure, rule, melody."

11. Papias, ed. cit., sig. M3^{ra}: "Harmonia modulatio vocis et consonantia plurimarum vocum pars musicae est quae [*l.* qua] discernitur inter acutum et grave." In the Venetian eds. of 30 June 1485 "per Andream de Bonetis de Papia," 17 Mar. 1491 "per Theodorum de Ragazonibus de Asula," and 19 Apr. 1496 "per Philippum de pincis Mantuanum," the lemma is spelled *Armonia* and registered under A, as in Florentius's index; his own (or Verrazzano's) spelling varies but here is *Harmonia*. The entry ends "quem [*sic*] discernit acutum et graue"; compare s.v. *musica*, 1476 sig. [Qq11]^{rb} "harmoniaca [*sic: harmonica*] quae discernit in sonis acutum et gravem."

12. Isidore, *Etym.* 3.20(19).2. "Fitting together" (*coaptatio*) translates Greek *harmonía*.

13. In fact *Musica enchiriadis* 9.

14. *Lucidarium* 5.5.4, quoting *Analytica posteriora* 2.2, 90^{a}18–19 (of *symphōnía*). *Armos* is pseudo-Greek; *harmonía* is derived from *harmóttein* or *harmózein*, "to fit."

15. Isidore, *Etym.* 3.20(19).4; the next sentence blends an attempted emendation (*a melosa* for *et melos a*) of Isidore's "This and *melos* are so called from sweetness and honey" with matter from Marchetto.

16. *Lucidarium* 5.3.3, where the etymology is falsely attributed to Isidore; see Herlinger, p. 205.

17. See the chapter summary of 13.21 "sonitus vocum atque verborum iuncundioris, quae a Graecis εὐφωνία dicitur"; in the earliest editions, after the Greek word, Theodore Gaza's gloss is added "idest vocalitas consonantiaque." *Voculatio* is Nigidius Figulus's term for "accent," cited at 13.6, 13.21.1, 3. There is nothing to the point in Book I, but early editions prefix it with Gellius's list of chapter headings (originally appended to the preface, which before 1651 was printed as an epilogue).

18. Ed. cit., sig. [Z6][ra], a conflation of Isidore, *Etym.* 3.20(19).2–3; see §7 below.

19. See *Sermo de duobus filiis ex Evangelio* 9, ed. Germain Morin, *Miscellanea agostiniana* (Rome: Tipografia poliglotta vaticana, 1930–31), 1:261.

20. *Lucidarium* 5.5.2–3.

21. *Etym.* 3.20(19).3.

22. Ed. cit., sig. Qq2[ra] "Melodia dulcedo cantus: suavitas vocis vel meloclama vel a convenientia chordarum tanquam membrorum: quae græci Τα μελη vocant." The Venetian editions insert a colon after *dulcedo*, making *cantus* nominative instead of genitive, and for the nonword *meloclama*, with its suggestion of *clamor*, the no less unfamiliar *melodama* (before which the 1496 edition adds *a*); see *melodiama* in Hugutio, *Derivationes*, M 74. 1 (Cecchini 2:748). *Mélos* is Greek for both "melody" and "limb."

23. That *dulcis* agrees with *cantilenae* and not *sonus* is suggested by Osbern, *Derivationes*, M xlii (under *mel*) "melos indeclinabile, .i. [= id est] dulcis cantus, unde hec melodia -e et hoc melodioma -is" (*Osberno, Derivazioni*, ed. Feruccio Bertini and Vincenzo Ussani Jr. [Spoleto: Centro Italiano Studi sull'Alto Medioevo, 1996]), 1:423; see ibid., 437, no. 228: "melos, dulcis cantus, quod et melodia et melodiama dicitur; melus, dulcis, quod et melodus et melicus dicitur."

24. Papias, loc. cit.

25. See ibid., sig. Qq1[va].

26. Pseudo-Censorinus 12.1.

27. *Etym.* 3.20(19).7. However, here Isidore is speaking about the modes, not the whole tone.

28. Music theorists, as opposed to writers at large.

29. This part of the definition goes back to *Musica enchiriadis* 9; see Marchetto, *Lucidarium* 2.1.3, p. 106 Herlinger; Ciconia, *Nova musica* 1. 22, p. 98 Ellsworth.

30. See Anon., *Species plani cantus sunt terdecim,* in MS Girona, Arxiu Capitular 91, fol. 118^{r} "Semitonus est collectio duarum vocum imperfectum <sonum habens>, sicut mi fa vel fa mi. Tonus est collectio duarum vocum plenum sonum habens, et dicitur de 'tono, -as,' et capitur ubicumque est intervallum vocum duarum coniunctarum, exceptis mi fa" (ed. Gümpel and Sachs, 193); evidently an abbreviated form, from no earlier than the second third of the 15th cent. (ibid., 205) of Arnaldus's text or its source.

31. *Postposito* here means "dispensed with," not "postponed," as in the common medieval command formula *omni mora postposita,* "without delay."

32. That is the verb "I thunder, thou thunderest."

33. A commonplace in late medieval music theory; the adjective *semus* entered actual use.

34. Not so: Boethius records this as an older usage, specifically in Philolaus (*De inst. mus.* 3.5), but himself employs the term for the enharmonic quartertone (1.21).

35. *Micrologus* 4.5.

36. In Greek and Latin not a letter like English *y* capable of being either a vowel or a consonant, but a continuant, capable of indefinite prolongation like a vowel but functioning in the language as a consonant, e.g., *l m n r s.*

37. Literally "in letters"; the ancient notion of a letter comprises name, shape, and sound.

38. Macrobius ought to have said that the ratio 9 : 8 cannot be divided equally by two rational numbers in geometrical proportion; the pure

semitone would be 3 : 2√2, which was beyond the capacity of an arithmetic that dealt only in ratios of integers.

39. Literally "leftover." *Comm.* 2.1.20–23. This is the difference between the ditone (81 : 64) and the fourth (4 : 3).

40. *Perfectas* here means "completed," not "perfect"; the translation is influenced by Browning, "Abt Vogler," 52.

41. Boethius, *De inst. mus.* 1.3, p. 189.15–23 Friedlein.

42. That is, the intervals are melodic not harmonic; the etymology follows the ancient principle of seeking a word's *étymos lógos* or "true principle," vaguely similar words that expressed its supposed meaning.

43. Ibid. 5.5.

44. Ibid. 3.10, p. 283.6–9 Friedlein.

45. See Klaus-Jürgen Sachs, *Der Contrapunctus im 14. und 15. Jahrhundert: Untersuchungen zum Terminus, zur Lehre und zu den Quellen* (Beihefte zum Archiv für Musikwissenschaft, vol. 13 [Wiesbaden, 1974]), 65–122.

46. I.e., has no other factors but 1, is prime.

47. See Boethius, *De institutione arithmetica* 2.4, p. 87.8–13 Friedlein: "Cum enim quinque volumus demonstrare, facimus quinque virgulas ducimusque eas hoc modo ·IIIII· et cum septem totidem, et cum decem, nihilo minus, quia naturalius est quemlibet numerum, quantas in se retinet, tot unitatibus adsignare quam notulis [= numerals]." For *bis unum* see 2.28, p. 119.8 Friedlein.

48. *Comm.* 2.2.12.

49. That is, we shall recognize that the octave has the same qualities as the unison, the ninth as the second, and so on.

50. The three Latin comparatives are used for superlatives: compare Italian *migliore* "best," *peggiore* "worst," from Latin *melior* "better," *peior* "worse."

51. A twenty-fourth (= three octaves and a major third) above G (= Γ) is *b″*, which makes a sixth with the last note on the hand, *d″* (= Dlasol). *Citra*, "this side of," may mean "without," of something not used; all the

same, *extra* would have been easier. Tinctoris says *praeter* (*Diffinitorium musices* 6, p. 26 Panti).

52. To judge from the above list, Florentius is imagining an instrument that encompasses seven octaves, far more than described in any contemporary description of a clavichord (what he means by "monochord"), harpsichord, or organ.

53. The examples for chs. 8–12 are on fol. 68^v.

54. See the Commentary for Florentius's assertion that the two semitones in the octave are major and minor.

55. In the abridgment presented by the Girona manuscript (p. 193), the size of the semitone is understood and not specified.

56. Florentius ought to say that the contrapuntist will make the minor third major, not the semitone.

57. I.e., the major and minor semitones are placed between the same syllables as in the minor third; see the next chapter.

58. The Greek *dià pasôn* means "through, across all [strings]."

59. This is incorrect: Boethius, *De inst. mus.* 2.31, p. 265.14–18 Friedlein, specifically states that the diapason comprises five tones and two minor semitones. Simple arithmetic confirms: since the generating ratio of the octave is 2 : 1, and that of the tone 9 : 8, the difference between the octave and five tones will be $2 \times 8^5 : 9^5 = 2^{16} : 3^{10}$, the square of $2^8 : 3^5 =$ 256 : 243. But this was beyond the author of 3.15–20.

60. See ch. 7 above.

61. Boethius, *De inst. mus.* 2.28–30; Macrobius does not mention the apotome, but for the minor semitone see *Comm.* 2.1.22–3, cited at 2.4.10 above.

62. The sense ought to be that the generating ratio of the whole tone is 9 : 8 (the lower number being placed before the higher as at Macrobius, *Comm.* 2.1.22), and that it is made up of the leimma (256 : 243) and the apotome (2187 : 2048); but Florentius's awkward language appears to say that the major semitone is to the minor as 9 to 8.

63. Lit. "reason dictates all this."

64. Normally this would be a major semitone, but Florentius must have meant between ♭ and ♯, which would be the Pythagorean comma (531441 : 524288). See the Commentary.

65. That is, a fourth may be used against the tenor, provided that another voice sings a note a fifth below the tenor.

66. Yet again the Latin is strangely expressed. It would have been simpler to say that a composition should begin and end on a perfect consonance; imperfect consonances create ambiguity.

67. It is only in perfect consonances that *fa* in the contrapuntal voice should not coincide with *mi* in the plainchant and vice versa; in an imperfect consonance there is no objection to (e.g.) *F* in the plainchant against *a* in the contrapuntal voice. Moreover, the offending interval may be either a tritone (e.g. *B–f*) or a diminished fifth (e.g. *f–b*).

68. That is, the perfect consonances to which they naturally tend, as the sixth to the octave.

69. This rule cannot apply to two-part counterpoint, which is what Florentius has been discussing in this chapter. A fourth is permitted between the contrapuntal voice and the plainchant only if a third voice takes a fifth beneath the plainchant.

70. Or "by a third, fourth, fifth," by the postclassical use of distributive for ordinal, as later in this chapter.

71. Literally "in what order we shall use these things": Latin prefers the indirect question where English idiom prefers a relative clause.

72. In fact, he does so at once, unfortunately without providing musical examples; we supply them in the Commentary. Florentius does not specify whether the contrapuntal voice begins above or beneath the tenor. With two exceptions in rule 4, when the tenor ascends the contrapuntal voice begins beneath it.

73. These rules are highly abbreviated compared with the others, which offer several possibilities starting at the unison, fifth, third, and sixth.

74. The natural sense of the Latin is a fourth down, but Florentius means (or should mean) up.

75. *Subire* may mean "go under" a thing, but not "go down"; as at 1.7.7 it means "rise," suggested by the following *quoque* ("too") and required by the context, since "descend" would be possible only for the step, not for the fourth.

76. Literally: "The descent of the same [notes] (has itself thus =) is in the following state." Florentius clearly finds the exposition of these rules rhetorically challenging.

77. Here *vocem* seems to be used hypercorrectly for *unam vocem*.

78. Literally "it is possible to be climbed," a good Latin idiom, and so in the next sentence with *ascendi;* unfortunately *morari,* being deponent, breaks the construction, and requires a personal subject.

79. In this instance the contrapuntal voice must begin beneath the tenor. Florentius could also have said that the contrapuntal voice may descend a tone.

80. Florentius, in search of yet another way to say "go up," fails to do so, though that is what he means. Even so, the octave is wrong. Again, in the last example the contrapuntal voice must start beneath the tenor.

81. That is, the cantus firmus.

82. Literally "between two [singers]," *duos* being masculine.

83. This heading is appropriate only to the first paragraph of the chapter; moreover, the species of 2.17 are the genera of 2.16.3 (observe the unblushing confusion at §7), and have their own *species specialiores*. Whatever else Florentius learned from Romerus it was not philosophy.

84. The second species of fauxbourdon, with a contratenor altus or bassus, is similar to what Guilielmus Monachus describes as "gymel" in three voices, in which the superius and tenor proceed in parallel sixths, with the bass in thirds or fifths under the tenor, or the superius and tenor move in parallel thirds, with the contratenor bassus in octaves and tenths beneath the tenor or sometimes above it in parallel thirds; see the examples in Brian Trowell, "Fauxbourdon," *New Grove II*, 8:619, and Ernest H. Sanders, "Gymel," ibid. 10:612. We wish to thank Brian Trowell for his observations.

85. Florentius perhaps has in mind the canonic rubric "Decimas do omnium quae possideo," used by Obrecht and Isaac to indicate a second voice in parallel tenths. While we indicate some possibilities here, this section will be the subject of a study by Bonnie Blackburn.

86. An example might be the Agnus Dei I of Josquin's *Missa Malheur me bat,* in which all the notes smaller than a semibreve are to be ignored; however, the tenor is taken from a chanson, not a plainchant, and Josquin provided a canonic inscription, "De minimis non curat praetor." Ramos describes a canon in his (lost) Requiem with the inscription "Ut requiescant a laboribus suis," indicating that *ut* and *re* are not sung (*Musica practica,* ed. Wolf, 92).

87. That is, find by trial and error.

88. Florentius seems to be referring to compositions based on a *soggetto cavato dalle vocali,* as Zarlino will later refer to it, such as Josquin's *Missa Hercules dux Ferrariae,* with its cantus firmus based on the vowels of the title. If this indeed is the composition he has in mind, and especially in view of the "messa cantata" that Ascanio sent to Ercole in 1486, as shown above, p. xi, it offers an important lead on the dating of the mass, which has variously been put at 1480–81, 1487, and 1501–4.

89. This appears to be a rising or falling ostinato, or interval canons at the fourth or fifth.

90. For example, the untitled mass by Standley in MS Trent 88, fols. 314v–322v, edited in *Sacred Music from the Cathedral at Trent: Trent, Museo Provinciale d'Arte, Codex 1375 (olim 88),* ed. Rebecca L. Gerber (Monuments of Renaissance Music, vol. 12 [Chicago: University of Chicago Press, 2007]), no. 106, based on the anonymous motet *Que es ista.* In both mass and motet the canonic voice must sing the tenor, omitting all pitches beneath *b♭*.

91. These are compositions in which one or more voices must be sung in retrograde motion, of which there are a number of examples in the late 15th cent.

92. Such as in the Gloria of Obrecht's *Missa Fortuna desperata,* where the tenor progresses to the middle, then reverses.

93. That is, the voice should be sung in inversion, another ubiquitous technique at the time.

94. The voice is sung in proportional diminution or augmentation, a technique particularly used in so-called isorhythmic motets of the earlier fifteenth century.

95. Properly thus, in which case "pluries" will (incorrectly) mean "the *n*th time," but possibly used to mean "once, twice, or thrice." Florentius seems to have in mind mensuration canons, where a line of music is sung under duple and triple mensuration of various kinds.

96. Despite Florentius's "in many instances," few examples have so far been identified. One might be the tenor of Isaac's *Palle palle,* in which the notes outline the shapes of the lilies and balls on the Medici coat of arms. See Allan W. Atlas, "Heinrich Isaac's *Palle, palle:* A New Interpretation," *Analecta Musicologica* 11 (1974): 17–25.

97. Florentius's discussion is rather elliptic. His intention is to distinguish imitation from *fuga,* where one voice-part follows the other exactly; with imitation changes may be made in the course of the melodic line, and it becomes less exact at a cadence.

98. The future indicative *inserviet* of the manuscript yields the unsatisfactory sense "when . . . shall render," or in normal modern English "when . . . renders."

99. Florentius stresses that the modes are applicable to polyphony as well as to chant.

100. 'Here' must be polyphony, which Florentius has not yet discussed.

101. Papias, sig. $O3^{vb}$; *vel cantus* is Florentius's gloss on *cantilenae.*

102. See 2.3.8, on melody.

103. Florentius allows himself here the term in common use, even though he disapproves of it.

104. "Neuma" is a term Florentius had used earlier without defining it. On its various meanings see the Commentary. "Cadentia," in the sense of *clausula,* is first found in Florentius and his contemporaries Jean le Munerat and Guillaume Guerson; see Leofranc Holford-Strevens, "Humanism and the Language of Music Treatises," *Renaissance Studies* 15

(2001): 415–49 at 430; *Lexicon musicum Latinum medii aevi,* ed. Michael Bernhard (Munich: Bayerische Akademie der Wissenschaften, 1992–), 3:280–81. The first citation for this sense of *cadenza* in the *Grande dizionario* 2:438 is from G. B. Marino (1569–1625).

105. That is, to end a sentence of the text with a cadence fitted to its mensuration, the final note of which should fall at the beginning of a measure.

BOOK III

1. *Boethius Geometrie II: Ein mathematisches Lehrbuch des Mittelalters,* ed. Menso Folkerts (Wiesbaden: Franz Steiner Verlag, 1970), 114. 25–8, 115. 33–4; see Euclid, *Elements* 1, definitions 14, 13, 15, 18.

2. Sánchez has not been traced; however, the word-order supports taking *sanctius,* despite its lower-case initial (the precise shape recurs only at fol. 74v, l. 12, in the second *semibreve* of 3.6.3), as a proper name rather than as the comparative adverb *sanctius,* "the geometer" being either any geometer in general or Euclid in particular: it is hard to see how this statement can be more venerable than the others, and even as "very venerably" the adverb, rendered yet more emphatic by its position before *geometra,* would be more suited (despite Plato's reported statement that "God ever practices geometry": Plutarch, *Quaestiones convivales* 8. 2) to a moralist or a legislator than to a geometer, even Euclid, who in any case is not even quoted accurately.

3. This combines Euclid, *Elements* 1, definitions 2 and 3: "a line is a length without breadth," "the ends of a line are points" (in "Boethius" rendered "Linea vero sine latitudine longitudo est. Lineae vero fines puncta sunt"), but misleadingly implies that a line cannot be infinite and has only one extremity.

4. Pseudo-Censorinus 7.1.

5. Inserting *et* before *semicirculo.* That is to say, from the figures peculiar to it (the notes) and the geometrical figures that it uses (the mensuration signs).

6. That is, what gives it luster.

7. *Ars practica mensurabilis cantus secundum Iohannem de Muris: Die Recensio maior des sogenannten "Libellus practice cantus mensurabilis,"* ed. Christian Berktold (Bayerische Akademie der Wissenschaften, Veröffentlichungen der Musikhistorischen Kommission, vol. 14 [Munich: Verlag der Bayerischen Akademie der Wissenschaften, 1999]), 1–2.

8. Not a quotation from Aristotle, though it is implicit in his use of *eláchiston* ("smallest"); but see *Regulae cantus mensurati secundum Johannem Otteby,* in Johannes Hothby, *Opera omnia de musica mensurabili; Thomas Walsingham, Regulae de musica mensurabili,* ed. Gilbert Reaney, CSM 31 (Neuhausen-Stuttgart: Hänssler Verlag for the American Institute of Musicology, 1983), 51–59 at 58: "Et ideo semibrevis partes minimas appellavere per gradum superlativum, dicentes ultra minimum minus dare poterit nemo"; ["And they called the parts of the semibreve minims in the superlative degree, saying that beyond what is smallest no one can supply something smaller."] Nicasius Weyts, *Regule,* ed. Coussemaker, *Scriptores,* 3:263 "Partes immediate semibrevium sunt minime. Partes immediate minimarum non sunt in arte, quia ultra minimum non est dare minimum; sed tantum sunt in usu quia tantum sunt due semiminime et quatuor cromata." ["The immediate parts of semibreves are minims. There are no immediate parts of minims recognized in theory, since beyond what is smallest it is impossible to supply something 'smallest'; but they exist only in actual usage, since there are only two semiminims and four *crome.*"]

9. Aristotle asserts in several places that a continuum is infinitely divisible: e.g. *Phys.* 3.7, $207^{b}16$–17, 6.2, $232^{b}24$–5 (compare $232^{a}23$), all available in the medieval *Auctoritates Aristotelis,* ed. Jacqueline Hamesse, Philosophes médiévaux 17 (Leuven: Publications universitaires; Paris: Béatrice-Nauwelaerts, 1974), 148 (2.108), 154 (2.171; compare 168). Since Aristotle uses the present, *fore* is so taken here, though the classical future would not be impossible.

10. On these note shapes see the Commentary.

11. That is to say, notes below the semibreve, which have no mensuration of their own, may count indifferently toward mode, tempus, or prolation.

12. *The Berkeley Manuscript*, ed. Ellsworth, 150.28–152.22 (the readings are closer to the Catania MS). This part of Goschalcus's treatise is based on Johannes de Muris's *Libellus practice cantus mensurabilis*.

13. The examples are collected at the end of the book. As will become evident, not everything discussed in the text is illustrated in the examples, nor does Florentius place them in logical order: in the text he treats first the signs for perfect values, then for imperfect values, whereas the examples move from larger to smaller note values. Florentius's terminology does not agree with Goschalcus's, though he does not call attention to the difference (he exchanges the normal meaning of *maior/minor* and *perfectus/imperfectus* with respect to mode), and there are discrepancies in his description of the mensurations (on this, see the Commentary). In the modern transcriptions, the maxima and long have been presented as tied whole notes to facilitate understanding whether the breve is perfect or imperfect, and when imperfection and alteration apply. The examples are multipurpose, for they also illustrate instances of imperfection and alteration before these concepts have been discussed; Tinctoris never commits this fault.

14. 'Perfect major mode in the maxima" is a pleonasm, and "the same in the long" a *contradictio in adiecto;* but since Florentius's major and minor mode are the normal perfect and imperfect and vice versa (see previous note), it is "perfect" here, not "major," that is rendered redundant by "in the maxima," and "major," not "perfect," that is intended by *eundem.* The sentence would be clearer if Florentius had written simply *modum maiorem,* but there is a similar, and similarly confusing, *perfectum* in 3.5.2.

15. In these mensurations the circle and semicircle normally indicate whether the breve is perfect or imperfect.

16. Florentius appears to share Tinctoris's opinion (echoed by Gaffurius) that the sign indicates an acceleration of the measure by an inexact amount. See Tinctoris, *Proportionale* 1.3.11–12, p. 52 D'Agostino.

17. The stroke indicates that the breve is to undergo diminution by half, or duple proportion; each semibreve becomes equivalent to a minim in perfect prolation. Florentius's language is far from clear.

18. Three notes in the time of two. Florentius should have specified that this happens when the mensuration changes from imperfect to perfect in the course of a piece.

19. "Imperfect mode halved in the maxima" is an odd way of putting it: he means that the circle now indicates a perfect long. Theoretically, these "modus cum tempore" signs indicate mode and tempus, but in practice they result in diminution. On these signs see Anna Maria Busse Berger, *Mensuration and Proportion Signs: Origins and Evolution* (Oxford: Clarendon Press, 1993), 148–63.

20. On these signs, see ibid., 24–25.

21. See above, n. 13.

22. That is to say, what are written as two breves will, in counting time, be equivalent to two undiminished semibreves. So too at the end of the next sentence.

23. The reversed semicircle normally indicates a sesquitertian relation, but can also mean diminution by half; see Busse Berger, *Mensuration and Proportion Signs*, 29–32.

24. These are the *modus-cum-tempore* signs, which were written with the circle or semicircle, denoting mode, and the figure 3 or 2, denoting tempus.

25. None of these examples shows alteration, and the last two do not incorporate longs (apart from the final note, which by convention is a long without mensuration).

26. *Eodem modo* here of course has nothing to do with "mode" in any musical sense.

27. These two sentences refer to diminution by half (either by circle or semicircle with a stroke, or by *modus-cum-tempore* signs).

28. Curiously, Florentius does not introduce the characteristics of ligatures frequently stated by theorists: propriety (*proprietas*) and perfection. The primary (conceptual, not visual) form of the two-note ligature is breve–long, which is considered to have propriety and perfection. The various permutations are achieved by adding tails or changing the form of the last note to an oblique. Moreover, all internal notes are breves, un-

less the first two notes have an ascending tail on the left, when they are breves "with the opposite propriety," in this case semibreves. Essentially, Florentius is showing how to read a ligature, not how to understand it.

29. This is not well expressed: Florentius means "except when we put a long after them" (see below).

30. In these ligatures the last note is turned back over the previous one, making it a long rather than a breve.

31. Florentius's language echoes the condemnation of a heresy; similarly Jacques de Liège, *Speculum musicae*, ed. Roger Bragard (Corpus Scriptorum de Musica, vol. 2 [Rome: American Institute of Musicology, 1961]), 7:403, 409.

32. The objection to the first two stems from their shape: while a descending oblique is normal, and the proper form for descending semibreves, an ascending oblique is not. These ligatures are called "alpha" or "alfados" in Spanish sources. They appear in Goschalcus, though he does not use the name (*The Berkeley Treatise*, ed. Ellsworth, 172–76); Guillermus de Podio (*Ars musicorum*, fols. 54–55) accepts them as normal. They are also found among Tinctoris's music examples in the *Tractatus de notis et pausis*, though he does not name them. The origin of Florentius's extremely negative attitude is puzzling.

33. Examples of both in *Pomerium*, ed. Vecchi, 7.3.

34. *The Berkeley Treatise*, ed. Ellsworth, 126–28. Florentius should have said "with ascending *and* descending tail," which is what Goschalcus shows. There is no mention of Parisian doctors, however.

35. Lit.: "by what procedure they are perfected or imperfected"; in such constructions Latin prefers indirect questions where English and Greek use relative clauses. Florentius's exposition is extremely abbreviated, compared with Goschalcus's (*The Berkeley Treatise*, ed. Ellsworth, 152–65).

36. This includes the sense "is proved to be perfect," but even so the sense is obscure.

37. The Latin has *minori cum*, yielding "by the smaller completion of a perfection together with," which makes no sense.

38. Florentius does not define a "point of value," but he implies it is the same as the point of addition, shown in measure 9 of Ex. 3.11.

39. The six causes are shown in order in Ex. 3.11, though one would have expected a dot of perfection after the fifth breve. The example does not fit the alternative version in major prolation, where the value of a semibreve is lacking in the tenth measure.

40. Florentius offers four.

41. Ex. 3.12 shows two pairs of semibreves divided by a *punctus divisionis*, each imperfecting the breve next to it; the first is the semibreve already used to illustrate the second way. It appears that *comparatio* is here used to mean "making a pair."

42. Again, the same example does not work for both major and minor prolation; in the latter there is one semibreve value too many, if we follow Florentius's rule that two smaller rests indicate that the previous note is perfect. This is not an infallible rule; Eloy ignores it in his *Missa Dixerunt discipuli*.

43. The version in imperfect prolation has a superfluous semibreve value.

44. For the construction compare *maiores nostri* and *our betters*.

45. That is, to show that they remain imperfect; the dot of addition affects only imperfect notes by making them the equivalent of perfect notes, which Florentius loosely expresses as "increase perfection." Surprisingly, he does not mention the *punctus perfectionis*, which is placed to insure that a note remain perfect when the case might be doubtful; perhaps he is thinking pragmatically, not bothering to distinguish two kinds of dot that both mark a note three times the next smaller.

46. Normally, color substitutes for alteration; the third blackened breve should have been a blackened semibreve, as we have transcribed it. However, this appears not to be an error, because Florentius goes on to specify that the second appearance of coloration in Ex. 3.16 shows that color removes half the value. We have not seen this doctrine elsewhere.

47. Removal of a quarter in the third pair of blackened notes applies to the smaller blackened note in so-called "minor color," when these patterns are interpreted as dotted rather than the normal sesquialtera. The

change took place during the latter part of the fifteenth century. See Ronald Woodley, "Minor Coloration Revisited: Okeghem's *Ma bouche rit* and Beyond," in *Théorie et analyse musicales 1450–1650/Music Theory and Analysis. Actes du colloque international Louvain-la-Neuve, 23–25 septembre 1999*, ed. Anne-Emmanuelle Ceulemans and Bonnie J. Blackburn (Louvain-la-Neuve: Département d'histoire de l'art et d'archéologie, Collège Érasme, 2001), 39–63. Florentius is the earliest theoretical witness for this practice; Woodley found unequivocal testimony only in sixteenth-century theorists (p. 43).

48. Normally called "reduction," when two blackened notes are separated by a group of notes in void notation. In Florentius's example, however, the last three notes are blackened to show that the semibreves belong with the long; the value of the semibreves themselves is not affected.

49. Thus a breve may be altered before a long, but not before a maxima, a breve, or a semibreve.

50. That is, having calculated the number of notes according to their mensuration. In Ex. 3.14 it will be a question of which semibreves group together to make up the value of a breve and which imperfect the preceding or following breve.

51. According to the description, the penultimate note should have been a semibreve, which would undergo alteration. The caption mentions only the first and second examples of alteration. Florentius has neglected to mention Ex. 3.15, which shows how coloration can substitute for alteration, indicated by a dot of division (see the beginning of Ex. 3.14).

52. I.e., the imperfect long. Florentius ought to have said that maxima rests are indicated by three long rests in perfect major mode, by two in imperfect, and that long rests occupy three spaces when perfect and two when imperfect.

53. Florentius or Verrazzano forgot to include the semiminim rests in Ex. 3.17.

54. Smaller rests do exist, since there need to be equivalent rests for every note value; in 3.2.2 Florentius has discussed notes smaller than a semiminim.

55. One would expect Florentius to state this principle at all four levels, maxima, long, breve, and semibreve; but the continuation shows that he has only semibreves in mind.

56. We should understand "in simple or florid counterpoint."

57. That is, when we treat them as if they were minims, and so in the next sentence.

58. See Boethius, *De inst. arith.* 2.40, p. 137.13–14 Friedlein: "Proportio est duorum terminorum ad se invicem quaedam habitudo"; from Nicomachus of Gerasa 2.21.3.

59. The MS has "of two quantities," anticipating §2.

60. Florentius conflates Boethius's *proportio* (Nicomachus's *lógos*, our "ratio") with *proportionalitas* (*analogía*, "proportion").

61. *Denarius* has nothing to do with the silver coin of late Republican and early Imperial Rome (whose name was revived for the Carolingian penny), for comparison with Nicomachus shows that numbers are intended; understand *numerus . . . numero*.

62. *De inst. arith.* 1.21 (p. 45.12–16 Friedlein), from Nicomachus 1.17.3.

63. Ibid. (ll. 20–1), translating Nicomachus 1.17.4: "the equal exists in one and the same manner."

64. Ibid. (ll. 26–9), from Nicomachus 1.17.6.

65. Ibid. 1.22 (p. 46.6–17), from Nicomachus 1.17. 7–8; but the names of the last two species are taken from the *Scolica enchiriadis* 3.56–59 (*Musica et scolica enchiriadis*, ed. Schmid, 119; 72 Erickson), displacing Boethius's *submultiplex superparticularis* and *submultiplex superpartiens*. The latter are also found in the *Tractatus de proportionibus* compiled by a pupil of Johannes de Muris, which in several manuscripts precedes the *Musica* <*speculativa*>, and to which Florentius's discussion in chs. 16–20 bears some resemblance while omitting all reference to music.

66. See *De inst. mus.* 2.4–11 (pp. 229–41 Friedlein; 54–65 Bowers).

67. Not in the *Enchiriadis* proper, but in the *Scolica* 3.17–57 (pp. 118–30 Schmid; 72–9 Erickson).

68. *Johannis de Muris Musica* <*speculativa*>, bk. 1, "Proporcionum musicalium theorica," 16–22, ed. Fast, 12–14.

69. This appears to be a misunderstanding of *De arte musicae breve compendiolum* 5.7, ed. André Gilles in *Philippi de Vitriaco Ars nova*, ed. Gilbert Reaney, André Gilles, and Jean Maillard CSM, vol. 8 ([Rome]: American Institute of Musicology, 1964), 88: "et sic patet quod minima praeponitur et quod hic quasi minor numerus praeponitur maiori," "and thus it is clear that the minim precedes and that this as it were smaller number precedes the greater," where the musical note is likened to a number. Florentius ought to have written "minorem numerum, vel quasi numerum."

70. *Sesqui-*, or *sesque-*, from *semis*, prefixed to the ordinal of a number n, is the regular Latin means of expressing the ratio $(n + 1)/n$. Florentius, or Verrazzano, spells it with *x* instead of *s*, but would have pronounced an *s* both here and in derivatives of *sex*.

71. See Marchetto, *Lucidarium* 4.4.5 "Et dicitur sesqualtera a sesqui, quod est totum et altera pars" ("And sesquialtera is so called from sesqui, which is the whole and the second half"); the "second half" is that of the second whole. *Idem* is neuter, used idiomatically for "and also."

72. The feminine form *hemiolia*, familiar from musical discourse, is found more than once in Boethius; the Greek for "the ratio 3 : 2" is masculine, *ho hēmiólios lógos*.

73. "A half" is *hḗmisu*; the compounding form "half-" is *hēmi-*.

74. Neuter *hólon*.

75. This is Florentius's own spelling; *sesqualter, sesquialter, sexqualter*, and *sexquialter* are all attested in other authors.

76. In Greek *epítritos* has no separate feminine, but *epitrita* is found in Latin from Boethius onwards.

77. "In addition to" is one of the meanings of Greek *epi* as preposition and prefix.

78. The Byzantine and modern pronunciation of *trítē*, feminine of *trítos* "third"; however, the Greek for "one-third" as a fraction is *tritēmórion*.

79. The MS has 39 : 36, which would be *proportio sesquiduodecima,* 13 : 12.

80. See the Commentary.

81. This ought to have been "mode."

82. These are scarcely English words, but no equivalents exist.

83. That is, "two units" (see §3); see next.

84. The transmitted reading, 10 : 6, which is the same ratio as 5 : 3, results from giving *duas partes* here its idiomatic meaning of "two-thirds" rather than "two unitary parts"; in that of 5 : 3 the two interpretations had come to the same thing. However, since the third ratio is 9 : 7 not 15 : 9, we should have expected 7 : 5.

85. This is carelessly added, for though 4 is not an aliquot part of 6, the ratio is the same as 5 : 3, which is superbipartient; but Florentius continually forgets to cancel down.

86. These terms have been left in Latin for want of English equivalents.

87. This and the subsequent definitions properly belong to the third mode; the names should denote any superpartient ratio whose consequent corresponds to the fractional. See Commentary.

88. The stated definition is satisfied by 9 : 5 alone.

89. The MS exhibits *superbipartiens quartas* (also below) and *superbipartiens quintas;* the former would be an improper name for 6 : 4 (the superparticular ratio 3 : 2), the latter a legitimate name for 7 : 5 (Dionysius van Ryckel, *De arte musicali, prima pars: Musica speculativa,* MS Ghent, Rijksuniversiteit, 70 [71], fol. 82^r; Tinctoris, *Proportionale* 1.9.11, p. 52 D'Agostino). However, since Florentius is again concerned only with $(2a - 1) : a$, and the names in §7 are correct, we have (perhaps overcharitably) ascribed the error to the copyist.

90. This last example ought not to be there, since the five units by which 12 exceeds 7 are not sixths; the proportion would rather be *superquinquepartiens septimas,* but ratios of the form $(2a - 2) : a$ lie outside Florentius's purview. It seems safer to suppose an untimely recollection that $12 - 7 = 11 - 6$ than to emend *xii* into *xiii* and supply a definition of *supersexpartiens septimas* or 13 : 7, which was not mentioned in §6.

91. Other sources speak of *dupla sesquialtera* etc., but to render "double sesquialter" would obscure Florentius's singularity.

92. One would have expected 10 : 4.

93. This translates the meaning of the Latin, that Florentius is listing the species of this genus in another way; what he is trying to say, however, is that the following are subspecies of another species (*tripla* as opposed to *dupla*) of this genus.

94. The MS inappropriately presents 25 : 4; since $25 = 6 \times 4 + 1$, the ratio is *sescupla ad sesquiquartam*.

95. Florentius appears to have developed a sudden and inappropriate scruple against predicating a singular complement of a plural subject.

96. Which is the same ratio as 14 : 3, *quadrupla superbipartiens*.

97. Rather than suppose this paragraph to have escaped from the discussion of superpartient ratios in the second mode at 3.18.5, we should understand *superpartiens* as a term covering all multiples of all species of superpartient, the *species specialissima* being designated by the fractional, e.g. *dupla superbipartiens tertias* = 8 : 3.

98. Florentius has in mind Italian *cifre*, "(arabic) figures"; compare *Oxford English Dictionary* s.v. cipher, cypher *n.*, sense 3. Whereas in theoretical discussions proportions may be written in roman numerals, in notating music only arabic figures are used; they are called "arithmetical letters" because in arithmetic they serve to write numbers, as in grammar letters are used to write words. Tinctoris in his *Proportionale* regularly uses *cyphra*.

99. That is, notes in coloration can create *sesquialtera* proportion.

100. I.e., signs of perfect tempus also apply to the breves contained in longer notes or divided into shorter ones; so *mutatis mutandis* to signs of perfect major or minor mode and major prolation.

EPIGRAM

1. Or: "which is mighty in the marvelous art."

2. Florentius does not use the word *suspendere;* in view of *pausa* in line 7, it presumably does not refer to rests. Or does Tranchedini mean "to hang one voice over another," i.e., to improvise counterpoint *super librum,* explained in Book II?

3. I.e., whether the perfect or imperfect was used; "what tempus is," i.e., what it means, would be *quid tempus.*

4. Perhaps "what all the singable notes are" (*figurae* are usually note shapes).

5. The Guidonian hand.

Commentary

1.14.13. Examples of the older notations

Florentius promises examples of Boethius's notation, along with those of the *Musica enchiriadis*, Guido, Hucbald, and the moderns; he then presents the example of the principal protus in Book I, chapter 8, of *Musica enchiriadis*, with the ambitus *d–a*.[1] Guido's notation turns out to be not the solmization syllables traditionally associated with him, but a blending of the two notations attested in his writings,[2] namely letters written over the text as in the *Micrologus*,[3] but above or below a single line like the notes of the *Epistola de ignoto cantu*,[4] thus affording a recourse *ad fontes* in the humanistic manner. Hucbald is represented not by his simplified Boethius (see below) but by longs, apparently replacing the *virgae* of some neumed manuscript, together with a *pes* and a *clivis*;[5] the notation of the moderns appears in the following chapter. The "Boethian" notation comprises in distorted form the paired Greek symbols, vocal to the left, instrumental to the right, for lichanos hypaton diatonos, hypate meson, parhypate meson, lichanos meson diatonos, and mese set out in the table at *De institutione musica* 4.4 and already exploited by Hucbald.[6] However, poor Florentius, brought up in an age when lichanos hypaton and *D sol re* were synonymous, did not realize that for Boethius the names were, and the note shapes were not, dependent on the *modus*; it is as if a modern compatriot of Florentius did not realize that *sol* was not always the pitch-class that the Germanic peoples call G. As Boethius had explained in the previous chapter, the correspondences in the table are specific to the Lydian *modus*, that is to say, to the double octave from *d* to *d″*, in which the sequence of pitches from lichanos hypaton diatonos to mese is that represented by

these symbols, namely *g a b♭ c′ d′*. The pitches intended by Florentius, which would have required to be notated with quite other note shapes, belong to Boethius's Hypolydian, the double octave from *A* to *a′* (4.15–16). Still, he was a pioneer in his attempt to recover the ancient practice.

1.10.5; 1.11.1; 2.18.3. Florentius's remarks on fitting the text to the music

It happens rarely that theorists of the fifteenth century venture to say anything about what has become a modern concern: how to underlay the words to the music.[7] In practical sources the words are often placed under the notes in a very approximate position, with only occasional separation of syllables. The end of Book I, ch. 10, promises to tell us just what we want to know: "In all modes, attention must be paid to the words very often underlaid to the notes. For they show very well that those notes bfa♮mi are sung as *fa* or *mi* whether there are signs or not. So much for this; let us add a little about the words to be underlaid to the notes." What chapter 11 discusses, however, is not how to underlay the text but how the words tell us whether B♭ or B♮ is to be sung, a proposal that seems to be unique to Florentius. This is a most intriguing idea. The whole system of mutations (which Florentius has just discussed) was devised to enable singers to tell when to sing a flat and when a natural on B. How should the text be of any help?

Florentius proposes that the text, whether in plainchant or a polyphonic composition, should be read through first. It should then be decided (on the basis of the hexachordal structure of the melody) which of the notes on B should be sung as *mi* and which as *fa*. These syllables should then be matched to the corresponding syllables of the text. For example:

This example illustrates an exception to Gonzalo Martínez de Bizcargui's rule that "Every melody that rises from *f* to *b* or rises to *b* and returns to *f* is sung with B♭, to avoid a tritone" (cf. Florentius 1.10.2). Exceptionally, "if the passage coincides with a clausula on the note *a* at the end of a word, B♮ is sung, even if a tritone ensues."[8] Following Florentius's method, the singer will fix in his mind that the B on the syllable *sti* is to be sung with a natural; perhaps he will say to himself, *sti* = *mi*. The advantage of this method, though it takes some preparation, is that there will be no hesitation in singing, if the singer has fixed the notes to the syllables in his memory. Moreover, Florentius says, it is a great help in cases where the clef changes in the middle of the staff. If the singer loses his way between lines and spaces, he will remember where *mi* and *fa* should fall because he has mentally attached them to the words of the text.

Florentius mentions the text again at 2.18.3 in connection with cadences, suggesting that the structure of the text should match that of the mensuration, so the end of a sentence coincides with a cadence, which should fall at the beginning of a perfection (a mensural unit in perfect or imperfect time). Theorists from the time of Guido and earlier stress the importance of linking neumes according to the text, "per cola et commata et periodos," but Harrán found only one (anonymous) theorist who did so in the fifteenth century.[9]

1.16. The coniuncta

The earliest full account of the theory of *coniunctae* is by Goschalcus, in the first treatise of the Berkeley manuscript.[10] Goschalcus

is evidently the fountainhead of its diffusion in Spanish sources;[11] he is not, however, cited by Florentius, who leans on the Abbas Populeti and Arnaldus Dalps. Before Florentius gets to his chapter on *coniunctae*, given especial prominence by the scribe because the title is in capital letters, he has already mentioned the word in chapters 8 and 9, giving contradictory explanations. First he quotes the Abbas Populeti (1.8.3), who says that some call *permutatio*, the change from B♭ to B♮ or vice versa, a *coniuncta*, which he describes as "an accidental attribute of song." Two paragraphs later Florentius explains that the *coniuncta*, also called *musica ficta*, arises from the placement of ♭ and ♮ in the hand on notes other than B; indeed his reason for preferring the term *coniuncta* is that it "connects" these accidentals with the syllables *ut, re, mi, fa, sol, la*, thereby indicating that the hexachords can be begun on degrees other than C, F, and G.

The chapter on *coniunctae* (1.16) begins with two definitions: "For a *coniuncta* (as Arnaldus says) is an acquired actual attribute of singing, in which one may make a semitone out of a tone, or vice versa. Alternatively: a *coniuncta* is the intellectual transposition of some property or *deductio* from its proper place to that of another below or above." These definitions match those in Goschalcus, though here they are credited to Arnaldus Dalps.[12] Florentius then proceeds to name them one by one. Goschalcus states that some claim there are seven *coniunctae*, others eight or more, but his opinion is that there are ten. Florentius has twelve. His first transposed hexachord begins two steps beneath Γut and ends on Cfaut, and *fa* is placed on Are. It is not certain whether by "duabus vocibus" below G he means *E* or *E*♭, and thus whether the *fa* on Are is *A*♭ or *A* is *fa* by virtue of a G♯, and this is true of all his other examples of *coniunctae*. Goschalcus, however, is more explicit in his descriptions. His first transposed hexachord begins on *F*: "the first *coniuncta* is taken between A and B *graves*; it is signed on B with the sign b, and its hexachord begins (they say) lower,

below Γ, so that fa is sung on B *gravis*."[13] Moreover, Goschalcus illustrates all the *coniunctae* with examples taken from chant, as do many other theorists who follow him. Florentius, although he had promised that "they will not be lacking below in examples" (1.8.6), fails to do so. We may assume, however, that he agrees with Goschalcus that the *coniunctae* are at *B*♭ (which is a true *coniuncta* since the medieval system allowed only a *B*♮), *c*♯, *e*♭, *f*♯, *a*♭, *c*♯′, *e*♭′, *f*♯′, *a*♭′, and *c*♯″. He names them differently, however, always specifying where *fa* falls in the hexachord, never *mi*. *Fa* falls on Are, ♮mi, Dsolre, Elami, Gsolreut, Alamire primo, Dlasolre, Elami secundo, Gsolreut, Alamire secundo, Dlasol, and Ela. The two additional *coniunctae* are therefore *A*♭ and *e*♭″, and they were surely conceived with polyphony, not plainchant, in mind, even perhaps organs. Moreover, he states that he could list very many more, but these will suffice. Whether these are outside the normal vocal range, or he intends notes such as G♯, D♯, or D♭, is not clear.

2.10–12. *The major and minor semitone*

Florentius flies in the face of traditional music theory by insisting that the two semitones B–C and E–F do not have the same size. The first hint at this oddity occurs in 2.9.1, where he describes the interval of a third: "The minor (third) comprises a tone and a semitone, whether major or minor." He then labels that interval with the minor and the major semitone both as *re fa* and *mi sol*, citing Arnaldus Dalps: "For the third, which also exists in an imperfect form, although simple in number, nevertheless beginning from unity is twofold in respect of tones and semitones, one kind major, one minor, and so forth." By "major" and "minor," however, Dalps is referring to the interval of a third, not the major and minor semitone, as is clear from the grammatical case. Be that as it may, Florentius argues the difference in other terms, in an explanation tacked on to the end of chapter 12, on the diapason.

He acknowledges Boethius and Macrobius for the division of the whole tone into two unequal semitones, apotome (major semitone) and diesis (minor semitone). However, he says, it is difficult to see them in the hand, so they require more discussion. He continues: "It is established that the semitone *mi–fa* is sung everywhere, but yet it is sometimes greater, sometimes smaller; few have grasped where it is (one or the other). For it makes a great difference whether *mi–fa* is ♮ C or E F, as stands to reason. The notes are not equal in the case of ♮ and ♭ as they are in that of E, even though they are on the same line or in the same space; therefore the higher semitone [♮ C] [see Ex. 2.15] there naturally makes less of an interval to *fa* than elsewhere, but the latter [E F] is lower, from which a greater interval must follow [see Ex. 2.16]."

Where did Florentius get the notion that the intervals B–C and E–F have different sizes? He knows that the whole tone A–B is divided into two unequal semitones, but at E–F there is not a whole tone in the Pythagorean system. Still, this does not answer the question why E–F should be a major semitone. For this we need to turn to one of his Spanish contemporaries and his ongoing controversy with Guillermus de Podio.

In his treatise of 1511, *Arte de canto llano y contrapunto y canto de organo con proporciones y modos,* Gonzalo Martínez de Bizcargui argued, against Boethius and Guillermus de Podio, that *mi–fa* is "semitono mayor cantable" (sig. a4^{v}) and is found in the diatessaron and diapente (i.e. E–F), and not the other (the smaller), which is "incantable" (sig. b4^{v}). Although he maintains that the tone is divided into nine commas, of which the major semitone contains five and the minor four, he seeks proof in practical experience: the sense of hearing and the strings on an instrument: "hallamos ser contrario a nuestros oydos por la pratica que es la esperiencia dela cuerda" (ibid.). The reference to an instrument clarifies the reasoning behind his idea: in meantone tuning the fifths and fourths are tempered and the pure major third is divided

into two equal whole tones, with the result that the flats are higher than the sharps. Juan Espinosa, in his *Tractado de principios de musica practica y theorica sin dexar ninguna cosa atras* (1520), chided Martínez for this "diabolical statement," contrary to mathematics and dependent on the fallible ear. In the 1538 version of his treatise Martínez responded truculently at great length, pointing out that one can even *see* the difference on the monochord (i.e. clavichord) and organ.[14]

How did Florentius come across this doctrine? It certainly would not have been through the learned Abbas Populeti, and—uncharacteristically—he cites no authority for it. We suspect that musicians in Naples must have convinced him of the truth of the argument, based on musical instruments.

2.14–15. *Florentius's rules on counterpoint*

After Florentius describes the intervals, he takes up the rules of counterpoint, by which he means the devising of a contrapuntal voice against a chant melody (the definition would have come at the beginning of Book II, which is missing). In 2.14 he lists eight rules, but in a general manner; many of these are familiar from the contrapuntal teachings of the time. The rules are codified in a more specific sense in 2.15, based on the melodic progression in the tenor. His method is quite different from that of Tinctoris, who starts out with a unison between the contrapuntal voice and the tenor, then shows how it may be followed by another unison, a third, a fifth, and an octave, depending on how the tenor voice moves.[15] Florentius has four rules, each based on a different tenor pattern: up and down a step, up and down a third, up and down a fourth, and up and down a fifth. The contrapuntal voice thus begins in different places. For example, when the tenor rises by a step, the counterpoint may begin in perfect intervals at the unison, fifth, octave, or imperfect at the third or sixth. This is perhaps a

more useful procedure for singing "super librum," over the (chant) book, as it was called, for the singer has the tenor in front of him and has to think which intervals would be appropriate. In any case, whichever method is used, the student is to memorize every possibility in order to call it to mind quickly while singing. Certain patterns in the tenor will suggest the most likely progression in the discant. For example, a descending step in the tenor, especially at a cadence, will often call for a sixth in the discant rising a step to create an octave with the tenor.

While one could not criticize Florentius's method, his practical application leaves much to be desired, and chiefly because he entirely omitted to show the progressions in musical examples—nor does he even promise them. Following his instructions (15.3–7), the following examples have been extracted. The tenor voice is shown as a black whole note, the contrapuntal voice as a white whole note; the pitch has been chosen at random. Florentius does not state whether the contrapuntal voice, when not starting on a unison, begins above or beneath the tenor. As Rossi observes, the transcription shows that when the tenor ascends, the counterpoint is beneath, and vice versa (with two exceptions when the tenor descends a fifth). Florentius does not list every possible progression.[16]

RULE I

Tenor ascending a step

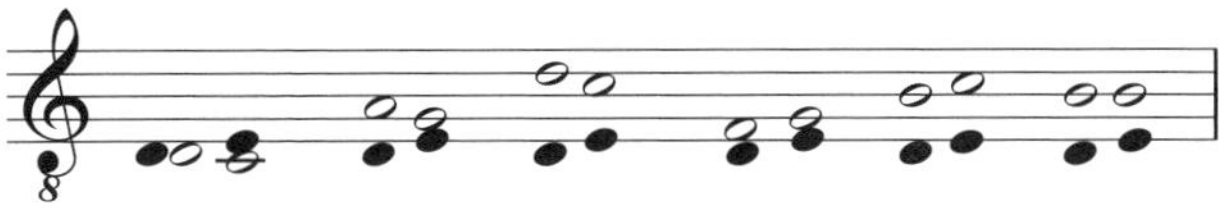

Tenor descending a step

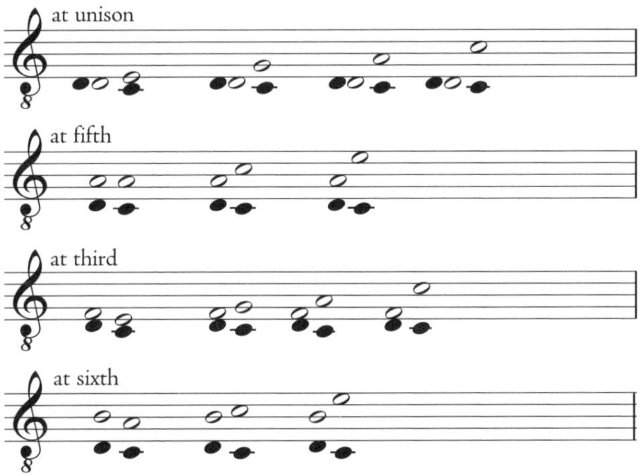

RULE 2

Tenor ascending a third

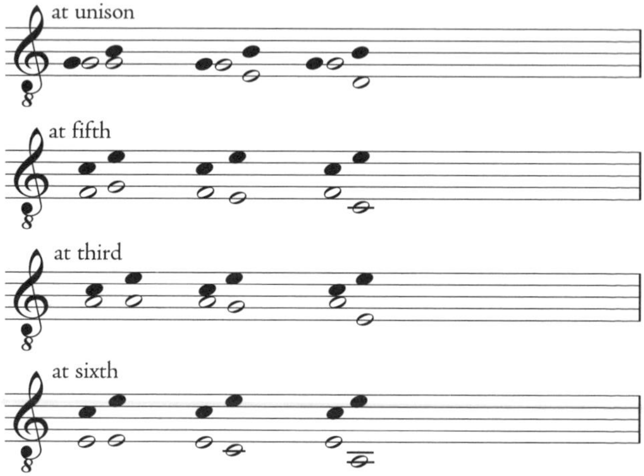

Tenor descending a third

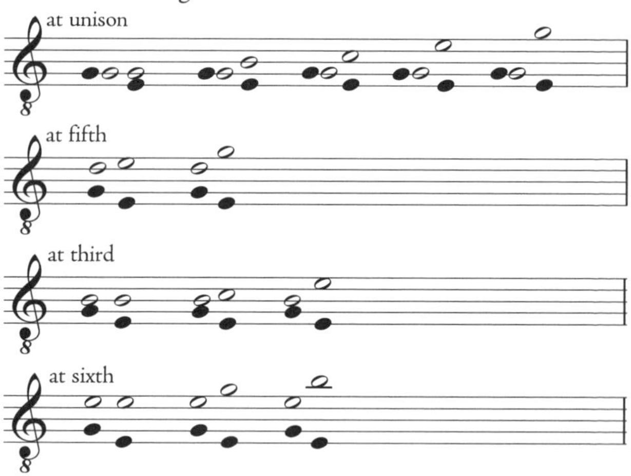

RULE 3

Tenor ascending a fourth

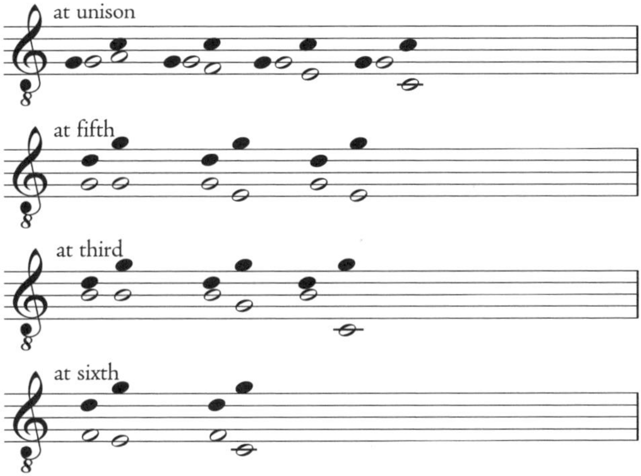

Tenor descending a fourth

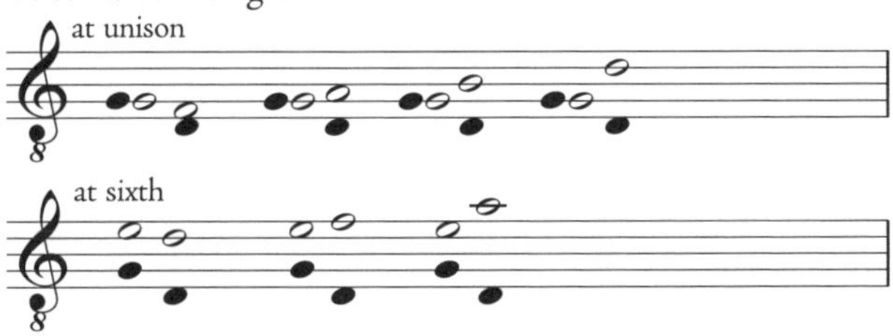

RULE 4

Tenor ascending a fifth

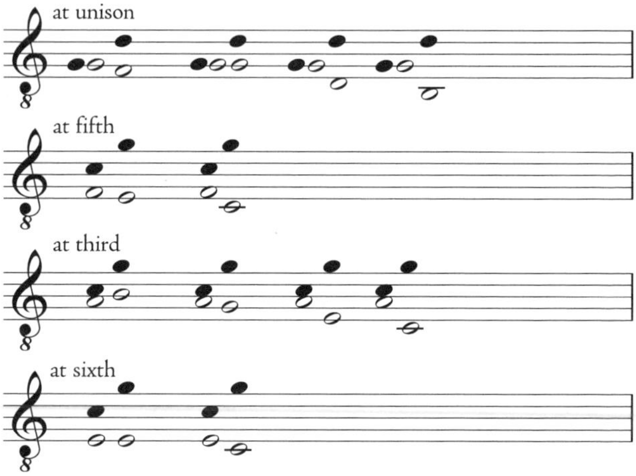

Tenor descending a fifth

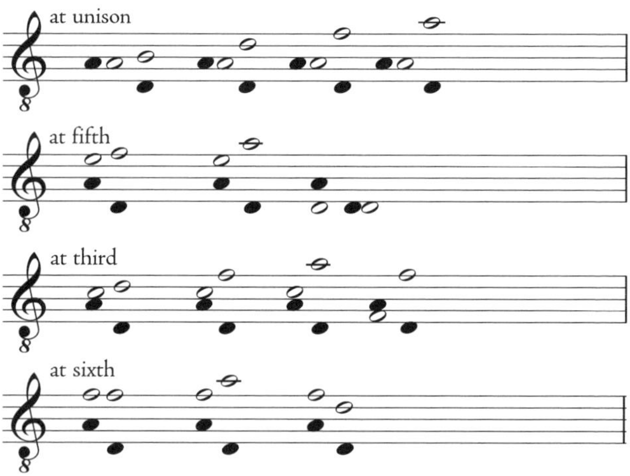

2.18.1. *The neuma*

"Neuma" is another of the terms that Florentius uses before he gets around to defining it. At 1.12.6 he mentions a number of chant genres, which he says "may be composed in alternating *neumae* of all the modes. But of this elsewhere." In the rules of counterpoint at 2.14 and the description of composition at 2.16–17 he employs the word without gloss. Finally, at 2.18, he devotes a chapter to the neume and cadence. As usual, he starts out with a definition from one of his classical or medieval sources, in this case Papias's *Vocabularium*: "Many people say that the neume is a part of the song or chant that is made by the doubling of notes." He continues with an unsourced remark, "Some say that it is the sweetness of the song, or a sweet song,"[17] but then gets down to the technical musical meaning: a neume is "those notes that we know were devised in assembling songs in order that one tone should differ from another, and which are contained by aggregation or segregation in the same modes. In the vernacular it has been called a cadence. Composers use it mostly like a clausula when the verbal sentence is finished." The examples show five examples of a *neuma* for the first mode in chant notation (Ex. 2.1) and then four cadences (actually clausulae to be fitted against a tenor), two in triple meter and two in duple meter (Ex. 2.2–3). The *neuma* for Florentius, therefore, is a cadential pattern in chant and polyphony.

3.2.2. *Note values shorter than a minim*

Some theorists (such as Tinctoris and Francisco Tovar) do not wish to recognize any note that is smaller than a minim, hewing to the dictum attributed to Aristotle, "ultra minimum non est dare minimum." Since such durations exist in practice, it was necessary to call them minims in duple and quadruple proportion. Floren-

tius is quite happy to accept the smaller notes, some of which are familiar from other theorists (occasionally under different names), but others are new. Since he does not discuss Italian notation, which was obsolete by the time he was writing, all these notes should represent the next smaller division in the French mensural system of mode, tempus, and prolation.

The semiminim, represented as a blackened minim, has the normal form and name and is the equivalent of quarter-note in American English and crotchet in British English.

What Florentius calls the semiseminimin () is the equivalent of the eighth-note in American English and quaver in British English. Hothby calls it *croma* (still the modern Italian name). Ramos calls it "cursea sive cursuta aut crocea."[18] "Corchea" (sometimes "corcheo") is what the Spanish theorists use; *corchea* is still the modern Spanish word, related to French *croche* as *corchetes* ("brackets") to *crotchets*. Goschalcus, however, calls it "seminima," and gives it two shapes, one with an R-shaped flag like Florentius's *crossuta* and the other where the flag turns back on the stem.[19]

Florentius's *crossuta* (), clearly the same word as Ramos's *cursuta,* would appear to be the same as his semiseminimin, except that he writes it with a different flag. Unfortunately, he does not explain the exact relationship of the notes, nor does he include them in any of his music examples. He had clearly found the *crossuta* in Spanish sources, and perhaps did not realize that it was equivalent to half a semiminim.[20]

The *semicrossuta* () is logically half the *crossuta,* and thus a 16th-note or semiquaver (Italian *semicroma,* Spanish *semicorchea*). Ramos and Durán call it a "minaria." We have not seen this rather fanciful shape elsewhere.

The *fugiela* (), looks similar to the semiseminimin, which is what *fusiel* means in the anonymous German treatise *De vera et compendiosa seu regulari constructione contrapuncti;*[21] but if Florentius is consistent in halving note values it will be a 32nd-note or

demisemiquaver (*biscroma* in Italian, *fusa* in Spanish; *New Grove II* 18:200 gives a Latin name *fusella*). Ramos and Diego del Puerto call it a *fusea*,[22] Tovar a *fuseta*. For Goschalcus, the *fusa* is a black minim with and upward and downward stem.[23]

The *semifugiela* (𝅘𝅥𝅲) would be a 64th-note or hemidemisemiquaver (*semibiscroma* in Italian, *semifusa* in Spanish; *New Grove II*'s *fusellala* is obviously an error for *fusellula*).

Although Florentius claims that all these notes are singable, the smallest note value found in practical sources is the *semifusa* in its Latin sense of 16th-note or semiquaver. What are we to make, then, of his *fugiela* and *semifugiela?* Perhaps he simply listed all the notes and note names he had found in theoretical or musical sources, putting them in what he thought was descending order. However, there is another possibility for these last signs: they look very much like the signs one finds in lute and keyboard tablatures (sometimes with stems only). If one is accustomed to vocal music, keyboard music appears to be very much faster because of the use of double- and triple-flagged notes; however, they are generally equivalent to semiminim and fusa (in its Latin sense of quaver) in vocal music.

3.3–7. Major and minor mode

Florentius begins his exposition of the mensural system with a quotation from Goschalcus explaining *maior modus*, the measurement of the maxima, and *minor modus*, the measurement of the long. Either of these two notes can be perfect or imperfect, yielding four different mensurations at this level. *Maior modus perfectus* has three longs in the maxima; *maior modus imperfectus* has two longs in the maxima. *Minor modus perfectus* has three breves in the long; *minor modus imperfectus* has two breves in the long. The measurement of the maxima is rarely used in practical music, and is not always mentioned by theorists; nevertheless, since Florentius

has found signs for it in earlier treatises he wishes to discuss it. However, without saying so, he departs from Goscalchus's terminology, using "major/minor" for the usual "perfect/imperfect" and vice versa:

	Goschalcus (and others)		Florentius	
	Triple	Duple	Triple	Duple
Maxima	Perfect major	Imperfect major	Perfect major	Perfect minor
Long	Perfect minor	Imperfect minor	Imperfect major	Imperfect minor

The reader who has not recognized this will suppose him constantly in error; but in fact, within the text Florentius is consistent, applying "maior" to signs with the circle, indicating triple mensuration, and "minor" to signs with the semicircle, indicating duple; "perfect" mensurations have three dots in the sign, indicating a maxima, "imperfect" two, indicating a long. However, Ex. 3.3, illustrating perfect minor mode, clearly exhibits a long containing three breves, as is normal, not a maxima containing two longs, as Florentius ought to have made it. Even Ex. 3.4, of imperfect minor mode, is pedagogically inept, because it could equally well show perfect longs that had been imperfected by the following breve.

Tinctoris was the first theorist to demonstrate that there are sixteen possible combinations using duple or triple values for the maxima, long, breve, and semibreve.[24] Florentius, unfortunately, is not so systematic, and he does not state which notes under modus signs with the semicircle are perfect or imperfect. When he says that these signs "allow perfect minor mode where circles do" (3.6.3), he implies that the long and breve are perfect, but when he goes on to say that perfection applies only to the semibreve and alteration only to the minim, the long and breve must be imperfect.

The source of Florentius's terminology is puzzling; we have not found it in any other theorist. Clearly he did not learn men-

sural notation from the Abbas Populeti, who is not cited in Book III.

3.16–20. Terminology of ratios

In this section Florentius abandons music for arithmetic; his *Liber Musices* discusses ratios entirely in their own right, without reference either to the musical intervals they may generate or to their realization in rhythm, though the latter is partially illustrated in Exx. 3.21–6. In this it is unlike not only the *Tractatus de proportionibus* and Tinctoris's *Proportionale musices*, but even the tradition represented by Nicomachus of Gerasa's *Introductio arithmetica* of the second century AD, Boethius's *De institutione arithmetica* (largely translated from it), and Johannes de Muris's *Arithmetica speculativa* (an abridgment of the latter), which all end by considering both the mathematical and the musical relations of the numbers 6, 8, 9, and 12.

This Nicomachean tradition divided inequality into the greater, in which the antecedent of the ratio was greater than the consequent (e.g. 2 : 1), and the lesser, in which it was less (e.g. 1 : 2): each genus was then divided into five species, those of the lesser inequality being each the inverse of the corresponding species of the greater. Since Florentius says nothing of the lesser inequality and its species beyond recognizing their existence, we shall concentrate on the greater, setting out their names and forms. In what follows a, k, and n stand for integers greater than 1:

Multiple	$a : 1$
Superparticular	$(a + 1) : a$
Superpartient	$(a + k) : a,\ k < a,\ k \nmid a$
Multiple superparticular	$(na + 1) : a$
Multiple superpartient	$(na + k) : a,\ k \nmid a$

The first two cause no difficulty; we need note only that ratios need not be stated in their simplest terms (so that 4 : 2 is recognized as duple and 6 : 4 as superparticular even before being canceled down to 2 : 1 and 3 : 2) and the superparticular proportions are named in Latin by prefixing *sesqui-* to the ordinal of the consequent.

The superpartient ratios may be subdivided according to the difference k between the antecedent and the consequent: when $k = 2$, the relation is superbipartient, when $k = 3$ it is supertripartient, and so on. However, both Nicomachus and Boethius, having listed the superbipartient ratios 5 : 3, 7 : 5, 9 : 7, 11 : 9, and so on, thereafter concentrate on the special case of $k = a - 1$, yielding the ratio $(2a - 1) : 1$: supertripartient 7 : 4, superquadripartient 9 : 5, superquinquepartient 11 : 6, etc.; this accords with the Greek, Latin, and English idiom whereby "n parts" denotes the fraction $n/(n + 1)$. These ratios could be more fully expressed by adding the fractional of the consequent; thus in the Greek of Nicomachus's commentator Iamblichus 5 : 3 is *epidimerȇs trítōn*, literally "with two parts over of thirds," in Boethius's Latin *superbipartiens tertias*, apparently "which over-twy-divides thirds."[25] Likewise 7 : 4 is *epitrimerȇs tetártōn/supertripartiens quartas* and 9 : 5 *epitetramerȇs tetártōn/superquadripartiens quintas*.

Florentius, however, claims to present three species of superpartient ratios, designated respectively by k, by a, and by both; thus 5 : 3 is *superbipartiens* because $5-3 = 2$; it is *superpartiens tertias* because the unitary parts of the difference are thirds; it is *superbipartiens tertias* by combination of the two nomenclatures. These are not true species but modes of classification; perhaps Florentius was attempting to compile a comprehensive account by combining sources.

In discussing the first classification, he does not, unlike Nicomachus, Boethius, de Muris, and the *Tractatus de proportionibus*, confine himself to the special case, but recognizes as super-

tripartient such ratios as 10 : 7 and 11 : 8 (he forgets 8 : 5, mentioned by Tinctoris, *Proportionale* 1.7.6, p. 54 D'Agostino), and similarly 11 : 7 and 15 : 11 as superquadripartient; unfortunately, he constantly forgets to cancel down, so that he also counts as superquadripartient 10 : 6, which is the same superbipartient ratio as 5 : 3 and has already been given under that head.

The second mode, designated by fractionals alone, is found in Prosdocimo de' Beldomandi, *Brevis summula proportionum* 9; it ought to group together all ratios with the same consequent that meet the conditions for superpartiency, namely that the difference neither exceed nor divide the consequent, so that while *superpartiens tertias* and *quartas* would still be single-member sets (5 : 3, 7 : 4, respectively), 7 : 5, 8 : 5, and 9 : 5 would all count as *superpartiens quintas*. However, Florentius exhibits total confusion, concentrating on the special case of $k = a - 1$, and then producing inappropriate examples.

The third mode combines the other two designations, by both difference and fractionals; however, unlike Prosdocimo he considers only the special case and not (despite some confusion at least in the manuscript) such ratios as 7: 5, *superbipartiens quintas*, although he does contrive to reckon 12 : 7 as *superquinquepartiens sextas* instead of *septimas*.

The multiple superparticular ratios do not call for especial comment, except that Florentius prefers to call them *dupla ad sesqualteram*, etc. rather than the usual *dupla sesquialtera*, perhaps because it suggests $2 \times 3 : 2 = 3 : 1$ rather than $(2 + 3) : 2 = 5 : 2$. No such scruple affects the naming of multiple superpartient ratios, which are *dupla superbipartiens* and so on; however, all those beyond multiple superbipartient are recognized only in the case $(ka + k) : a$, e.g. *tripla supertripartiens* = 15 : 4, 18 : 5, etc., *quadrupla superquadripartiens* = 24 : 5, 32 : 7. At the end of the chapter he appears to state, somewhat elliptically, that the fractional of the consequent may be appended to specify the ratio; that is, that we may

call (e.g.) 32 : 7 *quadrupla superquadripartiens septimas*. Such names are known to Tinctoris (whose exposition is a model of clarity), though he goes no further than *dupla quadripartiens quintas* = 14 : 5; but as in musical matters Florentius is an amateur attempting to punch above his weight.

NOTES

1. See *Musica et scolica enchiriadis*, ed. Schmid, 16. He uses the same melody for all four examples.

2. This was pointed out by Dr Jeffrey Dean in a seminar at Oxford.

3. 17 (Smits van Waesberghe, 190, 192). Also in the *Regule rhythmice;* see *Guido d'Arezzo's "Regule rithmice," "Prologus in Antiphonarium," and "Epistola ad Michahelem,"* ed. and trans. Dolores Pesce (Musicological Studies, vol. 73 [Ottawa, Ont.: The Institute of Mediaeval Music, 1999]), 374.

4. In *Guido d'Arezzo's "Regule rithmice,"* ed. Pesce; see the additional examples on p. 545, which are also found in the *Micrologus*, ed. Smits van Waesberghe, 213. A line is not shown in either edition, and Smits van Waesberghe does not indicate if the pitches are heightened.

5. See the examples from Brussels, KBR 10078/95 in *Hucbald, Guido, and John on Music: Three Medieval Treatises*, trans. Babb, ed. Palisca, 13–42. Moreover, Hucbald's version of the staff has six lines representing six strings; the syllables are placed only between the lines (ibid., 23). Michel Huglo commented succinctly on Florentius's example: "un homme de la Renaissance qui ne comprend rien" (pers. comm.).

6. *Musica* 47, ed. Chartier, *L'Œuvre musicale d'Hucbald*, 198 = *Scriptores*, ed. Gerbert, i. 118 (trans. Babb 38).

7. For the one fifteenth-century source that addresses the problem see Don Harrán, *Word–Tone Relations in Musical Thought from Antiquity to the Seventeenth Century*, Musicological Studies and Documents, vol. 40 (Neuhausen-Stuttgart: American Institute of Musicology and Hänssler-Verlag, 1976), 67–75.

8. *Arte de canto llano* (1538 ed.), sig. c4^{v}.

9. *Word–Tone Relations,* 388–91. Later theorists, such as Zarlino, stress the importance of paying attention to the syntax when setting a text, but this is at a point where it is expected that words can be understood. See ibid., 392–96.

10. *The Berkeley Manuscript,* ed. Ellsworth, 48–67.

11. On this see Karl-Werner Gümpel, "Gregorian Chant and *Musica ficta:* New Observations from Spanish Theory of the Early Renaissance," *Recerca Musicològica* 6–7 (1986–87): 5–27.

12. *The Berkeley Treatise,* ed. Ellsworth, 50, 52.

13. Ellsworth, 55.

14. Sig. e2^{r}–e7^{r} at e4^{v}. Martínez (whose treatise had first been published in 1508) had been criticized earlier by Francisco Tovar, *Libro de musica practica* (1510), who pointed out to the "insipient" theorist that tempered instruments were a purely practical expedient and the ear is not a true judge of music (fols. 12^{r}–13^{r}).

15. *Liber de arte contrapuncti* 1.3, pp. 148–52 D'Agostino.

16. For a comparison of his rules with those of Tinctoris, see Rossi, "Un manuale di musica," 267–70.

17. Cf. Papias on *melodia* and *melos suave,* cited at 2.3.8.

18. *Musica practica,* ed. Wolf, 79.

19. *The Berkeley Treatise,* 126. Guillermus de Podio, *Ars musicorum,* sig. 50, calls the term "omnino falsum."

20. However, Diego del Puerto, in his *Portus musice* (Salamanca, 1504; repr. Madrid, 1976), sig. a6^{v}, lists ten note shapes, naming the last five "seminima, semiminima, corchea, semicorchea, fusea." The "seminima" is the black minim, the "semiminima" a black minim with flag. The next two notes, however, are white minims with one and two flags, respectively, and the fusa is a black minim with an upward and downward hooked stem. For Durán, *Sumula de canto de organo* (sig. a3) they are seminima, corchea blanca (white flagged minim), corchea negra, minaria blanca (white double-flagged minim), and fussea.

21. See *Anonymi Tractatus de cantu figurativo et de contrapuncto (c. 1430–1520)*, ed. Christian Meyer, Corpus scriptorum de musica, vol. 41 (Neuhausen: American Institute of Musicology; Hänssler-Verlag, 1997), 58–65 at 60, 61.

22. Diego del Puerto, *Portus musice*, sig. a6[v]. The note shapes are lacking in Ramos's original treatise; they have been added by hand in one of the exemplars and incorporated by Wolf. For this note he gave a black minim with upward and downward flagged stem, though that is not found in the French notation that he is expounding.

23. *The Berkeley Treatise*, 126. He also says that two of these are equivalent to three minims, or three to four minims. Goschalcus also talks about red notation, which Florentius never mentions.

24. *Tractatus de regulari valore notarum*; *Opera theoretica*, ed. Seay, 1:125–38.

25. We resort to this unlikely compound in order to bring out the participial force of *partiens*, "dividing." *Twy-*, or *twi-*, is the historic combining form of *two*, standing to it etymologically as *bi-* to *duo*.

Florentius's Language

Florentius's Latin is a strange brew of classical and unclassical, elegant and incoherent. On the one hand, we find the historically correct accusative plural of *-i* stems in *-is* still sometimes used by Vergil (e.g. *omnis* 1.14.7, 2.5.2), wrongly extended (as in the late Republic) into the nominative (e.g. *omnis* 1.5.12, 16), and the gerundive of third-conjugation verbs in *-undus* still sporadically attested in classical authors and retained in certain legal formulae (e.g. *faciunda* Pr. 15). The dative *cantu* (1.11.1) for *cantui* is the rarer form but perfectly correct. At 2.14.4 the periphrasis *reddet effectum* = *efficiet* is pre-classical.

On the other hand, we find such post-classical usages as *singuli*, properly "one each," used for "all," *vel* (nonexclusive "or") for *et* ("and"), *attamen* ("yet even so," "at least") for *verum* ("however"), *enim* (causal "for") for *autem* ("but"), *fore* (future infinitive) for *esse* (present infinitive), *sibi* for *eis*, *suus* for *eorum*, *ipse* as little more than a definite article, distributives for ordinals, *hic* for *is* (and, e.g., *hosdem* for *eosdem*), *poesia* for *poesis*, *utillimus* for *utilissimus*, along with *nec . . . quidem* for *ne . . . quidem*, which was not definitively exposed as an error till the nineteenth century. *Inquam*, which correctly follows the beginning of a sentence to show that it is quoted, is used before a quotation at 1.2.4, with the adverb *ita* at 1.2.4, 1.4.18, and with a pronominal object at 1.1.14, 2.5.7; at 2.10.1 Florentius uses the medieval *acuitio* for "sharping," rather than Pliny's *exacutio* (used of literal sharpening).

POETICISMS

Sometimes Florentius uses constructions more appropriate to poetry than to prose, such as singular distributive for cardinal (1.6.4

ternam proprietatem for *tres proprietates*) and the *apo koinou* construction *circulos quosdamque semicirculos* (3.9.1) in which the common qualifier of two substantives is placed between them. Poetic too is the perfect infinitive in 1.13.1 *ostendisse conantur,* used instead of the present without any perfective implication; but at 2.14.3, where *solius* is used for *unius solius,* imitation of Statius, *Thebaid* 6.533 *ferre manu sola,* "to carry in one hand," is less likely than a hypercorrect omission of the numeral as if it were an indefinite article as in Italian and occasionally in later Latin, for at 2.15.7, where *solam* again means *unam solam,* he also writes *vocem* for *unam vocem.*

MORPHOLOGY

Florentius commonly forms the ablative singular of the substantivized *-i*-stem adjectives *brevis* and *semibrevis* not in *-i,* the adjectival ending, but in *-e,* on the analogy of true substantives such as *civis* and *ovis;* but at 3.21.12 *semibrevi* is parallel to §13 *semibreve.*

SYNTAX

The construction of noun or pronoun and gerundive for an action being performed on an object is used incorrectly at Pr. 23 *Verba sub notulis ordinanda,* 3.12.1 *omnes figuras alterandas compellunt;* at 2.16.3 *illud autem tertium genus . . . temptandum modis perspiciemus* the gerundive seems to serve as a present participle passive. The future participle is used for the infinitive at 1.1.31 *novum opus me scripturum coegit.*

Florentius is fond of using the future perfect as the perfective future: 3.4.2 *cucurrerit* (contrasted with *habebit*), 3.5.2 *cecinerimus.*

In the dedication, §2, Florentius writes *Non enim eo ingenio, ea arte, eaque altitudine rerum res edita est, qua ingenii tui acumen, et admiranda tuae naturae disciplina in legendis emendandisque libris uti soles;* the second person ought to be third, either *solent* or more elegantly *solet* agreeing with the nearer noun (compare *qua* rather

than *quibus*), but Florentius seems to be treating *ingenui . . . disciplina* as a periphrasis for *tu*.

There is constant confusion of tenses in the subjunctive. At 1.1.28 *demonstrarim* the perfect subjunctive appears in a final clause instead of the present, and at 3.5.1 for the imperfect; conversely, at 1.10.3 the imperfect replaces the perfect. At 1.5.15 *augerentur* appears to be used as a potential, 'there could be'; at 1.10.3 *esset* ought to be plain *est*. Confusion between future indicative and present subjunctive we have taken, perhaps overcharitably, for scribal error: *descendamus* for *descendemus* 2.15.5 and conversely *inserviet* for *inserviat* 2.17.7 (possibly a persistence error after *inveniet*), *ostendent* for *ostendant* 3.4.tit.; but we have left *tribuerunt* at 3.6.tit., where even the perfect subjunctive *tribuerint* would be inappropriate for the present *tribuant*.

Deponents are treated as passives, e.g. 2.16.6 *scrutari;* conversely, at 2.18.1 *differatur* is put for *differat*. At 1.14.12 intransitive *patebunt* stands for causative *patefacient*.

MISCELLANEOUS ABNORMALITIES

The preposition *e* or *ex* is sometimes used in the sense of *de* to introduce the thing spoken of: 1.1.8 *ex eiusdem effectis*, 1.1.18 *ex ipso et Arione*, 1.5.14 *e quibus Macrobius Saturnaliorum libro*. At 2.5.7 *per* is used for *ad*. At 2.7.3 *petere* "make for" is constructed with *ad* instead of a direct object; in the same sentence *citra* is hard to interpret. Particles are also misused: at 2.12.3 *Nam magni interest mi fa ♮ c quam e f* we expect *utrum mi fa ♮ c an e f sit;* at 2.14.3 *secus* takes the place of *sed*. At 2.14.8 *alterutrum* "one of the two" is used for *utrumque*. *Utpote* "as might be expected" is misused for *utputa* "for instance" (1.6.5, 2.4.3, 2.14.6).

Florentius often strains language in his attempts at variation (e.g., 2.15.5); at 1.6.9 *eaedem in figurativo non coloris id est atramento plenae* the two possible constructions of *plenus*, with genitive and

ablative, are awkwardly combined. At 2.14.7 *e quinta uocem vel unam, vel quartam ascendi, vel ibidem morari* cardinal is paired with ordinal, impersonal passive with deponent; for downright ungrammatical conflations see 1.1.1, 2.10.1, and also 3.7.2, unless we emend *quaelibet* to *quamlibet*.

Syntax also breaks down at 1.5.7, 1.10.9, 1.16.1, 2.14.6; and at times Florentius's Latin is incoherent to the point of incomprehensibility, as at 1.6.9, 1.10.1.

VERNACULAR INFLUENCE

Whereas in classical Latin the perfect participle passive constructed with *habere* meant that the object, after undergoing the action, was at the subject's disposal, in proto-Romance it came to form the perfect tenses of the active; at 2.16.2 Florentius writes *inventum . . . habebant* for *invenerant*. Constructed with *esse*, it classically expressed the perfect tenses of the passive, but the perfect sense was lost, so that the tense of the compound verb matched that of the auxiliary; this underlies the presents passive *formata est* "is formed" (1.4.1), *tali sunt figura scripti*, "are written with the following shapes" (3.3.5) for *formatur, scribuntur*.

Lost too was the distinction between comparative and superlative: the former is put for the latter at 2.6.2 *ab ima, id est graviori vel inferiori, voce ad altiorem*, 2.15.8 *ut potero brevius*; the latter for the former at 1.5.7 *optimas vel deteriores*.

At 1.5.14, where *neque satis elatas* means not "nor high enough" but "nor very high," Latin *satis* takes on the sense of Italian *assai*; likewise at 2.14.7, 2.15.5 *firmare* is used to mean "stop" as if it were Italian *fermare*. At 3.20.9 *et fiat denominatio respectu minoris numeri*, one will not miss the echo of the scholastic tag *a potiori fiat denominatio*, but the resumption by *erit* suggests the future indicative meaning of older Italian *fia* or *fie*. Hence, when the first person plural of the imperfect subjunctive is twice used for the future in-

dicative, *nesciremus* 1.11.1, *formaremus* 3.16.4, we may invoke the influence of Italian *-remo* rather than Spanish *-remos* or Catalan *-rem*. At 3.5.1 *ut opinio horum extat*, stating the reason why Florentius will discuss signs he has not seen, *ut* seems to represent Italian *come* in the sense of *poiché*,[1] even though the sense is more familiar in Spanish *como (que)* and indeed French *comme*. *Is* is used like *quello* with an qualifying genitive, adjective, or participle: 1.1.45 *ea Boethii*, 1.1.8 *id maius vel minus*, 3.8.3 *earum . . . sine causa existentium*, 3.13.1 *ea . . . minimae*.

There is indeed a Hispanism at 1.1.45 *organicam* [sc. *musicam*], 1.16.1 *cantu . . . organico*, meaning not instrumental music but polyphony, in Spanish *canto de órgano*, in Catalan *cant d'orgue*; we may suspect Florentius had the term from Romerus, whose *ad aliud significari* cited at 1.5.3 instead of *ad aliud significandum* shows the influence of Spanish *para* or Catalan *per a* + subject + infinitive. On the other hand, the use of *subire* for "rise, climb" at 1.7.7, 2.14.5, though it survives in Castilian *subir*, is perfectly classical.

Explicit reference is made to the vernacular at 2.17.1 *Eandem vernacula lingua cadentiam vocitarunt* and 3.21.1 *arithmeticis characteribus vel litteris vel (ut lingua vernacula utar) cifris*.[2]

NOTES

1. See *Grande dizionario della lingua italiana*, ed. Salvatore Battaglia, 3 (Turin: Unione Tipografico-Editoriale Torinese, 1954), 350, sense 7. Latin *ut* may express the cause of an unsurprising or inevitable result, but not as here the motive for a human choice.

2. In fact, *cadentia* has already been used several times (2.14.8, 2.17.7, 2.18.tit.).

Bibliography

PRIMARY SOURCES

Anon. *Species plani cantus sunt terdecim* [*sic*] (MS Girona, Arxiu Capitular 91). Edited by Karl-Werner Gümpel and Klaus-Jürgen Sachs. In "Das Manuskript Girona 91 und sein Contrapunctus-Traktat." *Archiv für Musikwissenschaft* 45 (1988): 186–205.

The Berkeley Manuscript: University of California Music Library, MS. 744 (olim *Phillipps 4450*). Edited and translated by Oliver B. Ellsworth. Lincoln, NE and London: University of Nebraska Press, 1984.

Boethius, Anicius Manlius Severinus. *De institutione arithmetica libri duo; De institutione musica libri quinque.* Edited by Gottfried Friedlein. Leipzig: B. G. Teubner, 1867.

——*Fundamentals of Music.* Translated by Calvin M. Bower, edited by Claude V. Palisca. New Haven: Yale University Press, 1989.

Censorinus. *De die natali,* with *Anonymi cuiusdam epitoma disciplinarum* [Pseudo-Censorinus]. Edited by Nicolaus Sallmann. Leipzig: BSB B. G. Teubner Verlagsgesellschaft, 1983.

Cicero. *De re publica.* Edited by J. G. F. Powell. Oxford: Oxford University Press, 2006.

[Pseudo-Cicero]. *Ad C. Herennium de ratione dicendi* (*Rhetorica ad Herennium*). Translated by Harry Caplan. Loeb Classical Library. Cambridge, Mass: Harvard University Press; London, William Heinemann Ltd., 1954.

Ciconia, Johannes. *Nova Musica* and *De Proportionibus.* Edited by Oliver B. Ellsworth. Lincoln, NE and London: University of Nebraska Press, 1993.

Durán, Domingo Marcos. *Comento sobre Lux bella.* Salamanca, 1498. Reprint. Madrid: Joyas bibliográficas, 1976.

——*Lux bella.* Seville, 1492. Reprint. Madrid: Joyas bibliográficas, 1976.

Escobar, Cristóbal. *Este es una introduccion muy breve de canto llano.* [Salamanca, ca. 1496]. Reprint. Madrid: Joyas bibliográficas, 1978.

Guido d'Arezzo. *Guido d'Arezzo's* Regule rithmice, Prologus in Antiphonarium, *and* Epistola ad Michahelem. Edited and translated by Dolores Pesce. Musicological Studies, vol. 73. Ottawa, Ontario: The Institute of Mediaeval Music, 1999.

Hucbald. *L'Œuvre musicale d'Hucbald de Saint-Amand: Les compositions et le traité de musique*. Edited by Yves Chartier. Cahiers d'études médievales, Cahier spécial nº 5. [Saint-Laurent, Québec]: Bellarmin, 2005.

Hucbald, Guido, and John on Music: Three Medieval Treatises. Translated by Warren Babb, edited by Claude V. Palisca. New Haven: Yale University Press, 1978.

Isidore. *Isidori Hispalensis episcopi Etymologiarum sive originum libri XX*. Edited by W. M. Lindsay. 2 vols. Oxford: Clarendon Press, 1911 and reprints. References are to the chapter numbers of this edition.

——*Isidore de Séville, Étymologies, livre III*. Edited and translated by G. Gasparotto and J.-Y. Guillaumin. Paris: Les Belles Lettres, 2009. (A critical advance on Lindsay; but note that the chapter numbers of the section on music are one lower than his, because the spurious ch. 14, which immediately precedes them, has been omitted from the count as well as the text.)

Macrobius. *Saturnalia* and *Commentarii in Somnium Scipionis*. Edited by James Willis. 2 vols. 2d ed. Leipzig: BSB B. G. Teubner Verlagsgesellschaft, 1970.

Marchetto of Padua. *The Lucidarium of Marchetto of Padua: A Critical Edition, Translation, and Commentary*. Edited and translated by Jan W. Herlinger. Chicago: University of Chicago Press, 1985.

——*Pomerium*. Edited by Joseph Vecchi. Corpus Scriptorum de Musica, 6. [Rome]: American Institute of Musicology, 1961.

Molina, Bartolomé. *Arte de canto lano llamado lux videntis*. Valladolid, 1503. Reprint. Madrid: Joyas bibliográficas, 1977.

Muris, Johannes de. *Johannis de Muris Musica <speculativa>*. Edited by Susan Fast. Musicological Studies, 61. Ottawa: The Institute of Mediaeval Music, 1994.

Musica Enchiriadis and Scolica Enchiriadis. Translated by Raymond Erickson. Edited by Claude V. Palisca. Yale University Press: New Haven and London, 1995.

Musica et scolica enchiriadis una cum aliquibus tractatulis adiunctis. Edited by Hans Schmid. Bayerische Akademie der Wissenschaften, Veröffentlichungen der Musikhistorischen Kommission 3. Munich: Verlag der Bayerischen Akademie der Wissenschaften, 1981.

Papias, *Vocabularium*. Milan: Dominicus de Vespolate, 1476.

Peter of Spain (Petrus Hispanus Portugalensis). *Tractatus afterwards called Summulae logicales*. Edited by Lambertus Marie de Rijk. Assen: Van Gorcum, 1972.

Podio, Guillermus de. *Enchiridion*. Edited in Karl-Werner Gümpel, "Das Enchiridion de principiis musice discipline des Guillermus de Podio." *Gesammelte Aufsätze zur Kulturgeschichte Spaniens* 27 (1973): 359–96.

Prosdocimus de Beldemandis. *Brevis summula proportionum*. Edited by Jan Herlinger. Lincoln, NE and London: University of Nebraska Press, 1987.

Pseudo-Censorinus, *see* Censorinus.

Puerto, Diego del. *Portus musice*. Salamanca, 1504. Reprint. Madrid: Joyas bibliográficas, 1976.

Ramos de Pareja, Bartolomé. *Musica Practica*. Edited by Johannes Wolf. Leipzig: Breitkopf & Härtel, 1901.

Scriptores ecclesiastici de musica sacra. Edited by Martin Gerbert. 3 vols. Saint-Blaise: Typis San-Blasianis, 1784. Reprint. Milan: Bollettino bibliografico musicale, 1931.

Scriptores de musica medii aevi. Edited by E. de Coussemaker. 4 vols. Paris: A. Durand, 1864–76. Reprint. Milan: Bollettino bibliografico musicale, 1931.

Spañón, Alfonso. *Introducción de canto llano*. N.pl., ca. 1504. Reprint. Madrid: Joyas bibliográficas, 1976.

Tinctoris, Johannes. *Diffinitorium musices: Un dizionario di musica per Beatrice d'Aragona. Edited and translated by* Cecilia Panti. La tradizione musicale, 8. Florence: Edizioni del Galluzzo, 2004.

——— *Opera theoretica*. Edited by Albert Seay. CSM 22. [Rome] and Neuhausen-Stuttgart: American Institute of Musicology, 1975–78.

——— *Proportionale musices. Liber de arte* contrapuncti. Edited and translated by Gianluca d'Agostino. Florence: Edizioni del Galluzzo, 2008.

Tractatus de proportionibus. Edited in Christian Meyer, " . . . per venerandae memoriae magistrum Iohannem de Muris . . . La tradition parisienne de l'enseignement de Jean de Murs." In *Gedenkschrift für Walter Pass*, ed. Martin Czernin, 217–34. Tutzing: H. Schneider, 2002.

Uguccione da Pisa. *Derivationes*. Edited by Enzo Cecchini *et al.* Florence: SISMEL: Edizioni del Galluzzo, 2004.

SECONDARY SOURCES

Bologna, Giulia. "Un fratello del Moro letterato e bibliofilo: Ascanio Maria Sforza." In *Milano nell'età di Ludovico il Moro. Atti del Convegno internationale 28 febbraio–4 marzo 1483*, 1:293–332. 2 vols. Milan: Archivio Storico Civico e Biblioteca Trivulziana, 1983.

Grande dizionario della lingua italiana. Edited by Salvatore Battaglia *et al.* 21 vols. and supplements. Turin: Unione Tipografico-Editoriale Torinese, 1962– .

Holford-Strevens, Leofranc. "Humanism and the Language of Music Treatises." *Renaissance Studies* 15 (2001): 415–49.

——— "The Erudition of Florentius de Faxolis and Blasius Romerus." In *Uno gentile et sottile ingenio: Studies in Renaissance Music in Honour of Bonnie Blackburn*, ed. M. Jennifer Bloxam, Gioia Filocamo, and Leofranc Holford-Strevens, 751–59. Turnhout: Brepols, 2009.

Lexicon musicum Latinum medii aevi. Edited by Michael Bernhard. Munich: Bayerische Akademie der Wissenschaften, 1992– .

Lowinsky, Edward E. "Ascanio Sforza's Life: A Key to Josquin's Biography and an Aid to the Chronology of his Works." In *Josquin des Prez: Proceedings of the International Josquin Festival Conference . . . June 1971*, ed. Edward E. Lowinsky with the collaboration of Bonnie J. Blackburn, 32–75. London: Oxford University Press, 1976.

Motta, Emilio. "Dell'autore probabile di un prezioso codice musicale della Trivulziana." *Bollettino storico della Svizzera italiana* 21 (1899): 76–77.

New Grove Dictionary of Music and Musicians. 2d ed. Edited by Stanley Sadie and John Tyrrell. 29 vols. London: Macmillan, 2001.

Pellegrini, Marco. *Ascanio Maria Sforza: La parabola politica di un cardinale-principe del rinascimento.* 2 vols. Rome: Istituto Storico Italiano per il Medio Evo, 2002.

Rossi, Francesco Rocco. "Un manuale di musica per Ascanio Sforza: Il *Liber Musices* di Florentius (Ms. 2146 della Biblioteca Trivulziana di Milano)." 2 vols. Doctoral thesis, Università degli Studi di Pavia, Dipartimento di Scienze Musicologiche e Paleografico-Filologiche, 2007.

——— "*Auctores in opusculo introducti:* L'enigmatico Florentius musicus e gli sconosciuti referenti teorici del *Liber Musices* (I-Mt 2146)." *Acta Musicologica* 80 (2008): 165–77.

Seay, Albert. "The 'Liber Musices' of Florentius de Faxolis." In *Musik und Geschichte/Music and History: Leo Schrade zum sechzigsten Geburtstag,* 71–95. Cologne: Arno Volk, 1963.

Index

Note: Lowercase roman numerals refer to page numbers in the Introduction, arabic numbers refer to page numbers in the Notes and Commentary, and multipart references indicate book, chapter, and paragraph numbers in the English translation.

Publication of this volume has been made possible by

The Myron and Sheila Gilmore Publication Fund at I Tatti
The Robert Lehman Endowment Fund
The Jean-François Malle Scholarly Programs and Publications Fund
The Andrew W. Mellon Scholarly Publications Fund
The Craig and Barbara Smyth Fund
for Scholarly Programs and Publications
The Lila Wallace–Reader's Digest Endowment Fund
The Malcolm Wiener Fund for Scholarly Programs and Publications